A LITTLE MANUAL FOR SERVANT LEADERS

A STUDY OF 1 & 2 TIMOTHY & TITUS WITH STUDY GUIDE

BY J.K. JONES & JIM PROBST

With great grace
J.K. Jones Jr.
1 Tim. 4:7-8

A Little Manual for Servant Leaders
A Study of 1&2 Timothy and Titus with Study Guide
Copyright © Eastview Christian Church

ISBN 978-0-987841-1-5

Published in 2014
by
College Press Publishing Co.
Printed and bound in the USA

All rights reserved. No part of this publication may be reproduced, stored in a retrieval system, or transmitted in any form by any means, electronic, mechanical, photocopy, recording, or otherwise, without the prior permission of the publisher, except as provided by USA copyright law.

All Scripture quotations, unless otherwise indicated are taken from *The ESV Bible* (The Holy Bible, English Standard Version), copyright 2001 by Crossway, a publishing ministry of Good News Publishers. Used by permission. All rights reserved.

TABLE OF CONTENTS

Acknowledgements *5*

Introduction *7*

Chapter 1 .... *11*
Watching Out for Self-Appointed Leaders

Chapter 2 .... *19*
What a Servant Leader Should Never Forget

Chapter 3 .... *27*
The Servant Leader's Highest Priority

Chapter 4 .... *39*
What Does a Servant Leader Look Like?

Chapter 5 .... *53*
Servant Leadership Paradoxes

Chapter 6 .... *61*
Servant Leadership's Hard Side

Chapter 7 .... *67*
The Servant Leader's Workout Routine

Chapter 8 .... *77*
Only Multi-Generational Servant Leaders Will Do

Chapter 9 .... *89*
Servant Leaders Beware

Chapter 10 .... *99*
Shaping the Servant Leader's Character

Chapter 11 .... *99*
Finding Your Servant Leadership Metaphor

Chapter 12 .... *109*
The Servant Leader's Long Obedience

Chapter 13 .... *119*
What Wise Servant Leaders Know

Chapter 14 .... *129*
What Kingdom-Driven Servant Leaders Look Like

Chapter 15 .... *135*
When Servant Leaders Must Step Up

Chapter 16 .... *143*
The Servant Leader's Dance with God

Chapter 17 .... *157*
Standing Tall as a Servant Leader

Chapter 18 .... *167*
Saying What You Mean as a Servant Leader

Chapter 19 .... *175*
The "Doing Good" Reminder of Servant Leadership

Chapter 20 .... *183*
Dying Daily as a Servant Leader

Conclusion *191*

Discussion Guides *203*

References *246*

ACKNOWLEDGEMENTS

Mike Baker, the senior pastor at Eastview Christian Church (ECC), Normal, Illinois, models the heart and soul of this book. He has been my faithful friend and constant brother in Christ for over two decades. He has faced criticism, threats, and naysayers with profound grace, often refreshing me when I have come under attack from those same critics. Over the past few years we have enjoyed the privilege of working side by side in this part of God's global enterprise. I thank God daily for him, as well as for his soul mate and most enthusiastic cheerleader, Mike's wife, Sara. Our lives are also immensely blessed by the good and faithful staff that shares this ministry. They are giants in my eyes. I particularly want to thank Tyler Hari, Jim Probst, Jason Smith, and Mark Warren, good spiritual brothers who comprise the pastoral leadership team that Mike directs, for their love, encouragement, and partnership. I am, by far, the least among these mighty men. One of my dearest friends and cherished partners at ECC, mentioned above – Jim Probst, has played a significant role in helping me to flesh out the small group discussion guide provided in the book. Thank God for him. Our Lord has used Jim to make me a better apprentice of Jesus.

I am grateful to those willing to read and coach me through this lengthy writing journey, in particular Susie Baker, Dr. Tom Tanner, and Dr. Don Green. These three friends have been enormously helpful. Julie Pond, editor-extraordinary, makes everyone she assists look better than they really are. Jim Probst and I are immensely grateful for her partnership in our writing ministry. I would also like to thank our Heavenly Father for the faithful elders of ECC who watch over us and who give themselves to the Word and prayer: BJ Armstrong, John Ashenfelter, Jim Connolly, Darrell Douglass, Rod Hoff, John Moses, Rick Schaumburg, Barton Shaw, Steve Wadhams and, of course, Mike Baker. These men, one and all, embody the meaning of this book. Praise the Lord. I would also like to make special mention of my friend, Jim Connolly, cited above. He is currently pursuing doctoral work and that long journey of completing an advanced degree has not allowed him to continue as an elder. We break bread together periodically and always seem to land on conversations about servant leadership. Good food and good fellowship around the Word have often fed my soul. Thanks, Jim.

A final word of gratitude is in order to my sisters in Christ who serve faithfully in their ministry of the Word through ECC and elsewhere. There are too many to list in detail, but a few have particularly blessed my life: Jackina Stark, Rhesa Storms, Kay Moll, Susie Baker, Sara Baker, Miriam Windham, Lisa Doran, April Kinzinger, Lisa Miller-Rich, Brooke Yarbrough, Sabrina Owens, and my daughters, Lindsey Clark and Chelsea Jones. Last, but in no way least, is my wife, Sue, who has taught me far more about the Jesus-following way than I have taught her. Her love makes me want to be a better man. Thank you, God. Thank you, Sue. A healthy leadership, after all, makes for a healthy church.

"Father, I have written this book as an offering to You. Whether others read it or not, Your eyes are enough. You are my audience of One, in Jesus' Name, Amen."

INTRODUCTION

"The central question is, Are the leaders of the future truly men and women of God, people with an ardent desire to dwell in God's presence, to listen to God's voice, to look at God's beauty, to touch God's incarnate Word and to taste fully God's infinite goodness" *(Nouwen, Henri. (2001).* **In the Name of Jesus: Reflections on Christian Leadership.** *(pp. 29-30). New York: Crossroads Publishing Company).*

Ephesus and Crete were not places for wimpy leadership. The Apostle Paul handpicked two servant leaders with unique callings and clear giftedness to meet the challenge. Paul chose young Timothy for Ephesus and seasoned Titus for Crete. Timothy was raised in a mixed-marriage home. His dad was Greek and his mother, Jewish Christian. He was led to Christ by his grandmother Lois and his mother, Eunice, and in words beyond explanation "was circumcised" by Paul (2 Timothy 1:5 and Acts 16:1-3). Titus, in contrast, was a Gentile by birth and apparently introduced to Jesus by Paul (Titus 1:4, and Galatians 2:1-5). He was spared "circumcision" when Paul refused to give into the demands of legalistic and erroneous Jewish Christians. Please note the significant contrast between Timothy and Titus: younger and older, Jew and Gentile, circumcised and not circumcised, Ephesus and Crete. So much is buried in those differences.

Consider their different locations of ministry. Ephesus was known as the religious center of the Roman Empire. Crete was known as a hedonistic Mediterranean island. Ephesus housed the famous temple of Artemis (Diana/Roman) where religion and sexuality blended together to form rampant superstition and flagrant sensuality. When Paul arrived there around 52 AD, he spent three years or so making disciples and changing the spiritual landscape. It was no easy task. The Temple of Artemis was one of the Seven Ancient Wonders of the World. I've seen what's left of it in my travels through Greece and Turkey. Paul encountered such strong opposition that a full-blown riot took place (Acts 19:23-41). What kind of chance would Timothy have in a ministry like that? Paul urged him to stay put (1 Timothy 1:3). Titus, on the other hand, was left behind in Crete by Paul to straighten out a mess of gigantic proportions (Titus 1:5). The Cretans were notorious for being dishonest, brutish, and gluttonous (Titus 1:12). How would Titus fare in a place like that? Two challenging locations were matched by two unique servant leaders.

This book is an attempt to explore Paul's wise counsel to each man. This is not another Bible commentary or one more leadership resource. Rather, the offering here is a concise combination of Biblical exposition, devotional rumination, and concrete application based on the exploration of three New Testament Letters written by Paul to Timothy and Titus and affectionately referred to since the eighteenth century as the Pastoral Letters (1 and 2 Timothy and Titus). Though I've never been comfortable with the name attached to these letters, because all New Testament Letters have a "pastoral" quality to them, I nonetheless embrace the term. I also know there are scholarly voices out there that are not fully convinced of Scripture's prescriptive value when it comes to leadership. Dr. Ruth Tucker has my attention when she cautions us about the use of Scripture as a text for talking about leadership:

"Does the Bible serve as a leadership text? Does God offer a template for leadership? Books and articles in abundance present the twelve steps or seven lessons of leadership found in the Bible...But I now have serious doubts about using the Bible as a leadership text – or even a leadership guide. I contend that it simply does not in any fashion present imperatives or rules or principles or guidelines for leaders – no more than it presents the imperatives for teachers or chiropractors or public speakers...We do well to avoid using the Bible as a manual for leadership...When it comes to leadership, however, we find the Bible most accessible and practical when we are mining its rich veins for illustrative material rather than hard facts and step-by-step-instructions" (2008, pp. 59-60, 67-68).

Perhaps this resource is simply my humble attempt to offer illustrative and descriptive material from Paul's correspondence with Timothy and Titus. Admittedly, I'm reading these three letters through the lens of servant leadership. The chapters of *A Little Manual for Servant Leaders* are tightly written "pastoral reflections" with emphasis on simplicity and clarity. The target audience is comprised of the pastor/elder who needs a refresher on the nature of servant leadership, the Jesus-follower who needs some inspiration to stay in a tough ministry context, and the hungry apprentice to Jesus who wants to explore and to grow into what it means to be a genuine servant-leader of Jesus Christ. I have intentionally looked into the faces of people I know as I wrote this book. I have asked myself, "How would my son-in-law, Matt Clark, hear this piece of 1&2 Timothy and Titus?" I have wondered, "How would my small group react to what I just said about 1Timothy 2:9-15?" I have, throughout the writing of this book, contemplated, "How will the ECC pastoral and administrative staff respond to this little book on servant leadership?" *A Little Manual for Servant Leaders* is primarily offered as a gift of love to the Eastview Christian Church, Normal, Illinois, elder team, staff, small group leaders, and to the larger world of servant leaders in God's vast Kingdom.

A Little Manual for Servant Leaders

CHAPTER 1
Watching Out for Self-Appointed Leaders
1 Timothy 1:1-11

"Perhaps the most obvious outcome of being humble is that you will learn, grow and thrive in a way the proud have no hope of doing. The logic is simple: people who imagine that they know most of what is important to know are hermetically sealed from learning new things and receiving constructive criticism"
(Dickson, John. (2011). **Humilitas.** *(p. 116). Grand Rapids: Zondervan).*

Bible students have asked me all kinds of questions over the years about servant leadership. Those inquiries are wide and varied. Here are some examples. Is there only one kind of leader in the Bible? How would I know God was calling me to leadership? What does that look like or sound like? What is the difference between human leadership and servant leadership? Is there one? Can women lead in the church? If so, where can they lead? If not, why not? Is managing people the same as leading people? Can someone be hesitant and reluctant and still be a leader God can use? Is there a profile in Scripture for what a leader should look like? How would you define servant leadership? Where are the leadership danger spots? What should servant leaders ask? Those few are a mere sampling. There are so many others. Suffice it to say, there is intense curiosity about this thing we call servant leadership. Let's simply start where Paul starts in his first letter to Timothy.

Probably around the mid-sixties AD, Paul wrote from Corinth, Greece or perhaps somewhere north of there in Macedonia to his much loved friend and ministry partner, Timothy. This book will not debate with Bible scholars and students who do not accept Paul's authorship. It is assumed here. He had just been released from his first imprisonment in Rome (think Acts 28). His concern for his "true son" in the faith is evident (1 Timothy 1:2). Timothy is probably in his late teens, maybe early twenties. Raised in Lystra, an out-of-the-way-town in Lycaonia, he has gained some ministry experience in his travels with Paul, but, in terms of concentrated and extensive work in the life of a local congregation, he is a greenhorn. Biblical advice and pastoral help from Paul is warranted. Ephesus is a universe away from Lystra. The difference is as stark as that of the tiny down-state village of Wapella, Illinois, and that of the sprawling metropolis of Chicago. Ephesus was the third leading city in the Roman Empire, behind Rome and Alexandria. It was free, saturated in Greek culture, and probably running about 250,000 in population. From the very beginning of the letter, Paul makes one central fact clear: ***watch out for self-appointed leaders.*** Note to all would-be-servant-leaders: one of the most dangerous people you will ever meet is a self-appointed leader. Remember that Timothy has walked into a ministry situation marked with very strong opposition. So, what do self-appointed leaders look like? Let's listen to Paul's opening words and then explore their meaning (1Timothy 1:1-11).

[1] *Paul, an apostle of Christ Jesus by command of God our Savior and of Christ Jesus our hope,*

[2] *To Timothy, my true child in the faith:*

Grace, mercy, and peace from God the Father and Christ Jesus our Lord.

> ³ *As I urged you when I was going to Macedonia, remain at Ephesus so that you may charge certain persons not to teach any different doctrine,* ⁴ *nor to devote themselves to myths and endless genealogies, which promote speculations rather than the stewardship from God that is by faith.* ⁵ *The aim of our charge is love that issues from a pure heart and a good conscience and a sincere faith.* ⁶ *Certain persons, by swerving from these, have wandered away into vain discussion,* ⁷ *desiring to be teachers of the law, without understanding either what they are saying or the things about which they make confident assertions.*
>
> ⁸ *Now we know that the law is good, if one uses it lawfully,* ⁹ *understanding this, that the law is not laid down for the just but for the lawless and disobedient, for the ungodly and sinners, for the unholy and profane, for those who strike their fathers and mothers, for murderers,* ¹⁰ *the sexually immoral, men who practice homosexuality, enslavers, liars, perjurers, and whatever else is contrary to sound doctrine,* ¹¹ *in accordance with the gospel of the glory of the blessed God with which I have been entrusted.*

Timothy is clearly loved by Paul in these opening words. Their relationship is solid and holy, marked by the three words that make all the difference in any relationship – grace, mercy, and peace. He offers his usual greeting, but seems abrupt and in a hurry to address the issue at hand. The wise apostle ("the sent one") counsels this young pastor with three specific profiles of what a self-appointed leader looks like.

First, **self-appointed leaders are more interested in what is different than what is Divine** (1:3-4a). Please notice the phrase in 1:3 "teach any different doctrine" (also see 6:3). It comprises a single word in the Greek New Testament – "heterodidaskaleo." It's probably a verb that Paul crafted to fit the occasion. The idea here is that some were "teaching a different Gospel" than Paul. He warned the Ephesian elders of this danger back in Acts 20:29-30: "I know that after my departure fierce wolves will come in among you, not sparing the flock and from among your own selves will arise men speaking twisted things, to draw away disciples after them." Paul's words proved to be prophetically accurate. A different teaching had infiltrated the church in Ephesus. We don't know the specifics, but what we do know is that it had something to do with conjecture – "myths and endless genealogies" (1:4). There was a group of people preoccupied with Jewish legends and names found in the Book of Genesis. The outcome of this speculative kind of teaching was controversy (1:4) rather than knowing Christ and making Him known. Perhaps this talk of myths and genealogies doesn't zing us in the twenty-first century, but certainly there is a preoccupation among Christians today with minor themes of Scripture and lesser known details that can move us away from Jesus. We can't afford to forget that we are caretakers of God's revealed plan as found in Christ alone.

The Gospel of Jesus Christ is formed by great grace, as well as great cost. Entrance into this relationship with Jesus is free, marked by faith in Him, and to gravitate toward the trivial and non-essential can be fatal. Discipleship at its very core is an on-going attachment to Jesus. The Gospel writer, John, describes it plainly; we abide in Him, and He abides in us (John 15:1-17). He is the Master Rabbi and we are His apprentices. Anything that would attempt to detach us from His life-giving nourishment, anything like health, wealth, and prosperity teaching; anything like do-it-yourself-salvation; and anything that would move us away from the Lordship of Christ and the Apostles' doctrine is to be shunned. Two fundamental questions can help any servant leader avoid the speculation or faddish Bible teaching that might seduce. Does this teaching match up with the clear and simple truth of the Gospel? Does this teaching promote unity and love among Christ-followers? Run from any self-appointed leader who majors in the different just to be different. Like the old-school preachers always said, "Keep the main thing the main thing."

Second, *self-appointed leaders are more interested in trivia than transformation* (1:4b-7). Paul made it perfectly clear to Timothy that the end of all real Christian teaching is a preoccupation with the love of Jesus and all of its implications and applications (1:5). Motives matter. The pursuit of Christ and His likeness is essential. The kind of motive that prompts the servant leader must be anchored in genuine love for others. When God's Word is rightly lived and taught, there are three obvious outcomes. The Word moves us to Jesus, restrains us from doing evil, and encourages us to live godly lives. It keeps us from wandering or swerving away from the truth (1:6). Some of Timothy's opponents had steered in a different direction and subsequently turned to "vain discussion" ("metailogia" in 1:6), like an inattentive driver who has lost control of the car and dangerously veered into oncoming traffic. There is no way to sugarcoat this truth. Some leaders are simply godless. Paul is describing a kind of Gospel accident that is waiting to happen due to senseless, empty, futile even trivial teaching. The end result is the glory of the teacher, not the glory of God.

Several years ago, I was confronted by a well-intentioned Jesus-follower about an innocent passing comment I had made in a sermon. I dared to suggest that bacon was created to be enjoyed. The person apparently had never read Acts 10:9-23 or weighed the implications of what happened on Simon the Tanner's seaside rooftop in Joppa. Granted, bacon may not be the healthiest food God allows us to eat freely. This person had a full-blown manuscript filled with proof-texts on why Christians cannot eat bacon. To quote a cherished friend of mine, "I kid you not." Nothing I said about the Gospel or the freedom we have in Christ made a dent in the trivial armor that person was wearing. The chief purpose of Scripture is to witness to Jesus, not our impossible list of legalistic rules. Be wary of teachers with a non-Gospel agenda. They have missed the mark and turned off the Jesus-following way. Avoid chasing "teaching rabbits" or the latest faddish thought. Stay in the Book, and preach, and teach the cross.

Third, *self-appointed leaders are more interested in having their way than living the Way* (1:8-11). Notice with me that Paul acknowledges the law is good (1:8), the issue is whether it is used "properly" (nominos – lawfully or rightly). The proper use of the law leaves us with no excuses to hide behind. It puts safety fences around us so that sin can't harm our relationship with Jesus. But more than anything, the law clearly reveals God's will to us. The Biblical law is to the Jesus-follower what traffic law is to the driver. There are speed limits that are not intended to rob us of pleasure, but to keep us from killing ourselves and others. The law cannot save us, but it can be a deterrent to fatal choices. It is a guide to direct us toward absolute trust in Jesus. Don't overlook how Paul creatively inserts five of the Ten Commandments in his conversation with Timothy. Honor your father and mother ("those who kill their fathers or mothers"), you shall not murder ("for murderers"), you shall not commit adultery ("for adulterers and perverts"), you shall not steal ("for slave traders" – practicing slavery is the same as stealing a human life), and you shall not bear false testimony ("for liars and perjurers"). Talk about understanding the Way. What Paul most cares about is the health and vitality of the local church grounded in "sound doctrine" that repeatedly points us to Jesus and His Way. Ultimately, God alone gets the praise (1:11).

I deeply appreciate the manner in which Eugene Peterson describes the Jesus Way:

> To follow Jesus implies that we enter into a way of life that is given character and shape and direction by the one who calls us. To follow Jesus means picking up rhythms and ways of doing things that are often unsaid but always derivative from Jesus, formed by the influence of Jesus. To follow Jesus means that we can't separate what Jesus is saying from what Jesus is doing and the way that he is doing it. To follow Jesus is as much, or maybe even more, about feet as it is about ears and eyes...It is significant that the primary term for identifying the followers of Jesus in the early church was "the Way"...Discernment of means adequate for living to the glory of God and

congruent with our identity as baptized Christians has always been demanding, which is why the biblical writers use the metaphor of *way* so frequently (pp. 22-23, 27).

Paul acknowledges to Timothy that this sacred Gospel has been entrusted to his care (1:11). So it is with us. Three questions are vital if we are to identify self-appointed leaders. First, do I believe there are biblical standards? If so, those will keep me grounded and ever vigilant. Second, do I believe Scripture changes people when rightly taught? If so, I won't place my trust in slick and seducing church fads. Third, am I willing to submit to God's grand purpose for my life? If so, I will fully embrace the stewardship of His Word and His Way. There is a remarkable chasm between a Savior-appointed servant leader and a self-appointed want-to-be. Be ever watchful.

A Little Manual for Servant Leaders

CHAPTER 2

"What a Servant Leader Should Never Forget"
1 Timothy 1:12-20

"I wish to bring back to mind my past foulness and the carnal corruptions of my soul. This is not because I love them, but that I may love you, my God" (Augustine. (1960). **The Confessions of St. Augustine.** *(p. 65). New York: Image Books).*

I like a good map. My iPhone comes equipped with *MapQuest*. It is a handy-dandy guide to most anywhere. However, I still like holding and studying the paper kind. I think my old-school ways come into play at this point. Several years ago, while enjoying some rest and reflection time in St. Louis, Missouri, with my wife, I shopped at a National Geographic Store. There I found a small, leather bound booklet of maps. Now when I travel, I often take it with me. I like tracking where I'm headed. I know there is a lot of debate over how long maps and map making (cartography) have been in existence. Some say that maps have been around for nearly 8,000 years, including the kind found on cave walls. Some say that maps have been around even longer than that. Regardless, many of us find maps invaluable in our everyday lives whether they are paper or digital. What is true of life in general, is true of life as it relates to being a servant of Jesus Christ. Most of us need a leadership map. We want a Global Positioning System (GPS) for servant leaders. In some ways, that GPS has been provided for us through our unique gifts, our one-of-a-kind personalities and passions, and our own sense of calling. I could even say the Holy Spirit is sufficient as our personal GPS (John 16:13).

Maps are essential to navigation, regardless of where we are headed. When it comes to servant leadership, the very best maps in the world can't help guide us if we forget two mega truths. Think about this in terms of ancient sea travel. Mariners relied upon staying close to the land. They watched for certain geographical markers to help guide them on their way. Eventually, the compass was created, and those who dared to go out into the deep blue sea could now get around by charting a course and tracking that course with a compass. The two ideas I want to unpack here are like land and compass for the servant leader. I find these two truths in 1Timothy 1:12-20.

> [12] *I thank him who has given me strength, Christ Jesus our Lord, because he judged me faithful, appointing me to his service,* [13] *though formerly I was a blasphemer, persecutor, and insolent opponent. But I received mercy because I had acted ignorantly in unbelief,* [14] *and the grace of our Lord overflowed for me with the faith and love that are in Christ Jesus.* [15] *The saying is trustworthy and deserving of full acceptance, that Christ Jesus came into the world to save sinners, of whom I am the foremost.* [16] *But I received mercy for this reason, that in me, as the foremost, Jesus Christ might display his perfect patience as an example to those who were to believe in him for eternal life.* [17] *To the King of the ages, immortal, invisible, the only God, be honor and glory forever and ever. Amen.* [18] *This charge I entrust to you, Timothy, my child, in accordance with the prophecies previously made about you, that by them you may wage the good warfare,* [19] *holding faith and a good conscience. By rejecting this, some have made ship-*

wreck of their faith, [20] *among whom are Hymenaeus and Alexander, whom I have handed over to Satan that they may learn not to blaspheme.*

The first mega truth is this: ***the grace of God is absolutely marvelous. It changes everything*** (1:12-17). One of the most revealing ingredients of true discipleship is gratitude. Paul never got so sophisticated in his Jesus-following life that he wandered away from God's grace. Grace not only made salvation possible, but it made the Jesus way possible. He thought about this grace day and night. The first six verses of this section of Scripture disclose for us Paul's reflection on his "before Christ" days as a blasphemer, persecutor, and violent man. The Apostle calls up in his memory how he had rejected Jesus as the Promised Messiah, how he had imprisoned and killed those who called themselves Christians, and how his life had been corrupted by the sin of prideful defiance ("Hybristes" – the Greek word from which we get our word "Hubris," translated here as "insolent opponent").

In the Greek/Roman culture of Paul's day, pride was not considered a negative trait. However, under the Lordship of Jesus Christ and the necessary humility required to "empty Himself" at the cross (Philippians 2:5-11), a new understanding began to form. Paul is looking back on his journey as a man immersed in deep humility. No longer is there room for self-exalting pride. He offers two mercy statements here that should not be overlooked (1:13 and 1:16). Paul's testimony is that he was "shown mercy." He did not get the punishment he deserved. God offered him what he could not do for himself. God offered him a way out of the mess of his life. This entire section is saturated with exceptionally personal self-awareness. Paul realizes he is a sinner saved by grace. Not only that, but he wants Timothy to know this specifically and sets it up with a sentence that he will repeat five times in his correspondence with both Timothy and Titus. He writes, "The saying is trustworthy and deserving of full acceptance" (See 1 Timothy 3:1, 4:9, 2 Timothy 2:11, and Titus

3:8). Paul's testimony is clear. God alone, by faith alone, in Christ alone, transformed Paul's life in unforgettable ways. The Gospel is at the center of all Paul's recollections. This Gospel is true, universal, salvation-driven, and more than anything, deeply personal. This personal nature in no way lessens the community or corporate piece of salvation. We don't travel alone, of course, in the Jesus following life. Paul is simply elevating his own story.

Stop and reflect for a while on the powerful words of 1:14. Paul describes this grace as "poured out on me abundantly." It paints a picture of a river overflowing its banks. Grace completely flooded every level of Paul's life. This small section of Paul's story sounds like a piece of music or poetry. It appears to be shaped by a formula of divine proportions. He offers two praises (1:12 and 1:17 – "I thank Christ Jesus our Lord" and "Now to the King eternal, immortal..."); three blessings (1:12 – "given me strength, considered me faithful, and appointing me to his service"); three descriptions of his past life (1:13 – "blasphemer, persecutor, and violent man"); followed with the two mercy statements already mentioned (1:13 and 1:16 – "I was shown mercy"). 2-3-3-2 and it all ends with a grand crescendo of confession and praise: "I am the foremost" and "To the King..." Talk about a life-changing conviction! Doxology is everywhere.

Doxology is what a servant leader offers to God when she encounters His radical grace. Doxology is what a servant leader gives to God when he comprehends the depth of his own broken life and the reconstructed life God offers without merit. It is why a servant leader like Paul describes God in four grace-filled ways (1:17). Paul tells Timothy this God of grace is eternal. He is beyond time. This God of grace is immortal. He is beyond death. This God of grace is invisible. He is beyond sight. This God of grace is the only God. He is beyond comparison. Paul never tires of offering his praise to this God who demonstrated His love for the Apostle in a very concrete way: while Paul was still a sinner, Christ died for him (Romans 5:8). Paul's witness to Timothy elevates the radical grace of God, not the wretched sin of his past. Praise Him from whom all blessings flow!

Anne LaMott is known for her beautiful writing and sometimes earthy speech. Like you and me, she still has a ways to go in her Jesus-following life. In her best-selling autobiography, *Traveling Mercies*, Anne describes her "Damascus-Road-like-encounter-with-God." Alcohol, drugs, and failed relationships had left her broken. She had been to church and run home to her houseboat crying. She explains in her own words, "I took a long deep breath and said out loud, 'All right. You can come in'" (1999, p. 50). Servant leaders give honor and glory to this great God of great grace.

The second mega truth a servant leader should never forget is this: ***The Jesus-following journey is really dangerous. It requires total alertness*** (1:18-20). The way is hidden with all kinds of improvised explosive tricks and temptations strategically placed by the enemy. This calls for keen watchfulness and spiritual awareness. Paul reminds Timothy that he is offering Timothy very specific "charge" (parangelia in 1:18). This word is translated the same way in 1:3 and 1:5 and is often found in military contexts outside of Scripture. Perhaps this is exactly what Paul had in mind. He wanted to place a sobering reminder in the heart and mind of his partner in ministry, his fellow soldier in Christ. The servant leader's life is one steeped in spiritual conflict. We don't exactly know what Paul meant by "in accordance with the prophecies previously made about you." Perhaps he was calling up a memory of Timothy's ordination ceremony when those early Christian leaders would have laid hands on him and prayed over him (consider 1 Timothy 4:14). What we do know is that Paul speaks directly of a "warfare " (strategon is used twice in 1:18). The Bible student can hear the word "strategy" in the Greek word "strategon." So Paul, once again, drawing on military combat language, says, "Strategize the good strategy." Know the tactics of the enemy. Remember that the Devil is like a roaring lion seeking to devour (1 Peter 5:8). Be ready. Don't fall asleep on post. Stand guard.

Paul doesn't leave Timothy defenseless. He mentions two weapons at Timothy's disposal: faith and a good conscience (1:19). They seem so important to Paul that he actually repeats them three times in the first letter (1:5, 1:19,and 3:9). Faith or "the" faith is absolute (pistis is used twice in 1:18 – no article in the first usage, but there is one in the second). Faith is complete trust in the finished work of Jesus at the cross. Paul invites and encourages Timothy to hold on tight to belief in the One True God who has the power and will to accomplish all that needs to be accomplished (Romans 4:20-21, Hebrews 11:1-6). "The faith" describes what might be vital Christian belief or basic Christian doctrine. Elsewhere Paul speaks of "the shield of faith" (Ephesians 6:16) that is able to extinguish all the flaming arrows the enemy can fire upon us. Again, Paul seems very intentional about describing a spiritual war that surrounds Timothy. The second weapon given to this young servant leader is a good conscience. We might think of it as a moral compass. A good conscience gives direction. It assists us in finding the right Jesus-following way. What grounds this in the practical world is the mention of two people who had not kept the Apostolic Faith or a good conscience: Hymenaeus and Alexander. We know nearly nothing about these two. We do know that Hymenaeus (assuming this is the same one) is mentioned again in Paul's second letter to Timothy (2 Timothy 2:17) and is falsely teaching that the resurrection has already taken place and destroying the faith of some. It sounds like Paul had the two men excommunicated from the church at Ephesus because they had "rejected" the faith and "shipwrecked" others' faith (1:19-20).

Remember the historical context. All of this is taking place in a city filled with at least fifty gods and goddesses. Temple prostitution and other sexual temptations are all around the city. Christian compromise lurks everywhere. These two men, Hymenaeus and Alexander, are casualties of a very real universal war. They deliberately and decidedly chose a wrong path and they are now missing in action. Don't overlook the point. The Christian life is one surrounded with spiritual combat. The word "rejected" (apotheo) means to walk away from something intentionally, to push away from it deliberately. "Shipwrecked" is an obvious word picture drawn from the life of a sailor. Paul mixes metaphors with military imagery and sailing imagery to make his point abundantly clear. The servant leader's life and ministry is grounded in the thick of battle. The call is to be alert always. Danger is everywhere.

I never experienced the horrors of actual military combat. My father did and some of my students have tasted the bitterness of war. I served, but spent the bulk of my tour stationed in Germany. My commitment included four years active duty as a security policeman in the United States Air Force and two years in the reserves. I entered the service toward the end of the Vietnam War. So many young lives were lost there. So many were wounded and are still recovering from scars that cannot be seen with the human eye. Subsequent wars in Iraq and Afghanistan remind us of this awful truth as well. The Vietnam War personifies the treachery and cunning of a spiritual enemy that is always seeking to masquerade as an angel of light (2 Corinthians 11:14). I have been, for the past thirty-eight years, a combat officer on the front lines of a global spiritual war that makes Vietnam look like a kindergarten playground in terms of devastation and loss of souls. Not to minimize physical war in any way, but to elevate the spiritual kind, this war has eternal consequences. I have witnessed the tactics of the enemy and have been spiritually wounded in combat myself. All true Jesus-followers have been wounded. In the meantime, even though our victory, our D-Day at the cross, assures our ultimate triumph, we go on fighting the good fight (1Timothy 1:18, 6:12). Wise servant leaders remain grateful and guarded. These two mega-truths sustain our commitment as servant leaders. Memorize them. Tuck them into your heart. You will need them.

A Little Manual for Servant Leaders

CHAPTER 3
The Servant Leader's Highest Priority
1 Timothy 2:1-15

"I am of the opinion that we should not be concerned about working for God until we have learned the meaning and the delight of worshiping Him"
(Tozer, A.W. (1985). **Whatever Happened to Worship?** *(p. 12).*
Camp Hill, PA: Christian Publications).

The servant leader's highest priority is not *telling* others what to do. Nor is the highest priority of the servant leader *knowing* what to do. The servant leader's highest priority, bar none, is *intimacy* with God, the vibrant worship of Him day by day. There must be holy space created to know God, to hear His friendly and life-changing voice, and to enter into whole-hearted offerings of praise. Only when our life is marked with worship of Him will He enable us to know what to say and what to do. Here's how Paul described this kind of intimacy to Timothy:

> ¹ *First of all, then, I urge that supplications, prayers, intercessions, and thanksgivings be made for all people,* ² *for kings and all who are in high positions, that we may lead a peaceful and quiet life, godly and dignified in every way.* ³ *This is good, and it is pleasing in the sight of God our Savior,* ⁴ *who desires all people*

to be saved and to come to the knowledge of the truth. [5] *For there is one God, and there is one mediator between God and men, the man Christ Jesus,* [6] *who gave himself as a ransom for all, which is the testimony given at the proper time.* [7] *For this I was appointed a preacher and an apostle (I am telling the truth, I am not lying), a teacher of the Gentiles in faith and truth.*

[8] *I desire then that in every place the men should pray, lifting holy hands without anger or quarreling;* [9] *likewise also that women should adorn themselves in respectable apparel, with modesty and self-control, not with braided hair and gold or pearls or costly attire,* [10] *but with what is proper for women who profess godliness—with good works.* [11] *Let a woman learn quietly with all submissiveness.* [12] *I do not permit a woman to teach or to exercise authority over a man; rather, she is to remain quiet.* [13] *For Adam was formed first, then Eve;* [14] *and Adam was not deceived, but the woman was deceived and became a transgressor.* [15] *Yet she will be saved through childbearing—if they continue in faith and love and holiness, with self-control.*

At the very start, let me warn you about the heading above 1Timothy 2:1 in most of our English Bibles. It typically reads *Instructions on Worship.* It is my contention that Paul is not talking exclusively about Sunday worship or the kind that would bring together a group of believers to honor and praise the Lord at a specific time and place. What Paul seems to have in mind is 24/7 worship, the kind that we are invited into 365 days a year. The life marked by prayer and praise is the one most able to carry out the high responsibility of servant leadership. Tozer, that prophetic voice of the mid-twentieth century, said what I'm trying to say. Read carefully:

> "I mean it when I say that I would rather worship God than to do anything else. You may reply, 'If you worship God you do nothing else.' But that only reveals that you have not done your homework. The beautiful part of worship is that it prepares you and enables you to zero in on the important things

that must be done for God. Listen to me! Practically every great deed done in the church of Christ all the way back to the apostle Paul was done by people blazing with the radiant worship of their God" (1985, p. 18).

My own life journey is one marked with the discovery of the necessity and priority of personal and corporate worship. Worship is the greenhouse for intimacy with God. It provides the just-right-conditions for knowing God and making Him known. There, in that profound place of submission to the one, great, and most deserving God is the servant leader's life most shaped. Paul has two concrete ways in which this intimacy is expressed. Let me identify and reflect on them with you.

First, *prayer is essential to our life of worship as servant leaders* (1Timothy 2:1-7). What Paul has in mind is not just any kind of praying, but the kind that is marked with a global heart. The faithful Apostle "urges" (parakaleo – 2:1) Timothy to pray. This is a strong word marked with the dual meaning of both exhortation and encouragement. "Parakaleo" blends confrontation with comfort. I know that combination sounds strange, even paradoxical. Notice that the Greek word reminds us of the third person in the Godhead, the Holy Spirit (Paraclete or Parakletos). The noun literally describes the Spirit as one who has been "called to someone's side." He is our Comforter or Helper. The word actually is drawn from the ancient Greek courtroom where someone would stand up as an advocate or defender for another. Paul, therefore, is coming up alongside of Timothy and putting his arm around his shoulder and encouraging him to persevere in this life of prayer as worship. The language "first of all" (2:1) is not an attempt to somehow list in importance the various parts of prayer, but rather it is Paul's intention to disclose to Timothy and us what is vitally important in this all-encompassing-kind-of-worship.

Note the various words he uses to explain to Timothy this large life of worship. All four words – supplications, prayers, intercessions, and thanksgivings – are pictures of intimacy with God. Admittedly, these pictures are hard to distinguish from one another. Let me take a swing at it. "Supplications" (deesis – used 19 times in the New Testament) describe the simple activity of praying for specific needs, even or especially our own. "Prayers" (proseuche – used 37 times in the NT) seems to emphasize a general kind of praying that might include requests, but often identifies a particular place of prayer like Jesus in Gethsemane. "Intercessions" (enteuxis – used only two times in the NT) is tough to specify. The background usage describes someone entering into the presence of a king and asking for something. Maybe this word is best thought of in terms of entering into the presence of God boldly and confidently in full assurance that He will hear our petition. "Thanksgivings" (eucharistias – used 15 times in the NT) is a picture of someone praying with a thankful spirit. I don't know if I completely grasp what Paul might be trying to distinguish here, but what I do know is that these four words help to identify this full life of worshipful intimacy. What pulls all four prayer words together is the next line – "be made for everyone." In other words, Paul encourages prayer of all kinds, for all times, for all people. Stop and consider the thought of the implications and especially remember the literary context that includes false-teachers like Hymenaeus and Alexander (1:20)! Prayers should be offered even for them. While we are pausing for a second, also consider the historical context. Nero is on the throne as Rome's Emperor (54 to 68 AD). He was not a leader easy to get along with and was especially hard toward those living the Jesus-following way. Whatever Paul is saying about this invitation into deep intimacy with God, he intended for Timothy to form a large and vibrant life of prayer and to teach others how to do that. Paul wanted Timothy to see the vastness of worship, as if peering into the Grand Canyon not a pot hole.

    The basis for this kind of intimacy is a right understanding of God. That's why Paul took time to offer some practical advice about prayer. He says there are at least three reasons for cultivating this kind of worshipful life (2:3-4). First, it gives *peace* a chance, especially in relationship with others. Second, it is *good*. Some things are good simply because they find their prompting in the heart of God and encourage peace. Third, it pleases God. The key, however, is not located in the practical prayer wisdom, but in the rich, deep, and large God-talk that Paul offers here. He speaks of "God our Savior" (2:3), "one God" (2:5), and "one mediator" (2:5). God, according to Paul, is in the salvation business, not in simply getting us to heaven or having heaven come to us (Revelation 21:2). God lovingly labors non-stop to reclaim the world – all of it – that was lost in the fall as told in Genesis 3. God is putting all of creation back together – our relationship with Him, His relationship with us; our relationship with others, their relationship with us; our relationship with creation, and its relationship with us. He is an all-purpose God. Because of this one true Savior and mediator, mankind is not an animal. God has created us in His image. Nature is not the ultimate authority. God alone is sovereign. Mankind is not inherently good. That distinction is reserved for God alone. We are fallen and fractured people in need of universal restoration. Progress is not inevitable. Science and technology will not win the day. Man has a purpose in God alone, by Christ alone, through faith alone. Worship marked by a healthy life of prayer is the place to begin for the servant leader who longs for intimacy with God.

No one can enter the life of a servant leader and not face some criticism, hurt, or even persecution. It is so easy to lose sight of the power of prayer to keep us attached to the one life-giving God. I have sometimes wondered about the hurtful words that people like Hymenaeus and Alexander might have thrown Timothy's way. I have been on the receiving end of poisonous anonymous letters. Voice messages have been left for me full of anger and hate. I have been assaulted with confrontational and accusing words by people who thought my preaching was in error. I once had an intoxicated man challenge me to a duel at the close of a Sunday morning worship service. It is so easy to forget 24/7 worship shaped by prayer. Prayer, the kind balanced with speaking and listening, is the line of communication that keeps us in direct contact with our Savior. Remember what we are exploring. The servant leader's highest priority is intimacy with God. Prayer is essential to that kind of life.

Second, ***praise is essential to our life of worship as servant leaders*** (2:8-15). Not just any kind of praise, but the kind that unites all believers. Now, this is perhaps one of the stickiest and thorniest sections of Scripture in the New Testament. A hermeneutical lesson might be in order before we try and make our way through the tall grass. First, all Biblical texts are bigger than any of us. This recognition requires a spirit of humility. Proper interpretation always begins here. Second, we must pay careful attention to the literary and historical "horizons" that shape Paul's instructions to Timothy. So many questions have to be asked. What is Paul really saying here? What's his purpose? Why is he saying it at this point in the letter? How did Timothy and the Christians in Ephesus understand this section of Paul's letter? What are the implications and applications for twenty-first century readers? How does this passage relate to other parallel passages (especially Galatians 3:28 and 1 Corinthians 14:33-35)? Not all of this can be answered here. For now, please don't overlook the obvious fact that praise is intended to unite men and women. Men are to praise God by lifting holy hands in prayer without anger and disputing (2:8), and women are to praise Him by dressing and living ("with good deeds" – 2:10) appropriately. Paul is not discouraging women from praying in public. 1 Corinthians 11:5 implies that women did pray and speak in public worship. So, why does Paul address the issue of outward appearance first? Before answering that question, let's do a little more background reflection.

Do you remember those fifty gods and goddesses I spoke of earlier that saturated the culture of Ephesus? The historical context invites us to recall that Ephesus was the religious center of the Roman Empire housing the infamous Temple of Artemis/Diana. The cult of Artemis/Diana was a female-led religion. The priests were all women! Scholars have debated for years the level of influence that kind of religious leadership and pluralism has on a culture. What we do know is that "in Christ" there is freedom (1 Corinthians 8:1-11:1 and Galatians 5:1ff), colossal freedom. Some Bible students have concluded that newly discovered freedom in Christ, shaped by a dominant female religious culture, invited openness toward speaking up in public worship. Some, overlooking this religious context, have suggested that women who never had a voice before, now in Christ, had discovered they too had total access to the Father and could know Him just as intimately, and therefore had something valuable to share in church. Others simply hear Paul's admonition for women not to speak in worship gatherings and overlook everything else he said.

Wherever we land in our interpretation of this passage, we must never forget that God designed men and women not only to carry out unique roles, but to share in complete access to Him. After all, part of what it means to be human beings is that we share in being created in God's image (Imago Dei – Genesis 1:27). Both are to pursue God's global purposes with equal passion. As image bearers of God, both men and women are called to know God and to make Him known. I so gravitate toward the wisdom and insight of Carolyn Custis James. In a remarkable book, *Half the Church,* she explores God's global place for women. Toward the close of her writing she reflects on this passage. Her words are helpful.

> "Since the late twentieth century two polarized groups – complementarians and egalitarians – have defined the evangelical landscape for women, particularly in the West. The debate between the two groups creates a fault line that runs straight through the body of Christ...Complementarians believe the Bible establishes male authority over women, making male leadership the biblical standard...Egalitarians believe that leadership is not determined by gender but by the gifting and calling of the Holy Spirit, and that God calls all believers to sub-

mit to one another...This stalemate, at the very least, ought to inject a hefty dose of humility into the discussion...Dr. John Stackhouse, a world-class evangelical scholar and a man who has served in both camps, arrived at a similar conclusion with what he describes as 'paradigm-shaking force.' After extensive research on 1Timothy 2:11-15, a passage he describes as 'easily one of the most obscure of the classic passages on this matter,' he writes, 'I remember quite clearly now – more than twenty years later – putting the book down on my lap and realizing this insight: Nobody could explain this passage.' The best scholars (even while tilting to one or the other side of this debate" will tell you these are complex passages and that it's a hermeneutical best practice to build your theological system on clear texts rather than passages that are subject to dispute" (2011, p. 154-156).

According to Paul, we must never stray too far from the creation story. Adam was created first and then Eve (2:13). I'm well aware of the explosive nature of that one idea. Ironically, so much division and hateful speech have shaped the way we hear Paul's words. Whatever we think of Paul, he was not, as some suggest, a male chauvinist marked by control issues. He was a man called by God, with apostolic authority, giving spiritual direction to a young servant leader in need of Biblical and practical assistance.

Back to our question: Why does Paul address the issue of a woman's outward appearance first, especially in a worship context? My study has led me to the following conclusion. Paul was always sensitive to Christian witness (Romans 1:16, 1 Corinthians 4:1, 2 Corinthians 4:5, Galatians 5:6, Ephesians 5:15, Philippians 1:18, Colossians 4:5-6, 1 Thessalonians 4:11-12, 2 Thessalonians 3:1, 1 Timothy 4:12, 2 Timothy 2:2, Titus 2:9-10, and Philemon 6). Every place he was sent and every letter he wrote was branded with his sensitivity toward those who did not know the Gospel and his passionate desire to win as many souls as possible (1 Corinthians 9:19-23). His concern in Ephesus is clear to me. He did not want pagan religious practices or unholy habits strolling into the church. I'm concluding that the Gospel had won some of the temple priestesses to Christ. As my friend, Jim Connolly, once remarked to me about this text, "God did not want a counterfeit practice walking its way into the life of the newly established church in Ephesus." The female leaders of the Artemis/Diana religious cult had distinctive dress, hairstyles, and general appearances. Paul did not want Christian women confused with temple priestesses. Even if the Gospel did not penetrate a single heart in the Artemis/Diana group, which I find hard to believe, Paul instructed Timothy to encourage Christian women to present themselves in a way that was Jesus-honoring. Look at some of the vivid language.

Paul specifically wanted women to "adorn themselves" with appropriate dress (2:9a – kosmeo). Their outward appearance, that is their "cosmetic" look, should not draw attention. He used two words to describe what every Christian woman was and is to aim for: "modesty and self-control" (2:9a – aidos and sophrosune). It is exegetically difficult to distinguish these words in Greek. They function as synonyms. Paul seemed to elevate a kind of female dress that would not embarrass the cause of Christ. He wanted Christian women to avoid any kind of appearance that might be sexually suggestive or sensual, any kind of adornment that might link those women to what happened at the infamous Temple of Artemis/Diana. His point is crystal clear – no clothes should be worn that would bring shame on the name of Jesus. Paul focused specifically on "braided hair" and expensive jewelry and clothing (2:9b). There is nothing inherently wrong with stylish hair, gold, pearls, or nice clothing. The problem surfaces when they become cultural symbols of prostitution and/or materialism. Paul emphasized the need for Christian character displayed through "good works" (2:10). This kind of practical witness is an act of worship according to the ever wise Apostle. The Bible does not advocate that a woman look like a "plain Jane" or "sad Sally." Apologies if your name is Jane or Sally. If the Bride of Christ, His church, is described as "beautifully dressed for her husband" then surely there is some grace and freedom in choosing jewelry and clothing that is not expensive, not extravagant, and not vain (Revelation 21:2). After all, "charm is deceitful, and beauty is vain; but a woman who fears the LORD is to be praised" (Proverbs 31:30). Whether it involved speaking or dressing, Paul did not want the newly established church of Christ to be confused with the ancient temple of Artemis/Diana.

The last verse of this section (2:15) is equally difficult to interpret. Whatever Paul was suggesting to Timothy about women and childbearing, he was not advocating a works-righteousness that made having babies a means through which women could be saved. That kind of thinking would violate the very essence of the Gospel. Childbearing is hard enough, ask any woman who has delivered a baby, without adding to it some morbid interpretation that has a woman at home, barefoot, and pregnant in order to be in a right relationship with God. Instead, Paul seems to be reminding us of a colossal Biblical truth. It was through the birth of a child, the Child, that the entire course of the universe was changed. Our Savior, in the fullness of time, was "born of a woman, born under the law, to redeem those who were under the law, so that we might receive adoption as sons" (and daughters – Galatians 4:4-5).

We began this exploration with a significant premise. A servant leader's highest priority is intimacy with God. The God-given duet of prayer and praise wrapped in a life of worship moves every Jesus-follower further and further into intimacy with Him. The most intimate communion with God is the one shaped through prayer and praise. Give yourself to the pursuit of Him wholeheartedly. Let the cultivation of life with Him be your supreme focus. Because of God's perfect design in the creation order, men have been given a sacred place of servant leadership, not selfish lordship. Women too have been given a sacred place of supreme service, not second-class subservience. Together, we are image bearers of

Him and invited into the very presence of God in order to know Him, to love Him, to worship Him, and, of course, to witness to Him. This intimacy, only possible through the mediation of Jesus Christ, is the servant leader's highest priority. Praise His Name.

A Little Manual for Servant Leaders

CHAPTER 4
What Does a Servant Leader Look Like?
1 Timothy 3:1-13

"At length they saw a man coming, of a low stature, bald on the head, crooked thighs, handsome legs, hollow-eyed; had a crooked nose; full of grace; for sometimes he appeared as a man, sometimes he had the countenance of an angel"
(Wake, William and Lardner, Nathaniel. (1996).
"Acts of Paul and Thecla." **Apocryphal New Testament.** *(p. 113).*
Whitefish, Montana: Kessinger Publishing).

I have often joked with students that Paul might have looked a little like Yoda of *Star Wars* fame. I have a twelve inch version of Yoda made of rubber that I found at some neighborhood garage sale. I've placed a Jewish kippah (sometimes called a "yarmulke") on the top of his bald head. My wife doesn't much care for it, but it paints a sweet picture for me that I like pondering. Regardless of what Paul looked like, God, in His colossal wisdom, saw the need to describe for us what a servant leader should look like. The passage in front of us is the ideal place to examine this portrait. The following words represent Paul's view of the mature servant leader:

¹ The saying is trustworthy: If anyone aspires to the office of overseer, he desires a noble task. ² Therefore an overseer must be above reproach, the husband of one wife, sober-minded, self-controlled, respectable, hospitable, able to teach, ³ not a drunkard, not violent but gentle, not quarrelsome, not a lover of money. ⁴ He must manage his own household well, with all dignity keeping his children submissive, ⁵ for if someone does not know how to manage his own household, how will he care for God's church? ⁶ He must not be a recent convert, or he may become puffed up with conceit and fall into the condemnation of the devil. ⁷ Moreover, he must be well thought of by outsiders, so that he may not fall into disgrace, into a snare of the devil.

⁸ Deacons likewise must be dignified, not double-tongued, not addicted to much wine, not greedy for dishonest gain. ⁹ They must hold the mystery of the faith with a clear conscience. ¹⁰ And let them also be tested first; then let them serve as deacons if they prove themselves blameless. ¹¹ Their wives likewise must be dignified, not slanderers, but sober-minded, faithful in all things. ¹² Let deacons each be the husband of one wife, managing their children and their own households well. ¹³ For those who serve well as deacons gain a good standing for themselves and also great confidence in the faith that is in Christ Jesus.

Perhaps a second reading of the verses above would be appropriate. I'll leave that up to you. For now, grasp the big picture. There are clearly two distinctive functions for servant leaders. Some function as shepherd-servants fulfilling large oversight (3:1-7). Others function as practical-servants completing specific tasks (3:8-15). Before we explore the contours of Paul's vision for the servant leader, let's identify the three shepherding terms that occur in the New Testament.

The first term to show up in 1 Timothy 3:1 is "overseer" (episkopos). The origin of the word comes from the ancient Greek city-state culture. It has often been translated "bishop" (King James Version, New American Bible, Amplified, Revised Standard, etc). Eugene Peterson, in

The Message, simply uses the term "leader." The picture originally described someone who was in charge or led city government. We might think of a person who served as a municipal officer or city supervisor. The New Testament elsewhere uses this word to speak of elders at Ephesus (Acts 20:28), leaders at Philippi (Philippians 1:1), some partnering with Titus at Crete (Titus 1:7), and our Lord and Savior (1 Peter 2:25). The ones I've listed for you are the only five occurrences.

The second term for elder is "presbuteros." You can hear our English word "Presbyterian" in the Greek word. Maybe that paints a picture for you. What you may already know is that this particular term comes out of the Jewish synagogue. A "prebuteros" was an older, seasoned, and spiritually mature leader. No qualifying age was ever given as far as I know. Scripture does use this term far more than "episkopos" or overseer. Some 66 occurrences are located throughout the New Testament. Sometimes it is used in the Gospels to point to the religious leaders in First Century Palestinian culture (Matthew 27:1, 3, 12, 20, 41; Mark 14:43 and 53; Luke 7:3, 9:22, 20:1; John 8:9, etc). "Presbuteros" is found throughout Acts and Revelation (consider Acts 15:2, 4, 6, 8, 22-23, and Revelation 5:5, 6, and 8). It is the very word James uses to describe one of the functions of these leaders in the life of the early church. When someone was sick, he was to call the "elders" of the church "and let them pray over him, anointing him with oil in the name of the Lord" (James 5:14). Specifically, in 1Timothy it shows up four times (5:1, 2, 17, 19) where Paul, on one hand, is speaking of older men in general (5:1-2) and, on the other hand, of particular spiritual leaders in the church at Ephesus (5:17-19). This is the very term John uses of himself in 2 John 1:2 and 3 John 1:2.

The third term is "pastor" or "shepherd" (poimen). Like "episkopos," "poimen" finds its origin in Greek culture, particularly in the area of agriculture. Travelers today can still see this ancient term in contemporary practice throughout places like Greece and Turkey. It may very well be the most beautiful and poetic of the three terms for elder/leader. This one simply implies caring for God's people like a shepherd with his sheep. It is predominantly located in the Gospels (fourteen times), but is also found in three other significant places – Ephesians 4:11, Hebrews 13:20, and 1 Peter 2:25 (note how both "overseer" and "shepherd" occur in the same 1 Peter passage to speak of Jesus). It does not occur in any of the three Pastoral Epistles. Now we can explore what Paul desired Timothy to grasp in 1 Timothy 3:1-13.

J. Oswald Sanders' *Spiritual Leadership* (1986) is a masterfully written book on the character required of all servant leaders. In a chapter entitled "Pauline Sidelights on Leadership" he lists six categories worth noting. These include social, moral, mental, personality, domestic, and maturity qualifications. My approach here might seem rather boring next to Sanders' superb slant, but allow me to attempt to label these six in a more rudimentary manner: positive traits for shepherding leaders, negative traits for shepherding leaders, positive traits for serving leaders, negative traits for serving leaders, positive traits for female servant leaders, and negative traits for female servant leaders.

1. Positive Traits for Shepherding Leaders.

Let's observe two preliminary statements before getting into the list of positive traits for shepherding leaders. First, notice with me that the sage Apostle calls what he is about to unfold to Timothy a "trustworthy saying." It is reliable. Remember, this is the second time we've heard this kind of talk (1:15). Second, Paul underscores a significant "heart" statement. He says, "If anyone *aspires* (orego) to the office of overseer, he desires a noble task" (3:1). There is a sacred hunger or pure desire elevated by Paul. He is not describing a person marked with self-ambition, but rather someone convinced by the Holy Spirit to serve the church. This leader is under some kind of divine compulsion. Paul's instruction to Timothy seems to be, "Look for the guy who has a holy conviction to shepherd God's flock." The word he uses to describe this kind of passion

What Does a Servant Leader Look Like?

for servant leadership literally means, "to stretch out your hand for it." A "want-to" is required. No arm-twisting or begging to lead is necessary. Apparently, there has been a Spirit-prompted recognition by the servant leader that this shepherding work includes a real giftedness, a passion for doing it, and a keen awareness of God's calling to care for His people. This servant leader is a volunteer, not a draftee.

In addition, Paul lists ten traits that mark this volunteer. Seven of them are located in 3:2, while the other three are found in 3:3, 3:4, and 3:7.

- *"above reproach"* – (anepilempton) the shepherd must be a person whose walk with Jesus is faithful and consistent. Paul is not speaking of perfection, but of on-going attachment to Jesus. The idea here is that a false accusation won't stick to the life of the servant leader. He is clothed with spiritual Kevlar.
- *"the husband of one wife"* – literally, Paul is saying this shepherd must be a "one-woman-man." I always smile when I think of what Paul is saying. It sounds like a country-western song. The clear point is that the servant leader must be faithful to his wife. So much argument and division has occurred over this one line. Some have suggested that a non-married man cannot be an overseer. Some have suggested that a divorced man, regardless of the circumstances, cannot be an overseer. Some would want to add "divorced and remarried" as the qualifying factor for elimination. Others have suggested that a polygamist cannot be an overseer, even though no evidence exists of early Christians practicing polygamy. Still others hear in this trait that a widowed man cannot be an acceptable shepherd. Whatever is being said here, I think the clearest and plainest interpretation is the best. Paul wants this servant leader to be exemplary (not perfect) in his marriage and family life.
- *"sober-minded"* – (nephalios) this word describes someone who is clear-headed, not fuzzy in his thinking. It only occurs here, 3:11 and Titus 2:2.

- *"self-controlled"* – (sophron) this is a picture of a person who is inwardly disciplined. He has, over a period of time, cultivated a life that is mastered by the Master.
- *"respectable"* – (kosmios) we have seen this word, or at least its stem, earlier in the letter (2:9 – "dress modestly"). Paul wants the outward life of this servant leader to be commendable. It contrasts nicely with the inward trait of self-control. I like thinking of this trait as exemplifying what a Christian gentleman would look like.
- *"hospitable"* – (philoxenia) speaks of a servant leader who is literally a "lover of strangers." The early church was constantly called upon to open their homes to traveling preachers, teachers, and followers of the Way. Because of the dangerous and immoral conditions that often existed in ancient inns or hotels, the safest and wisest place to stay overnight was in the home of a Jesus-follower. The overseer was to lead in this concrete act of love.
- *"able to teach"* – (didaktikos) underscores the required teaching gift of a shepherd. Nothing is said of how this particular trait could be portrayed. Some shepherds are able to teach in large group settings. Others find their giftedness and personalities best suited for small groups or one to one discipleship. The important piece here is that this servant leader has the ability to open Scripture, explain it well, and make appropriate applications to the life of the person being taught.
- *"gentle"* – (epieikeia) is a trait that might best be described as someone with a sweet spirit. Here is a servant leader who is able to get along with others well.
- *"manage his own household well, with all dignity keeping his children submissive"* – John Stott, in his superb commentary (*The Message of 1 Timothy and Titus*. (1996). pp. 97-98) calls this "domestic discipline." Here is a servant leader who is the priest-pastor in his home. He lives out the Jesus-following life in the most vital place of ministry. He is the same person in the privacy of his home that he is in the public life of the local church.

Because his leadership is exemplary behind closed doors, his wife and children love and respect him.

"be well thought of by outsiders" – non-believers respect this servant leader. What those outside of the family of God think of our leaders should matter. Paul is vitally interested in public opinion when it comes to shepherds of the Lord's flock (see Colossians 4:5 and 1 Thessalonians 4:11-12).

2. *Negative Traits for Shepherding Leaders.*

Without hesitation, Paul unpacks five negative traits that shepherding leaders must avoid. Four of these are located in 3:3, while one is located in 3:6. Some have observed in their study and reflection of these verses that all Christians should avoid these unseemly characteristics. True. However, there are those chosen by the Spirit and the local church to model all of the positive traits particularly and to lead out in avoiding all of the negative ones.

- *"not a drunkard"* – here again the Apostle does not say more than is necessary. He is not prohibiting alcohol consumption. He is condemning drunkenness. There is a difference. I know that many, like me, chose not to drink alcohol of any kind either because of their propensity toward addictive behavior or simply a holy decision of conscience. Regardless, moderation seems to be the important factor here. After all, the ever-caring Paul instructed Timothy to "stop drinking only water, and use a little wine because of your stomach and your frequent illnesses" (1 Timothy 5:23). In a culture that is prone to over-indulgence of various kinds, it would seem wise for the servant leader to model a consistent life of self-control with food and especially with drink. At a deeply personal level, I am fascinated by how Paul seems to be intentional in placing this prohibition alongside the ability to teach (3:2). The servant leader filled with the Spirit rather than alcohol is a useful instrument in the mighty hands of God.

- *"not violent"* – note the connection with the previous prohibition. People consumed with intoxicating drink are sometimes prone to a life of violence. This kind of destructive behavior does not fit the Jesus-following life. The servant leader useful for Kingdom purposes is not a bully. He does not think with his fists, but with a Jesus-saturated mind. His first reaction when disagreement ensues is not to punch another human being, but to understand before being understood.

- *"not quarrelsome"* – his pattern of servant leadership does not include trying to dominate others with words. This trait is in complete contrast to those false teachers who have attempted to infiltrate the church in Ephesus. Paul told Timothy that these counterfeit leaders have "an unhealthy interest in controversies and quarrels about words that result in envy, strife, malicious talk…(1Timothy 6:4). The servant leader who would shepherd God's sheep uses words to build up rather than tear down. He "leads…beside still waters" (Psalm 23:2).

- *"not a lover of money"* – simply put, this servant leader is not materialistic. He is not driven by a consumer mind set. His heart has been captured by the love of Christ. He does not think that "godliness is a means to financial gain" (1Timothy 6:5). The shepherd is well aware that "the love of money is a root of all kinds of evil" and knows its seductive lure, causing some to wander from the faith (1Timothy 6:10).

- *"not be a recent convert"* – (neophytes) those who desire the work of a shepherding servant leader are not brand new babies in Christ. They are seasoned. They have some spiritual roots. They have traveled with Jesus for a while. No age is identified by Paul. Some reach a level of trusted maturity sooner than others.

3. Positive Traits for Serving Leaders.

Before we begin our conversation about serving leaders, let's pause to reflect on the specific word Paul uses here. I know for some this word can be confusing. The word Paul inserts in 1Timothy 3:8 for a serving leader is "deacon" (diakonos). Remember the word for a shepherding leader in 3:1 is "overseer" (episkopos). Both are portraits of servant leadership. Both are vital to the life and witness of healthy congregations. The

What Does a Servant Leader Look Like?

deacon servant leader is entrusted with specific ministry tasks. Think of Acts 6:1-6 and the need for wise and Holy Spirit filled leaders to distribute food for the widows in Jerusalem. Seven servant leaders were chosen to "serve tables" (6:2). In contrast, the overseer servant leader is entrusted with the care of people, especially as that care relates to the Word and prayer (Acts 6:4). Think of Acts 20:17-38 and Paul's admonition to the Ephesian elders at Miletus. His mandate to them was to "be shepherds of the church of God" (20:28). I more than realize that there is a large debate among Bible students as to which of these words, "elder" or "deacon," best describes the role of vocational evangelist, minister, preacher, pastor, etc. The New Testament, I believe, gives us some freedom and flexibility. Some will even disagree with that premise. Regardless, my personal study has led me to the current conclusion that "elder" best describes the teacher/pastor, as long as this person serves alongside other elders. Some elders are paid and some are not (1Timothy 5:17-18). The N.T. seems to point us toward a plurality of elders in each local church. Ultimately, titles or labels are not important. Glory to God and healthy local churches trump titles. With that background, it is important to include one last item. There are six unique Greek words used in the New Testament for servant. A brief summary follows:

- Huperetes: originally described a slave who helped row a ship.
- Oiketas: referred to someone who worked as a household servant.
- Leitourgos: painted a picture of someone who served in the temple.
- Therapon: pointed to someone who served with dignity.
- Doulas: described a servant without rights or privileges. This is by far the most common of the five words in the New Testament and the one Paul often used of himself.
- Diakonos: literally referred to a servant who "waited on tables."

Now, back to 1Timothy 3. Paul includes six positive characteristics for deacons (3:8, 3:9, and 3:12).

47

- *"dignified"* – (semnos) elevates the idea of serving leaders who are dignified in their service or ministry. We are not talking about a Gloomy Gus, but a person who recognizes the truth of genuinely living out his faith. His behavior honors the Lord he serves.
- *"sincere"* – (dilogos) is one of those words in the New Testament that reminds us of the importance of our speech. Servant leaders seek always to be honest in what they say. Old school preachers often thought of "sincere" leaders as not "double-tongued." The leader means what he says and says what he means.
- *"hold the mystery of the faith with a clear conscience"* – describes for us a serving leader who is grounded in the Word. These deacons have embraced the mystery of the Gospel – Jesus' willingness to live in each believer. Their faith is not shaky. Contrast this trait with the description of false leaders who have not held on to faith and a good conscience, but have rejected sound Biblical instruction and shipwrecked their faith (1Timothy 1:19).
- *"first be tested"* – is profoundly sound advice and describes for us a period of scrutiny and examination. Here Paul calls Timothy to screen, to interview, and closely to monitor the initial probationary period of a serving leader. No time allotment is presented. The Holy Spirit can and will give guidance.
- *"husband of but one wife"* – points us back to 1Timothy 3:2. What is true of the overseer is true of the deacon.
- *"manage his children and his household well"* – this characteristic takes us back to 3:5. Both the shepherding leader and the serving leader are commissioned with the holy work of steering their homes and families in the way of Jesus.

4. Negative Traits for Serving Leaders.

There are three negative traits for deacons. Two of the three characteristics have already been discussed.

- *"not addicted to much wine"* – is addressed in 3:3 under "not given to drunkenness."
- *"not double-tongued"* – (diligos) the NIV translates this phrase as

"sincere." It is one of those words in the New Testament that reminds us of the importance of our speech. Servant leaders seek to always be honest in what they say. The authentic leader means what he says and says what he means.

- *"not pursuing dishonest gain"* – is discussed in 3:3 under "not a lover of money."

5. Positive Traits for Female Serving Leaders.

There are three positive traits listed by Paul for Timothy's consideration and instruction to female serving leaders. The word Paul uses here for deacons' wives has also been debated and discussed by Bible students. Some have suggested that Paul is not creating a special function here, but rather recognizing the simple truth that husbands and wives in love with Jesus serve side by side. I agree with the fact that Christian husbands and wives are yoked together in service, but it seems more likely to me, in light of the parallel between 3:8 and 3:11, that Paul is describing for us a unique function in the early church. If this were a simple reference to wives, why wouldn't he have done the same thing for elders and their spouses? It would have been so much easier for later interpreters if Paul had incorporated the same word he inserts in Romans 16:1 when describing Phoebe – "a servant (deaconess) of the church in Cenchrea." Maybe the ever-eager Paul intended to say something directly to wives and deaconesses. These female serving leaders, however we understand their role, have a legitimate place of leadership and, therefore, have specific character traits expected of them (3:11).

- *"dignified"* – recalls for us the serving leader's trait in 3:8. These women are to be just as dignified in their behavior as their male counterparts.
- *"sober-minded"* – references us back to the overseer in 3:2. Like the male shepherding leader, the female serving leader is to be marked with clear thinking.
- *"faithful in all things"* – summarizes a Jesus-following life that is absolutely saturated with integrity. The women being described by

Paul to Timothy can be trusted in any and every ministry situation.

6. Negative Traits for Female Serving Leaders.

Here is our final category. There is only one negative trait mentioned by the Apostle (3:11). This one characteristic may very well take us back to our discussion in 2:11 and the influence of the Artemis/Diana religious cult.

- *"not slanderers"* – invites us into a reflection on spiritual warfare. "Slanderer" or a malicious is a word linked to the noun "diabolos" or accuser (Satan), one of the names given to our enemy. The female serving leader is not someone who uses her words to accuse or attack. She disciplines her tongue and is fully aware of the challenges surrounding its control. "It is a restless evil, full of deadly poison" (James 3:8).

Let's make some final observations about these six lists. It is so easy to become overwhelmed by the detail of Paul's counsel to Timothy. I, perhaps like you, have spent a great deal of time studying, praying, and reflecting on these various leadership qualities. My constant question, beyond "what does this mean," has been "so what?" Why does this matter? What is at stake here? Perhaps these seven concluding observations will help:

Some servant leaders are called and gifted toward watching over the welfare of God's people. Thank God that, in His Divine wisdom, He saw the need to raise up godly leaders who could shepherd, protect, feed, guide, and provide for His flock.

Some servant leaders are called and gifted toward meeting practical needs of people. Praise God that, in His Divine wisdom, He raised up godly leaders who could address various needs that would arise among His children. What a great partnership between shepherding leaders and serving leaders.

- All of these servant leaders have characteristics that portray leadership maturity.

- These servant leadership lists were and are intended to help the church find the right people for the right places of service. Whatever Paul intended in passing them along to Timothy, he did not intend for them to be reduced to a "check list."
- Biblical leaders are, first and foremost, men and women soaked in Christian character.
- The chief objective of any Christian leader is to bring glory to God and bless His church. This is of utmost importance in any conversation about servant leadership.
- A Christian leader is someone who looks like Jesus in skin like ours. I'm constantly reminded of this when I read the cherished words of John Stott. His concluding paragraph is worthy of our attention. Consider our focusing question for this chapter one last time. What does a servant leader look like?

"The whole first half of this chapter (3:1-13) is a good example of the balance of Scripture. For, there is material here both to encourage the right people to offer for pastoral ministry and to discourage the wrong ones from doing so. The discouragement is that the required standards are high and the task is arduous. The responsibility of caring for 'God's church' is calculated to daunt the best and the most gifted Christians. But the corresponding encouragement is that the pastorate is a noble task, a beautiful undertaking, a laudable ambition. It involves giving oneself to the service of others. Besides, the words *episkopos* and *diakonos* are both applied to the Lord Jesus in the New Testament. Peter called Him 'the Shepherd and Overseer (*episkopos*) of your souls' (1 Peter 2:25), and he applied to Himself the verb *diakonein* (Mark 10:44-45). Could there be any greater honor than to follow in His footsteps and share in some of His *episcope* and *diakonia* which He is willing to delegate to us?" (*The Message of 1Timothy and Titus,* p. 102.)

A Little Manual for Servant Leaders

CHAPTER 5

Servant Leadership Paradoxes
1 Timothy 3:14-16

"Without churches so filled with the power of God that they can't help but spill goodness and peace and love and joy into the world, depravity will win the day; evil will flood the world. But it doesn't have to be that way. Strong, growing communities of faith can turn the tide of history. They can! Don't bother looking elsewhere. The church is it"
(Hybels, Bill. (2002). **Courageous Leadership.** *(p. 22).*
Grand Rapids: Zondervan).

I love the church. I really do. Even during my prodigal years, I never got so far away that I rejected her entirely. Yes, I judged her. Yes, I considered her out of touch. Yes, I doubted her effectiveness, but inevitably I came to embrace her as the imperfect Bride of Christ and the only hope for this fractured world. One of the most soul-shaping experiences in my young adult life was attending Lincoln Christian College, now Lincoln Christian University. Fresh out of the military and eager to get on with my life, I began the extensive journey of preparation for life-long ministry. Among the many professors and classes, one instructor and one course will forever standout. Charles Mills, an exceptional church history professor, taught a stuffy semester-long class called *Early Christian Centuries*. It was dreaded and feared. He was known for difficult exams and challenging questions. To describe Professor Mills as passionate is an understatement of gigantic proportions. He was a fifty-five gallon barrel of Red Bull. Think of him as a caffeinated Goliath. His bald head and rotund body made him look like a walking lighthouse. This man loved the church. So he began his memorable class in a baritone rich and strongly punctuated voice with, "I love the church." He would then commence reciting for us the old American hymn *I Love Thy Kingdom, Lord* by Timothy Dwight, grandson of Jonathan Edwards. Here are some of the words.

> I love Thy kingdom, Lord,
> The house of Thine abode,
> The church our blessed Redeemer saved
> With His own precious blood.
>
> I love Thy church, O God.
> Her walls before Thee stand,
> Dear as the apple of Thine eye,
> And written on Thy hand.
> (1968, # 313)

Unforgettable. I can still see Professor Mills' red face and neck as he unfolded in front of us his unembarrassed affection for the church. I think Paul felt the same way. Case in point. There is a tiny section at the close of 1Timothy 3 that often is overlooked when it comes to conversation about servant leadership. Found in this three-verse treasure are three magnificent descriptions of God's church. Behind each one is a servant leader paradox. Paul writes the following:

> [14] *I hope to come to you soon, but I am writing these things to you so that,* [15] *if I delay, you may know how one ought to behave in the household of God, which is the church of the living God, a pillar and buttress of the truth.* [16] *Great indeed, we confess, is the mystery of godliness: He was manifested in the flesh,*

vindicated by the Spirit, seen by angels, proclaimed among the nations, believed on in the world, taken up in glory.

According to the Apostle, he hoped to travel to Ephesus in order to be with Timothy (3:14), but, in the meantime, he wanted to offer some sound instruction on how Christians were to conduct themselves in *God's household* (3:15). The image or metaphor of the church as a household introduces the first paradox: ***Servant Leaders love God's household even though sometimes she acts like a dysfunctional family.*** Remember that a paradox is an upside-down truth. When a paradox is first encountered, one wonders if it is really true. Household (oikos) is one of those ordinary words that sometimes get used to describe extraordinary circumstances. A household is simply a word for a building or a family in a building. It paints a picture of people and places. When I was a child, we were taught a rhyme that went like this: "Here's the church, here's the steeple, look inside and see all of the people." We learned hand gestures that coordinated with the words. I can still recall the memory of making people appear inside a church with my little fingers. This same family image is sprinkled throughout 1Timothy 3. It shows up in 3:5, 3:12, and here in 3:15 – translated "household." Don't miss the obvious. If people were perfect, Paul would not need to advise Timothy on how they were to conduct themselves in the life of the church. Genuine servant leaders embrace and care for an imperfect people. Scripture never portrays the church as perfect, but it does remind us that God's household is priceless (Ephesians 5:25-32). Ironically, the church can be a very dysfunctional family.

Once again, the larger context of 1Timothy describes for us the imperfection of the church at Ephesus. False doctrine abounded (1:3, 4:1, 6:3), distracting conversations were everywhere (1:4, 1:6, 6:4), legalistic teachings were epidemic (4:3), and some were wandering from the faith (1:6, 6:21). Paul clearly marks out for this young servant leader the difference between godly living and the ungodly kind (1:9-10, 6:11).

It seems fashionable these days to bad-mouth the church. Some critics only see the dysfunctional nature of God's household. They describe her as hypocritical, judgmental, out of touch, anti-homosexual, dull, and deeply insensitive to the surrounding culture. I won't defend her imperfections. There are those who attempt to define for us accurately what some are saying about the church. David Kinnaman, in his well-researched book, *You Lost Me*, documents with sobering detail why some young Christians are leaving the church:

> "A generation of young Christians believes that the churches in which they were raised are not safe and hospitable places to express doubts. Many feel that they have been offered slick or half-baked answers to their thorny, honest questions, and they are rejecting the "talking heads" and "talking points" they see among the older generations. *You Lost Me* signals their judgment that the institutional church has failed them" (2011, p. 11).

Regardless of whether you accept that criticism or not, the church has never been described by the writers of the New Testament as perfect. Even an elementary reading of Paul's Letters to various congregations scattered throughout the Roman Empire will verify the church's lack of maturity. She is, however, God's greatest instrument for changing the world. I am filled with hope. Are you? I'm not arguing for a pie-in-the-sky view of the church nor am I hoisting a white flag in hopeless surrender to the culture. What I'm trying to share with you is the strangeness of the church. It is a paradox of gigantic proportions to acknowledge the malfunction of God's household while still holding on to her potential and promise. Servant leaders cling to that upside down truth.

There is a second paradox based on these three verses that servant leaders claim. ***Servant leaders love the church of the living God even though sometimes she appears dead.*** This second metaphor, located in 1Timothy 3:15 – ***church of the living God*** – is drawn from Old Testament imagery. The Hebrew Scriptures faithfully remind the reader that Yahweh is living and not dead (Deuteronomy 5:26, Joshua 3:10, 2 Kings 19:4 & 16, and Psalms 84:2). This essential characteristic of God was and is foundational for the Christian faith. God alone is able to care for all that He has created and to save it entirely because of who He is. His church is living because He is living. Whenever the church has a low opinion of God, it sinks to abysmal depths. Whenever the church has a high opinion of God, it is raised to mountaintop possibilities. I know it can sound heady to say that God lives in an eternal now, but it is true. Bring out the aspirin, but let this single truth be buried deep within the heart and mind of the servant leader. Our God is alive and well, and, therefore, He is able to sustain His church. The word that Paul uses here for church is drawn from the Greek word "ekklesia" which can be translated "the called out ones," a "gathering," or "meeting." Without God these "called out ones" or "gatherings" would resemble a local lodge or club, but with the living God, the church really is the hope of the world.

    I know it is painfully easy to grow disheartened with the local congregation sometimes. Sometimes she looks comatose. I was a young preacher serving a small rural church. I pastored and preached as faithfully as I could. I genuinely loved those people, and, in turn, they loved me and my wife. Admittedly, there were times when I wondered what God was doing. One of those occasions occurred on a memorable Sunday morning. I was in the middle of delivering the sermon when I smelled cigar smoke. Rising up behind the head of one saintly older lady, who liked having her hair styled in a light blue tint, was a pillar of smoke resembling Moses' signal to break camp and follow behind. The smoke wasn't so much a holy sign, but rather an indication that a saintly older man had forgotten where he was and had lit up a cigar to the glory of God! The smirks and laughter signaled that church was officially over as this older man's wife grabbed the cigar from his hand and tried to extinguish it quickly before anyone noticed. Too late. I recall leaving the building bewildered, stumbling home to the next door parsonage, and wondering if the Gospel of Jesus was making any impact in the lives of those well-meaning people. Since then, I have wondered about my own life too. Surely there were days when young Timothy had his doubts about the penetration of the Gospel in Ephesus. What kept him going and keeps me going is this grand truth: the-sometimes-dormant-church is intimately attached to the living God. What a paradox! Servant leaders don't forget it.

A third and final paradox arises out of this brief section of 1Timothy. ***Servant leaders love the church, which is a pillar and buttress of the truth, even though sometimes she appears in disrepair.*** It is hard to say what Paul had in mind exactly when he created this imagery. Suffice it to say the metaphor – ***a pillar and buttress of the truth*** – contrasted powerfully with the pagan Temple of Artemis/Diana. "Pillar" (stylos) paints for us a picture of large columns that would support a roof. The Temple of Artemis/Diana was world famous for its elaborate one hundred pillars that rose fifty feet in the air and surrounded the exterior of this great wonder. It was initially built somewhere around 800 BC. The Temple proper was three hundred feet long and one hundred and fifty feet wide. Think football field. Each pillar was polished marble and gleamed in the Ephesus sunshine as, together, they held up the massive marble roof. What a picture! Sunglasses required!

The word "buttress" or foundation (hedraioma) describes for us the supporting or stabilizing part of the Temple. "Footings" is the word we would use today. The ancient Temple was built in a very marshy area adjacent to the Aegean Sea. As I said earlier, I've seen what remains of that structure among the ruins of the old city of Ephesus. In order to build on these wetlands, layers of pressed charcoal were used, along with layers of sheep wool to absorb the moisture and to allow large stone slabs to be set. It always humbles me when I consider the available technology and engineering strategies that helped erect these ancient buildings. Paul's point in all of this pillar and foundation talk seems crystal clear to me. The church's two-fold purpose was and is to hold firmly to the truth of

Jesus Christ – that's our foundation – and to hold up the truth of the Gospel for everyone to see – that's our pillar. Ultimately, both purposes point us to Jesus. He is our foundation and pillar. Elsewhere, Paul eloquently spoke of this: "And He is the head of the body, the church; he is the beginning and the firstborn from among the dead, so that in everything He might have the supremacy" (Colossians 1:18). This notion so moved Paul that he devoted a few more lines to elevating the supremacy of Jesus (3:16).

Paul told Timothy, "Great indeed, we confess, is the mystery of godliness" (3:16). I take Paul to mean that the secret to a godly life is none other than Jesus. The Apostle then breaks into song and sings about the six major movements in our Lord's life. Each one is packed full of theology. The stanzas seem to be presented in chronological order.

1. "He was manifested in the flesh" – that's incarnation talk. He appeared in an actual body. Jesus put on flesh and lived among us. Bethlehem and manger come to mind.
2. "Vindicated by the Spirit" – that's resurrection talk. He arose from a borrowed tomb. Joseph of Arimathea, Nicodemus, and women like Mary Magdalene, Joanna, Mary the mother of James, soldiers, and others come to mind as participants and observers.
3. "seen by angels" – that's exultation talk. He returned to the Father. I love this reference to Angels. They praise and worship God; make and carry messages for God; guide and protect the people of God; serve and assist God in the final judgment; and struggle with and fight against spiritual forces in opposition to God. ***Angels saw God*** as a baby, defeat death on the cross, partner with people, save the world, and be worshipped.
4. "Proclaimed among the nations" – that's commission or proclamation talk. Consider Matthew 28:18-20.
5. "believed on in the world" – that's conversion or salvation talk. Some actually believed.
6. "taken up in glory" – that's glorification or ascension talk. All of heaven sang for joy. He will return again!

Jesus is the center of the universe. Without Him there is no creation, no conversion, and no church. Jesus simply matters. What's it like to see things from a different point of view? *Dead Poets Society* is a 1989 film by Peter Weir starring Robin Williams. It remains one of my favorite movies. There are so many memorable scenes, but one I am partial to is the occasion in which Robin Williams' character, Mr. Keating, an English teacher, invites the all-male class to stand on top of his desk and to see the world differently. Each student lines up to take a look at the world from an odd vantage point. Perspective matters. The way in which we see things shapes our vision and mission. Servant leaders must see God from a large and unique point of view. What the angels saw changed everything. What we as servant leaders see changes us.

CHAPTER 6
Servant Leadership's Hard Side
1 Timothy 4:1-5

"Leadership is a challenging way of life. Jack Welch defines an effective corporate executive as someone who can change the tires while the car's still rolling. Surely this describes effective leadership in any arena" (Bowling, John C. (2000) **Grace-Full Leadership.** *(p. 137). Kansas City: Beacon Hill Press).*

Servant leadership is hard. That's a fact. The reasons are numerous. Some of those reasons have already been mentioned in previous chapters. Other examples would include the pettiness often found in the local church, confusion over what it means to be called by God, difficulty in making and finding time for deep communion with God, and the reality of servant leadership as an iron man and iron woman race (2Timothy 4:6-8). The list of challenges could go on and on. Suffice it to say that servant leaders are shaped in community by community. Sometimes, that very community is seduced by false teaching and teachers. That's the underbelly of Paul's letter to Timothy. Here is how he described it to his young disciple and partner in ministry.

4 *Now the Spirit expressly says that in later times some will **depart***

*from the faith by **devoting** themselves to deceitful spirits and teachings of demons, ² through the insincerity of liars whose consciences are seared, ³ who **forbid** marriage and **require** abstinence from foods that God created to be received with thanksgiving by those who believe and know the truth. ⁴ For everything created by God is good, and nothing is to be rejected if it is received with thanksgiving, ⁵ for it is made holy by the word of God and prayer.*

I have highlighted four words. Those four are pivotal in defining and describing servant leadership's hard side. If forced to put this paragraph into one big idea, here is how I would say it. ***Servant leadership's hard side is found in the spiritual battle for truth.***

Let's start this conversation with the word "depart" (apostesontai). The particular word used by Paul here (4:1) literally means "will apostasize." The idea is that some people experienced alienation or removal from a relationship with Jesus. Specifically, Paul selected this word to show how some in Ephesus had given in to false teaching. The context is clear. Some were alienated from the faith. The Gospel seed had landed in the heart-soil of some and had not taken root. We don't know the details, but, when testing had come along, they abandoned the faith. The word can be used positively sometimes in the New Testament. For instance, in Luke 2:37, it is used to describe the devotion of Anna, the old prophetess, who "never left" the temple worshiping, fasting, and praying. She did not abandon her holy anticipation of the coming of the Messiah. Most of the fifteen occurrences of this word, however, speak negatively, like Luke 8:13, Acts 15:38, and Hebrews 3:12.

I wrote parts of this book out in the marketplace. Noise, as strange as it seems, now and then sharpens my listening skills. God can speak anywhere, even in the clanging and banging of everyday life. He communicates as I study, pray, reflect, and write. The practice of writing outside of the quiet of my study at home or the church keeps me grounded in the real world. One of those places included the International Plaza in Tampa Bay, Florida. My wife and I were on vacation there, and she enjoyed a day window shopping while I focused on finding some writing time. As strange as it sounds writing actually energizes me. I found a table next to a Starbucks kiosk. In the noisy environment of a mall, you can't help but eavesdrop on conversations that surround you. One of those conversations included an employment interview. I was amazed at how boldly and arrogantly the person applying for the job spoke of her accomplishments. Not one word of praise to the God who made it all possible appeared in her speech. Not one acknowledgement of the people who encouraged her along the way was mentioned. Not one ounce of recognition as to the place her family and friends might have played arose.

That interview reminded me that we are an immensely self-absorbed culture. Whether we are seeking a job, cultivating a relationship, hoping for recognition, or pursuing money, we are being constantly tempted toward abandoning a God-centered life. Ephesus was a place that dangled and jingled a life apart from the one, true Redeemer-God. Remember that Paul instructed Timothy to "stay there in Ephesus so that you may command certain men not to teach false doctrines any longer (1 Timothy 1:3-4). Ephesus not only housed the large temple of Artemis/Diana we have already discussed, but it also hosted a temple to Eros. Eros is the Greek word used to describe sexual or erotic love. The parallel between that ancient sexual selfishness and our own version of that same sin does not require much of an imagination. Timothy found himself ministering in a place of extreme wealth and hedonism much like the North American landscape, a place that makes it easy to abandon the faith.

The second word that helps to shape this picture of spiritual battle for the truth is "devoting" (4:1 – prosecho). It means to follow after. This demonic and diabolical conflict included for Paul the "paying attention to" or "coming to believe in" the dark side of life. Paul was looking past the surface of the Ephesian lifestyle of the rich and famous. He saw the enemy at work. Some apparently started out well with good intentions to follow Jesus and ended up actually following after deceiving spirits and demons. Like characters in John Bunyan's classic, *The Pilgrim's Progress,* some wander from the narrow way and pursue a life that appears more promising, but ends up enslaving and corrupting.

There is a remarkable illustration of this in the book of Acts. Philip, the evangelist, was sharing the Good News of Jesus in Samaria, and people "paid attention" (same word – prosecho) to what he was preaching (8:6). In contrast, a wicked sorcerer by the name of Simon was amazing people with his cunning and trickery. Many "paid attention" (prosecho – 8:10) to him. A spiritual battle ensued. In the end, Simon himself came to believe in Jesus and was baptized. Because, like me, Simon was a work-in-progress, Peter will have to confront him and set him on the right path once again (Acts 8:18-24)

Paul's third word is "forbid" (4:3 – koluo). It can be translated in a variety of ways: prevent, hinder, detour, or block a pathway. Like the two previous words, depart and devote, this one reveals another glimpse into the galactic size of spiritual warfare. A suffocating legalism or false asceticism clouded the Jesus following way in Ephesus. Two of the most basic appetites that most human beings have, marriage and food, were being legislated and controlled by some of the false teachers. Paul described these teachers as, "liars whose consciences are seared" (4:2). Their internal compass had been cauterized and now was unable to think correctly about God's original design of marriage – one man and one woman together for a life-time (Genesis 2). The bottom line truth is this – life-long celibacy is not holier than life-long marriage. Granted, some have been graced or gifted to remain celibate, but most of us haven't (Matthew 19:12). Paul does acknowledge in 1 Corinthians 7 that the single life can afford a person an "undivided focus" to serve God, but nowhere does he make the single life a command. I'm still amazed at the heavy-handed way some teachers of Scripture seek to control their hearers.

The fourth and final word Paul used to reveal the struggle for Gospel truth is "require" (4:3 – apokho). These same false teachers were commanding some to keep their distance from certain foods. A grocery list is not provided. Paul's approach to refuting this nonsense is fascinating. He tells Timothy that God created and gave us food that is to be received with a thankful spirit. It is so important to Paul that he repeats the truth that "God created" everything, including food, to be gratefully accepted (4:3-4). The Apostle is not saying that everything is good, but rather what God created for His purpose and glory is good. I agree with those who advocate that there are certain foods we should "require abstinence" or avoid because they are harmful to our bodies.

Examples of this kind of food might include processed food high in sugar, salt, artificial color, trans-fats, preservatives, or other additives. But what Paul is stating here goes beyond the debate of healthy vs. unhealthy food. Even the early church recognized that spiritual issues surrounded some food choices, like meat offered to pagan idols (Acts 15:20 and 1 Corinthians 8:1-13). Our freedom in Christ should never be used as a stumbling block for others (1 Corinthians 8:9). So, what is really at stake here? The issue is not marriage or food. Hunger for a relationship is good. Hunger for food is good. Both are God-given appetites with God-given boundaries. When hunger for marriage or food moves to lust or gluttony, it becomes destructive. I understand that and so do you. The issue here is rejecting God's goodness toward us. God's gifts come to us constantly. They come in the form of creation, homes, clothes, medicine, literature, freedom, and a myriad of other avenues, but especially in marriage and food. When we reject what He graciously provides and shape it in heavy-handed legalism, we disrespect the One who provides every good and perfect gift (James 1:17). Marriage and food are part of His good gifts to us. Servant leaders are called to model a gratefulness and stewardship of all that God lovingly provides. We do this primarily through a life of thanksgiving shaped by Scripture and prayer (4:5). This is the best weapon against false teachers and teaching that would manipulate and control the good and beautiful Jesus-following life.

Does anyone doubt that servant leadership can be hard? I was reminded of this several years ago when I was reading Reggie McNeal's fine book *A Work of Heart* (2000).. A friend of his came for a visit, and, like most of us, Reggie asked him how he was doing. Reggie's friend replied, "I wrote this yesterday. It pretty well says it all." He shoved a written prayer toward Reggie. Here's a slice of what he shared:

> "Dear Lord, I'm so tired. My strength is completely gone and so is my desire to continue on...I'm exhausted. I'm tired. I'm tired of giving to people who are never satisfied...I'm tired of demanding, thankless people. I'm tired of being abused. I'm tired of being talked about behind my back by people who are supposed to be my brothers and sisters. I'm tired of being ignored. I'm tired of comforting grieving people while my grief is ignored. I'm tired of bearing the burdens of others while I bear my burdens alone...I'm tired of feeding people when I'm starving to death. I'm tired of busybodies. I'm tired of people who never open their Bibles assuming that they know what God wants me to do...I'm tired of expectations...I'm tired of loneliness...I'm tired of serving and giving and feeding and comforting and teaching and encouraging and ministering. Lord, I'm so tired. I don't have anything left to give. I've got to rest. I can't go on. Lord, please let me quit" (pp.168-169).

All healing begins with a conversation with God. Honesty really is the best policy. Spiritual war can leave the bravest and most skilled soldier in need of rest and refreshment. The Word and prayer, anointed by the Holy Spirit, can rejuvenate any servant leader. The hard side of servant leadership is a constant reminder of our dependency on the One who has enlisted us in His service.

CHAPTER 7
The Servant Leader's Workout Routine
1 Timothy 4:6-5:2

"Strengthening the soul of your leadership is an invitation to enter more deeply into the process of spiritual transformation and to choose to lead from that place"
(Barton, Ruth Haley. (2008). Strengthening the Soul of Your Leadership. (p. 15). Downers Grove: IVP Books).

Physical exercise and spiritual training have a lot in common. Both require intentionality. Both call for persistence. Both involve a set of time-tested principles worthy of implementation. Neither is easy. Both are worth the effort. To put it simply, there are no shortcuts to good health, whether we are speaking of the physical life or the spiritual kind. The key ingredients are to eat right, to exercise appropriately, and to embrace a proper amount of rest. Most of us know this. It is the exercise part of this well-being-triangle that I want to talk about. ***Every servant leader needs a workout routine.***

Years ago, somewhere in Junior-High, I began to exercise regularly. Admittedly, I was a novice and didn't know much about appropriate exercise habits and workout routines. I stumbled around, now and then getting a little help from High-School coaches. Then, I entered military service, and physical health and maintenance took on a whole new meaning. Motivation is not a problem when a drill instructor is screaming insults about your mother and your family of origin. If you aren't smiling right now, my apologies. All the explanations in the world would not make the situation clearer. If you understand what I'm saying, you grasp the deeper truth that a drill instructor or a hard-nosed training partner eventually grows old, and, somewhere, you have to find more gracious and meaningful motivation. I began to lift weights on my own and to do some running on a regular basis. Not until I was in my early fifties did I broaden my walking/running routine and train for half-marathons and, eventually, a full marathon. Now, I find that I enjoy and value a regular life of physical exercise and training. I will never make the front cover of a fashion magazine or, like a friend of mine loves to say about my Clydesdale-like-running, "You will never be mistaken for a Kenyan." Still, I have uncovered a meaningful exercise rhythm. What has been true of my physical body has been true of my inner life. Ideally, strengthening the body and the soul go hand in hand. With that said, think of me as your personal trainer in this chapter.

About the same time I began to discover the benefits of faithful physical exercise, I experienced a spiritual awakening in my first year of military service. I providentially encountered the Navigators, an international discipleship ministry, committed to knowing Christ and making Him known. I began to experiment and to embrace certain Christian disciplines like Bible-intake, Scripture memory, prayer, witnessing, worshiping, serving, and fasting. Later in my long journey, I would encounter spiritual coaches and mentors among the great devotional writers of the past. People like William Law, Jeanne Guyon, Hildegard of Bingen, John Bunyan, Brother Lawrence, Evagrius of Pontus, Evelyn Underhill, Augustine, A.W. Tozer, and many others informed and encouraged my spiritual training. The Apostle Paul took on that very same role for young

Timothy. In the section of Scripture I want us now to read and explore, Paul identifies for his young disciple-in-training four life-long workout principles for all servant leaders. Allow me to repeat what I have already said: ***Every servant leader needs a workout routine.*** Here are Paul's own words to his son in the faith and his partner in ministry.

> [6] *If you put these things before the brothers, you will be a good servant of Christ Jesus, being trained in the words of the faith and of the good doctrine that you have followed.* [7] *Have nothing to do with irreverent, silly myths. Rather train yourself for godliness;* [8] *for while bodily training is of some value, godliness is of value in every way, as it holds promise for the present life and also for the life to come.* [9] *The saying is trustworthy and deserving of full acceptance.* [10] *For to this end we toil and strive, because we have our hope set on the living God, who is the Savior of all people, especially of those who believe.*
>
> [11] *Command and teach these things.* [12] *Let no one despise you for your youth, but set the believers an example in speech, in conduct, in love, in faith, in purity.* [13] *Until I come, devote yourself to the public reading of Scripture, to exhortation, to teaching.* [14] *Do not neglect the gift you have, which was given you by prophecy when the council of elders laid their hands on you.* [15] *Practice these things, immerse yourself in them, so that all may see your progress.* [16] *Keep a close watch on yourself and on the teaching. Persist in this, for by so doing you will save both yourself and your hearers.*
>
> [5] *Do not rebuke an older man but encourage him as you would a father, younger men as brothers,* [2] *older women as mothers, younger women as sisters, in all purity.*

I admire Paul for all kinds of reasons: his dependency on Christ alone, his complete transparency when it comes to his own life's struggle with sin, his awareness of how far the Lord had brought him in his journey, his studied mind and grasp of Scripture, his loving heart toward his children in the faith, his uncompromising boldness and dangerous witness. But nothing so draws me to this superb first century spiritual coach like his grasp of how to grow in life-long attachment to Jesus. Here are his four coaching tips for the servant leader's life-long workout routine.

First, ***creativity is good, but sticking to the basics is better (4:6).*** Stick to the basics. What are those basics? What "things" does Paul have in mind? What are the "things" Paul wants Timothy to "command and teach" (4:11)? What "things" does the older disciple want the younger disciple to "be diligent in" (4:15)? The word Paul uses in 4:6 for "things" gets translated two other ways in the ESV, "these rules," and "everything," depending upon the context. It actually shows up eight times in this letter (3:14, 4:6, 4:11, 4:15, 5:7, 5:21, 6:2, and 6:17). The concept Paul is communicating to Timothy is what we might refer to as the fundamentals, the essential basics, bottom-line practices, even the core teachings without which you cannot grow in Christ-likeness. Think Bible-intake and prayer (2:8, 3:9, 4:5). Consider the needed honing and refining one only gets through living in and growing with other believers, what we might call Christian community, accountability, or fellowship. Recognize the need to return repeatedly to the essentials of faith: trust in Jesus and in Him alone, the power of the cross, the central meaning of the life, ministry, death, burial, and resurrection of Jesus, ongoing cooperation with the Holy Spirit to form and change us to look more and more like Jesus, and, more than anything, a proper and ever-increasing understanding of who God is and what that understanding means to our everyday-Jesus-following-life. Core truths.

Paul does not describe elementary teaching. This is not spiritual Kindergarten. He does not refer to ideas mentioned in the Letter to the Hebrews: "instruction about washings, the laying on of hands, the resurrection of the dead, and eternal judgment" (Hebrews 6:2). The writer of Hebrews invites the reader to "go on to maturity" (6:1). So, for us, this invitation means to practice, live, and share the absolute central ingredients of what it means to be a life-long-apprentice to Jesus. Press on.

Never get so cocky or sophisticated in your journey that you fail to stay grounded in the essentials of a mature faith in Jesus. What cardio exercises like walking and running are to our physical well-being, soul exercises like unhurried Bible reading and reflection on the Jesus story are to our spiritual well-being. Silence and solitude are the sit-ups and push-ups of a vibrant inner world. There is nothing wrong with thinking creatively about working out with the Christian disciplines and tested holy habits, but nothing exceeds returning again and again to the central and foundational elements of the Christian life. Practice the other exercises, but keep the Gospel first and foremost in all that you are and do (1 Corinthians 15:1-3).

I find deep satisfaction in lifting weights. It refreshes me. I was a serious lifter for a while until my joints began to remind me that I could not continue to push heavy weight. Now I enjoy lifting lighter weight and doing more repetitions. When I first began, I could barely bench press 135 pounds. Those 135 pounds, one 45 pound plate on each end of the bar and the bar itself, taxed all of my strength. But through persistence, proper training techniques, and some sound advice, I began to grow as a weight lifter. So it is with the spiritual life. We progress. We stick with it. We grow. We keep the fundamentals. This leads us to another workout principle.

Second, *trying is good, but training is better (4:7-8).* Keep on training. The words "train" and "training" are used twice in this passage (gumnazo/gumnazia). We find our English word "gymnasium" here. Paul coaches Timothy to go to the spiritual gym continually. Train to be godly. Physical training is valuable and needed, but spiritual training has implications for this life and the one to come. Keep exercising. Stay at it.

Scholars have acknowledged the influence of the Greek/Roman athletic contests in Paul's use of this imagery. Every two years, an Olympic-like contest took place called the Isthmian games. Though younger than those in ancient Olympia, it rivaled those earlier games in popularity. Begun around 582 BC, it brought together gifted athletes and musicians. The three primary athletic contests were wrestling, boxing, and a short race of about 200 yards. The games honored the Greek god Poseidon and were held in the narrow strip of land that separated the Aegean Sea from the Ionian. It was located not far from Corinth, Greece, and was highly supported by sports-loving fans from Athens. The winner traditionally walked away with a crown made of wild celery or pine leaves. I know that doesn't sound as appealing as a gold medal, but it was passionately sought after in Paul's day. With all that said, the important question is this: Why does Paul emphasize training? Why doesn't he use the word "trying?" So much of the Christian Life has been framed by well-meaning spiritual coaches who advocate continual trying.

John Ortberg probably comes as close to a proper answer as any contemporary author I know. His splendid book, *The Life You've Always Wanted,* gets to the core issue of spiritual transformation. Ortberg says,

> "Trying hard can accomplish only so much. If you are serious about seizing this chance of a lifetime, you will have to enter into a life of training. You must arrange your life around certain practices that will enable you to do what you cannot do now by willpower alone. When it comes to running a marathon, you must train, not try…*There is an immense difference between* training *to do something* and trying *to do something*…Spiritual transformation is not a matter of trying harder, but of training wisely…Respecting the distinction between training and merely trying is the key to transformation in every aspect of life" (1997, pp. 46-48).

Notice with me that Paul never identifies exactly what these training methods or strategies should be. He gives Timothy and future readers plenty of freedom to work these plans out in accordance with our personalities, gift mixes, and unique callings. The Christian Disciplines can certainly be included in this discussion. Many Jesus-followers have found that the practice of incorporating into everyday life a routine of holy habits has been enormously soul-shaping. Jesus practiced these routines. He memorized Scripture. He prayed. He retreated for silence and solitude. He worshipped. He served. He witnessed. He shaped His life around attending to the Father's love and will. The spiritual disciplines help us do that.

The disciplines, as many have observed, cannot save us or change us to look like Jesus. God alone does the saving and changing. These practices are not for the elite among us. The disciplines are only tools that the Holy Spirit uses to strengthen and to transform any and all of us. They are our spiritual calisthenics. I, for one, am glad that Paul did not draw out a long list of spiritual exercises for Timothy. He left room for the Spirit to work the specific applications into Timothy's life. Scripture is clear. Spiritual training is the norm in a healthy relationship with Jesus (Hebrews 5:14 and 12:11). There is nothing wrong with trying, but it will not yield the desired results in the Jesus-following life. Training is best.

Paul offers another workout principle worthy of implementation. Third, ***youthful energy is good, but mature commitment is better (4:9-14).*** To state the principle even more succinctly, keep your commitment alive. The grace of God invites and encourages a response. The two words that most capture this idea are "toil" and "strive." Toil or labor (kopiao) describes what makes us grow weary, tired, and exhausted. Real training, the kind that is most beneficial, is depleting. Strive (agonizomai) is our response when we care about something deeply. We agonize over it. We pour ourselves into it. Again, I believe Paul is drawing on an athletic image. This word was used in ancient times to describe an athlete who left everything on the field. They, as we might say, "gave their all." Paul challenges Timothy to be an "example" (typos) among the other believers in five specific areas: speech, life, love, faith, and purity (4:12). The first two are exterior, or outer, life concerns. The final three are all about the inner world. Remember that Timothy is a fairly young servant leader. Paul is highly sensitive to this: "don't let anyone look down on you because you are young." It intrigues me that the Apostle prefaces all of this coaching talk with, "command and teach these things" (4:11). In that phrase is a muscular reminder that there are no short-cuts in this Christ-honoring life. Soul-strengthening requires a continual commitment. Paul marks out some very specific categories.

We "devote" (prosecho) ourselves to the public reading of Scripture (4:13). We passionately pursue a Word-directed life. We make Word-intake a holy habit. We preach and teach out of the overflow, regardless of where our "pulpit" is located, whether it happens to be in a public school classroom, an office cubicle, or in our own place of business. We keep our giftedness honed and ready to use (4:14). We are thoughtful and alert in this apprenticeship with Jesus. Where He goes, we go. What He says, we do. Our progress is self-evident (4:15). We pay close attention to our conduct and core values. We are people of the Book. We press on even when others refuse (4:16). That's commitment!

I was powerfully reminded of the value of lasting commitment during a graduation ceremony. Chuck Swindoll was the keynote speaker and he drew on a part of this very Bible passage we are exploring in this chapter. He entitled his message, "Signposts on the Road to Maturity." It has stayed with me all these years. Chuck raised five questions. All of them relate to the issue of mature commitment: Am I living an exemplary life (4:12)? Do I understand what is essential (4:13)? Am I capitalizing on my strengths (4:14)? Have I thrown myself into my calling (4:15)? Will I stay at it regardless (4:16)? At the close of that memorable sermon, Chuck told a story about Itzhak Perlman, the world-renown violinist. Perlman was in concert at New York City. One of his strings broke, but he played on. A second string broke, and he continued to play. Those attending to him walked on stage to hand him another violin, but he played on. Swindoll painted that picture for us and then asked, "How much music can you still play with what you have left?" I was riveted. If an invitation had been offered, I would have run to the platform. Chuck had captured the essence of what Paul was getting at in this third piece of workout wisdom. Genuine servant leaders have divine unction in their gumption. They've got boatloads of holy zippity-do-dah. They press on.

Fourth and lastly, Paul offers this piece of wise workout instruction. ***Keeping the big picture is good, but monitoring the details is better (4:15-5:2).*** Pay attention to the details. All smart coaches know this truth – how I practice determines how I play. Practice doesn't necessarily make the athlete perfect. What it does is make our patterns of practice permanent. The details matter. World class athletes monitor those details closely. Let me digress for a moment. Ponder what Paul is really encouraging Timothy (and us) to practice. Practice a godly example (4:12). Practice the public reading of Scripture (4:13). Practice exercising spiritual gifts (4:14). Practice intentional Christian growth (4:15). Practice self-watch (4:16). And, especially, practice authentic family life (5:1-2). We really are a "church family." How we treat older men as fathers, older women as mothers, younger men as brothers, and younger women as sisters reveals everything about whether or not we truly are monitoring the needed community details. Our task is to be present in what God is doing. We are coached to be spiritually alert and engaged. We, therefore, persevere. We bear up under the pressure that might undo us. We abide.

I've never been a great athlete. I wanted to be great, or maybe it is more truthful to say that I wanted to be famous, but I was never wired to be more than an average guy. A few years ago, I was invited to return to the small community where I had graduated from high-school. A homecoming parade was planned, and the organizers wanted to honor a group of basketball players that had left a lasting impression. That particular team still held the record for the most wins. I didn't want to go, but my wife "coached me" to attend. I'm sure any husband or wife reading this knows exactly what I mean. The parade was strictly a small town event, not Macy's of New York City. We sat on a typical small town float, waved at people we didn't know, and generally appeared to be a bunch of old guys past their prime. No one was happier to get off that float than me.

What I haven't told you is that our coach was in the same parade and on that same float sitting in a wheel chair. Disease and age had taken both of his legs. A good friend of mine and I had put him on the float and now were entrusted to take him off the float. Mission accomplished, and I started to walk away, but Coach reached out and drew me close to him. It was an awkward moment for a guy like me who values his space. With a Bobby Knight passion of earlier years, he pulled me into his face and said these memorable words, "You weren't my best athlete (gee, thanks for the encouragement, Coach), but no one gave me more heart than you." Then I cried. I mean, I really cried. I walked away, or maybe I floated away, pondering something that I have learned in my journey. Seldom do the best and brightest finish well. It is so often the most determined who do so. The truth of my story is that I am passionately average. Maybe you identify with me. In addition to being very average, I'm also a bottom line kind of thinker. So here is what I've been trying to say. Find a spiritual workout routine, and practice it for the rest of your life. That's what servant leaders do. It is exactly what our Lord did. He "endured the cross, despising the shame, and is seated at the right hand of the throne of God" (Hebrews 12:2). Amen.

CHAPTER 8

Only Multi-Generational Servant Leaders Will Do
1 Timothy 5:3-6:2

"A sect is accomplished by community reduction, getting rid of what does not please us, getting rid of what offends us, whether of ideas or people. We construct religious clubs instead of entering resurrection communities. Sects are termites in the Father's house"
(Peterson, Eugene. (2005). **Christ Plays in Ten Thousand Places.** *(p. 244). Grand Rapids: Eerdmans).*

One of the most troubling aspects of the contemporary church is the way she can tend to elevate youthfulness, discard seniors, carve away the undesirables, and homogenize God-intended uniqueness. If everyone in the church looks the same, we are probably not a true reflection of Christ's Church. It breaks my heart when I hear younger pastors describe the church they hope to plant. They describe their ideal church as young, vibrant, and absent of older folks. What a shame. What a warped view of the church. At the same time, one of the greatest challenges facing the contemporary church is learning how to meet such a variety of needs legitimately without turning the church into a shopping mall. Questions flood my mind. How do we discern who really is in need? How do we distinguish legitimate needs from illegitimate ones? What role does that person's family play in meeting needs? What is the church's legitimate responsibility? What responsibility do you and I have in meeting someone else's need? What responsibilities do the needy have? Is there a danger in meeting needs indiscriminately? Should those among us, who regularly meet needs, be paid? How do we protect a servant leader who regularly meets needs from frivolous accusations or criticisms? What responsibility do we have in meeting our own needs? How do we meet the needs of those who work in difficult places? None of the questions are easily answered. Paul takes his writing instrument in hand and by the Holy Spirit, begins to talk about meeting needs in a multi-generational church. Here's what he wrote.

> [3] *Honor widows who are truly widows.* [4] *But if a widow has children or grandchildren, let them first learn to show godliness to their own household and to make some return to their parents, for this is pleasing in the sight of God.* [5] *She who is truly a widow, left all alone, has set her hope on God and continues in supplications and prayers night and day,* [6] *but she who is self-indulgent is dead even while she lives.* [7] *Command these things as well, so that they may be without reproach.* [8] *But if anyone does not provide for his relatives, and especially for members of his household, he has denied the faith and is worse than an unbeliever.*
>
> [9] *Let a widow be enrolled if she is not less than sixty years of age, having been the wife of one husband,* [10] *and having a reputation for good works: if she has brought up children, has shown hospitality, has washed the feet of the saints, has cared for the afflicted, and has devoted herself to every good work.* [11] *But refuse to enroll younger widows, for when their passions draw them away from Christ, they desire to marry* [12] *and so incur condemnation for having abandoned their former faith.* [13] *Besides that, they learn to be idlers, going about from house to house, and not only idlers, but also gossips and busybodies, saying what they should not.* [14] *So I would have younger widows marry, bear children,*

manage their households, and give the adversary no occasion for slander. ¹⁵ *For some have already strayed after Satan.* ¹⁶ *If any believing woman has relatives who are widows, let her care for them. Let the church not be burdened, so that it may care for those who are truly widows.*

¹⁷ *Let the elders who rule well be considered worthy of double honor, especially those who labor in preaching and teaching.* ¹⁸ *For the Scripture says, "You shall not muzzle an ox when it treads out the grain," and, "The laborer deserves his wages."* ¹⁹ *Do not admit a charge against an elder except on the evidence of two or three witnesses.* ²⁰ *As for those who persist in sin, rebuke them in the presence of all, so that the rest may stand in fear.* ²¹ *In the presence of God and of Christ Jesus and of the elect angels I charge you to keep these rules without prejudging, doing nothing from partiality.* ²² *Do not be hasty in the laying on of hands, nor take part in the sins of others; keep yourself pure.* ²³ *(No longer drink only water, but use a little wine for the sake of your stomach and your frequent ailments.)* ²⁴ *The sins of some people are conspicuous, going before them to judgment, but the sins of others appear later.* ²⁵ *So also good works are conspicuous, and even those that are not cannot remain hidden.*

6 Let all who are under a yoke as bondservants regard their own masters as worthy of all honor, so that the name of God and the teaching may not be reviled. ² *Those who have believing masters must not be disrespectful on the ground that they are brothers; rather they must serve all the better since those who benefit by their good service are believers and beloved.*

    Widows were some of the most marginalized people throughout the Roman Empire. Though Paul does not speak of them here, orphans would have been included among the first century's socially ostracized. Scripture often places widows and orphans side by side (Deuteronomy 10:18, 16:11-14, 24:19-21, 26:12-19, 27:19, Job 24:3, Psalm 68:5, 109:9,

146:9, Jeremiah 22:3, Lamentations 5:3, Ezekiel 22:7, Zechariah 7:10, Malachi 3:5, and James 1:27). Widows, however, are the group Paul is most concerned with in this section of his letter to Timothy, though he will also take the time to address the issues surrounding paid elders and Roman slavery. For some reason, beyond my limited understanding, this passage moves my heart deeply, and I will try and not come across as an angry zealot or overly passionate do-gooder.

It should be noted that this is the longest section in the Scriptures for directly discussing the life situation of widows and the needed response by God's people. For now, this good insight about the plight of widows before the time of Christ from Bonnie Bowman Thurston might be helpful:

> "Throughout the ancient world, except in Egypt, the legal position of women was uniformly low. Women's legal status was always inferior to that of men, and widows had fewer legal rights than married women" (1989, p.17).

A widow or "chera" was, in the broadest definition, a woman who lived without a husband, but the term most often referred to someone whose husband was dead (Acts 6:1 and 9:39-41). What do we, as servant leaders, make of all of this widow-talk?

First, ***multi-generational servant leaders look like someone who knows when to care and how to care for marginalized people*** (5:3-16). Remember that Timothy is most likely younger than the majority of these widows. He needs practical wisdom to know how to handle this situation. Much of Paul's counsel is grounded in God's care for the widows throughout the Old Testament and an understanding of the heart and ministry of Jesus (Exodus 22:22-24, Deuteronomy 10:18, 24:17-22, 27:19, Psalm 68:5, Isaiah 1:17, Ezekiel 22:7, Mark 12:41-42, Luke 7:11-12, 18:1ff, and John 19:26-27). James 1:27 even says, "Religion that God our Father accepts as pure and faultless is this: to look after orphans and widows in their distress..." Paul, then, lays out for Timothy three clear classifications for ministering to these needs.

We can call the first group the true widows. These are women who need to be given "honor" or proper recognition (tima). This kind of care is shown through physical, emotional, and especially financial help. Paul talks about this care particularly in 5:3, 5-7 and 9-10. The second classification of widows are the ones not on the official "enrollment" or list. They have some other means of care; probably family members like their children or grandchildren were providing financial support like those in 5:4, 8, and 16. The third group includes those considered young enough to want to remarry. Paul addresses their situation in 5:11-15. Once again, I appreciate the insight of Bonnie Thurston:

> "Antiquity generally had high admiration for young, chaste widows. Not only here, but also in Titus 2:4-5 (where older women are to teach the younger women), the writer of the Pastorals stresses the traditional, domestic virtues that would be acceptable and praiseworthy in order that 'the word of God may not be discredited' (2:5b). Younger women are to follow the societal and legal requirements for women of their age so that the Christian reputation will be preserved. Remarriage is encouraged in spite of Paul's advice in 1 Corinthians 7 that 'she is happier if she remains as she is'" (1989, p.42).

Apparently, the younger widows were a challenge for Timothy due to their propensity toward being drawn to sensual desires and idleness (5:11-13). Early Church Fathers like Ignatius, Polycarp, and Tertullian wrote extensively on this issue of caring for widows. Paul's advice is clear. Honor, respect, and meet their needs. Perhaps Paul had in the back of his mind the story of Acts 6:1-7. Dr. Luke, after all, the writer of his own Gospel and the account of the Holy Spirit's work in and through the early church, was Paul's trusted friend and traveling partner. The point is clear for Timothy. Generational lines must be crossed in the name of Jesus. Servant leaders understand that part, but how are we to understand Paul's mentioning of a widow "enrollment" or list?

Twice, in 5:9 and 5:11, the Apostle speaks of widows being "enrolled." We assume there were certain widows who had exemplary reputations. Their names were recorded in some kind of booklet or catalogue. Those not included in this list were those who could not remain single or could not devote themselves to Christian service. Qualifications to be on this list were clear: an age of over sixty (hints of maturity and lots of life experience), modeled faithfulness to her husband, well known for good deeds, exemplary in raising her children, filled with hospitality, willing to wash feet, but especially devoted to doing all kinds of good deeds. Talk about down-to-earth-qualifications. Think Tabitha of Joppa in Acts 9:36-43 (Greek – Dorcas). She was widely known for "doing good and helping the poor." When she died, all the widows were crying and showing Peter the fine robes and other clothing she had made for them. She may have been the prototype woman on this official list. Timothy was to "put on," or enroll, (katalegestho) this kind of widow. It almost sounds like a particular kind of calling or official vocational ministry. If this is true, then Timothy was being instructed by Paul to look for older, more spiritually mature female partners in ministry. Who among us couldn't use an older and perhaps wiser Sister or Mother in Christ? Servant leaders willing to do the challenging multi-generational work in order to sustain a healthy church, grasp this. Servant leaders are always attentive to the marginalized. But that is not the end of the story. There is a second trait that marks out this sort of servant leader.

Multi-generational servant leaders look like someone who knows who to support financially and how to support them (5:17-20). Paul shifts gears. He now addresses the issue of elders who preach and teach. His superbly practical advice to Timothy is two-fold: 1. Pay them (Deuteronomy 25:4, 1 Corinthians 9:9, and Luke 10:7) and 2. Protect them from silly accusations. Substantiate, confirm, and handle all criticism toward an elder with deep maturity. If it proves true, rebuke the elder openly and lovingly. Please notice again the cross-generational lines

Timothy must travel. He is a young leader caring for older leaders. He is to "honor" them as he was called to "honor" leading widows. If you are a younger leader surrounded by older leaders, don't be intimidated (1 Timothy 4:11-14). Love them, bless them, and sustain them in the manner you would want done to you. Authentic servant leaders live out Matthew 7:12: "So whatever you wish that others would do to you, do also to them, for this is the Law and the Prophets."

I was compelled to confront an older servant leader in the life of one of the churches I once served. His pastoral visits seemed to target women who were home alone. Accusations began to surface of inappropriate behavior. I confronted him gently, and he denied it. More time went by, followed by more accusations, and I lovingly confronted him again. Eventually, the truth found him out, and he was asked to step down as a leader. What followed can only be described as a mess. Ultimately, he and his family left the church. The simple truth is that he could not be trusted to be alone with another woman. The church's reputation was harmed, and the clean-up took some time. That servant leader was far older than me and had extensive experience in ministry, but Scripture encourages and calls all servant leaders into multi-generational work. The hesitant need not apply.

There is a third piece in Paul's instruction to Timothy. ***Multi-generational servant leaders look like someone who knows what to do and what not to do about "self-care"*** (5:21-25). There is an earnestness and seriousness that is to shape the life of the servant leader. This section of Paul's practical advice almost sounds like an ordination service. Paul says, "In the presence of God and of Christ Jesus and of the elect angels I charge you to keep these rules..." (5:21). It sounds like pretty heady stuff. This part of servant leadership is extremely solemn. Timothy is called to show no favoritism or prejudice in carrying out his ministry. The particular term Paul uses here for "without prejudging" (prokrima) is a courtroom word. There should be no prejudice of any kind in Timothy's ministry.

Wow, have I blown that one a time or two! Even more, Timothy is to be very cautious about hurrying the process of selecting other servant leaders (5:22). Don't be too quick or hasty in ordaining anyone to ministry. Here's the practical piece: question, screen, and prayerfully deliberate any and all selections to servant leadership. When we fail to do that, we create far more problems and challenges in the life of the church and the work of other servant leaders. A part of our own "self-care" is the "servant-evaluation" of other would-be-leaders. I realize it can sound strange to our ears when we hear Paul tell Timothy in this very context, "Do not be hasty in the laying on of hands, nor take part in the sins of others, keep yourself pure" (5:22). However, the point is not hard to understand. We can easily become implicated in others' mistakes, and even in their sin, if we fail to screen future leaders thoroughly. Discernment is needed.

    That same discernment is required when it comes to the care of our own bodies. We don't know all the specifics that surrounded Paul's instruction to Timothy to "stop drinking only water." Maybe Timothy was prone to legalistic or ascetic practices. Sometimes well-intentioned servant leaders construct rule-fences around their lives to the point that they do more harm than good. The church has a long history of self-abusers. There is no place for that kind of practice in the life of the apprentice to Jesus. Servant leaders are free, under the Lordship of Jesus Christ, to drink wine as long as they model and practice moderation. I choose not to drink wine or any intoxicating beverage because of poor choices I have made in the past, as well as a long history of alcoholism in my family tree. Charles Spurgeon told his students that self-care started with being saved, then moved to being vigorous in personal piety, and finally blossomed into matching character with ministry. I like that. It is vital that all servant leaders take their spiritual temperatures periodically in order to discern spiritual health. Young leaders like Timothy, especially, must remember that older leaders and followers are monitoring their lives and decisions. Be wise.

There is one last slice of practical wisdom from Paul to Timothy when it comes to crossing generational lines. ***Multi-generational servant leaders look like someone who knows what to say and how to say it in difficult work settings*** (6:1-2). Paul has been working through the various social groups young Timothy will encounter in his ministry at Ephesus. Obviously, this part of our passage specifically deals with issues of slavery in the Roman Empire. Of course, many of these slaves would have been younger than Timothy and older than Timothy. This is a multi-generational group.

Two quick observations are necessary. First, there are those with clear anti-Bible agendas who have portrayed Paul as a racist and proslavery advocate. Nothing could be further from the truth. Paul is not condoning slavery. Second, slavery in the First Century Roman Empire was nothing like the atrocious and evil system that existed in the American South during the Eighteenth and Nineteenth Centuries. To make that leap is to defy accurate historical and cultural understanding. Slavery that seeks to demean and to own another human being is an evil of Satan and cannot be tolerated. Slavery of any form violates God's intended plan. It is a form of demonic oppression. I have often asked myself why Paul didn't openly condemn this wicked system. Once again, I deeply appreciate the wise words of the late John Stott:

> "Why, is it, then, that neither Jesus nor his apostles called for the complete and immediate abolition of this horror? Probably the main reason is that slavery was deeply embedded in the structures of Graeco-Roman society. All well-to-do people had slaves, and very wealthy people had several hundreds. They were regarded as essential, especially as domestic servants and farm laborers, but also as clerks, craftsmen, teachers, soldiers and managers. It is believed that there were more than fifty million of them in the Empire, including one third of the inhabitants of Rome. In consequence, to dismantle slavery all at once would have brought about the collapse of society. Any

signs of a slave revolt were put down with ruthless brutality. The fact is that 'monstrous evils' like slavery 'are not, like giants in the old romances, to be slain at a blow.' They are so firmly rooted that any attempt to tear them up may pull up the foundations of society with them. At the same time Paul enunciated principles which undermined the very concept of slavery and led inexorably to its abolition, even though Christians are ashamed that it did not happen sooner" (1996, p. 143).

What were those principles Paul identified to Timothy that might one day bring freedom to all slaves? First, show full-respect to all masters. My grandmother, and wise people like her, would sometimes say, "You can catch more flies with honey than with vinegar." Grandma meant that more is accomplished with love and respect than with meanness and force. "Honor" or full-respect is the same word we have encountered throughout this section of Scripture. It is the word for treating people with dignity (5:3, 5:17, and 6:1). Just as Timothy was to honor widows and elders, crossing generational boundaries, he was to teach Christian slaves to honor their masters, whether those masters were Christian or not. A slave's respect for his master might simply be the means through which that master was won to Christ. Some Bible students have observed, and I think rightly so, that much of slavery was more like military service. That doesn't mean that every master was pleasant and kind. No doubt some were abusive and sadistic. Paul simply understood the power of loving respect.

Second, it intrigues me that Paul instructed slaves to be a supreme example of Jesus to their masters. Timothy is to encourage this kind of submission. This is the call of being salt and light in a decaying and darkened world (Matthew 5:13-16). Surely, there were those Christian slaves who longed for their freedom. Perhaps they were even disrespectful to their Christian masters. There seems to be hints of that disrespect in 6:2: "They must serve all the better," Paul said. All employers deserve our very best, especially those who are a part of the Household of Faith.

Imagine the power of implementing Colossians 3:17 into the work place: "And whatever you do, in word or deed, do everything in the name of the Lord Jesus, giving thanks to God the Father through Him." If we are to be multi-generational leaders, we will have to build respect and construct bridges toward those who employ us, regardless of whether they are male or female, young or old, Christian or non-Christian. Masters and slaves are equal in God's eyes.

Here's the essence of what I think Paul was passing on to Timothy and what I want to pass on to you. Multi-generational leaders think of themselves less and teach others to do the same. They are alert to people who resemble widows and marginalized folks, alert to people who resemble elders and other key leaders in the life and witness of the church, and are alert to people who resemble slaves and masters, employee and employers, who must learn to use the workplace as a launching pad for the Gospel of Jesus Christ. None of this is small. The penetration of the Gospel into the culture never is.

Reading, especially the devotional classic kind, is a discipline that often refreshes my soul. Somewhere I read that Tertullian (160-230 AD – theologian from Carthage) said that pagans sometimes referred to Christians as "chrestiani" and not "christiani." "Christiani" is the Greek word for Christians, but "chrestiani" is the word for "kind ones." Apparently, the way in which those early Jesus-followers lived marked them as "the kindness people." Widows (and orphans), front-line leaders, and those who resemble ancient slaves need servant leaders who willingly cross generational chasms and embrace people with the kindness of Jesus. Only that kind of leader will do. It is the very kind of leader I want to be.

A Little Manual for Servant Leaders

CHAPTER 9

Servant Leaders Beware
1 Timothy 6:3-21

"When despair for the world grows in me and I wake in the night at the least sound in fear of what my life and my children's lives may be, I go and lie down where the wood drake rests in his beauty on the water, and the great heron feeds. I come into the peace of wild things who do not tax their lives with forethought of grief. I come into the presence of still water. And I feel above me the day-blind stars waiting with their light. For a time I rest in the grace of the world, and am free"
(Berry, Wendell. (2002). *"The Peace of Wild Things"* **Good Poems.** *(p. 426). Ed. Garrison Keillor. New York: Viking).*

What frightens you about servant leadership? What can keep you awake at night? I am not talking about some kind of unjustified phobia. The answer to my question is not found in the darkness of an unrealistic fear. It goes far beyond the anxiety of public speaking or being asked a question you cannot answer. Lifelong servant leadership is marked by something far more sinister. Before we come to this last passage in 1Timothy, stop and consider Paul's grand themes. He has written to Timothy about doctrine, worship, healthy leadership, vocational calling, multi-generational service, and other mega issues. Now we find ourselves in the very last part of this Epistle. What should Paul say? What's the final word to his young partner in ministry? Paul does what so many parents do when someone they love is about to head out on their own. My mother might say something like this: "Remember who you are. Behave yourself. Be wise. Work hard. Stay humble." You get the idea. Paul has a far more essential piece of farewell wisdom. Paul's counsel can be stated in a crystal clear sentence: ***Servant leaders need to beware.*** Some experiences are justifiably frightening. What should servant leaders realistically guard against? Here are Paul's closing words to Timothy:

> *Teach and urge these things.* ³ *If anyone teaches a different doctrine and does not agree with the sound words of our Lord Jesus Christ and the teaching that accords with godliness,* ⁴ *he is puffed up with conceit and understands nothing. He has an unhealthy craving for controversy and for quarrels about words, which produce envy, dissension, slander, evil suspicions,* ⁵ *and constant friction among people who are depraved in mind and deprived of the truth, imagining that godliness is a means of gain.* ⁶ *But godliness with contentment is great gain,* ⁷ *for we brought nothing into the world, and we cannot take anything out of the world.* ⁸ *But if we have food and clothing, with these we will be content.* ⁹ *But those who desire to be rich fall into temptation, into a snare, into many senseless and harmful desires that plunge people into ruin and destruction.* ¹⁰ *For the love of money is a root of all kinds of evils. It is through this craving that some have wandered away from the faith and pierced themselves with many pangs. But as for you, O man of God, flee these things. Pursue righteousness, godliness, faith, love, steadfastness, gentleness.* ¹² *Fight the good fight of the faith. Take hold of the eternal life to which you were called and about which you made the good confession in the presence of many witnesses.* ¹³ *I charge you in the presence of God, who gives life to all things, and of Christ Jesus, who in his testimony before Pontius Pilate made the good confession,* ¹⁴ *to keep the commandment unstained and free from reproach until the appearing of our Lord Jesus Christ,* ¹⁵ *which he will display at the proper time—he*

who is the blessed and only Sovereign, the King of kings and Lord of lords, [16] *who alone has immortality, who dwells in unapproachable light, whom no one has ever seen or can see. To him be honor and eternal dominion. Amen.*

[17] *As for the rich in this present age, charge them not to be haughty, nor to set their hopes on the uncertainty of riches, but on God, who richly provides us with everything to enjoy.* [18] *They are to do good, to be rich in good works, to be generous and ready to share,* [19] *thus storing up treasure for themselves as a good foundation for the future, so that they may take hold of that which is truly life.*

[20] *O Timothy, guard the deposit entrusted to you. Avoid the irreverent babble and contradictions of what is falsely called "knowledge,"* 21 *for by professing it some have swerved from the faith. Grace be with you.*

Some Bible students have noticed that the last part of this letter parallels the first part. Paul begins by talking about grace and concludes by talking about grace (1:2 and 6:20-21). He offers concrete instruction at the start and concludes with the same practical instruction (1:3 and 6:17-18). He speaks of straying, false teaching, ungodly characteristics, what his life prior to Christ was like, eternal life, Christ as immortal King, while commissioning Timothy to fight the good fight and to watch out for those who have shipwrecked their faith (1:6-20). With remarkable consistency, Paul comes back to those very same concerns at the close of the letter (6:3-21). This kind of chiastic structure is intended to be a memory device. One of the most vital ingredients in servant leadership is a good memory. With sparkling clarity, Paul marks out for Timothy four essential cautions.

First, ***beware of heretical teachers*** (6:3-5). What are they doing in Ephesus? These non-Gospel preachers are teaching *a different doctrine.* They are not Word-directed teachers. Notice with me all the descriptions of this warning in Paul's concluding instructions.

6:3 – "If anyone teaches a different doctrine and does not agree with the sound words…"

6:3 – "and the teaching that accords with godliness…"

6:5 – "deprived of the truth, imagining that godliness is a means of gain."

6:10 – "wandered away from the faith…"

6:21 – "swerved from the faith…"

This is the very same language we noticed in the first part of the letter. These false teachers have not been saturated by the Word. The Scriptures have not read them. Here are some mega questions for all servant leaders: Do I subject my thought to Scripture, or do I subject Scripture to my thought? Does the text master me? Am I growing in my submission to the Word? One of my deepest concerns for the contemporary church is her failed appetite for Scripture intake and the necessary yielding that is required. There is a famine in our land that goes far beyond physical drought, poverty, and hunger. It exceeds some of the worst conditions in places like Somalia and Haiti. There is a spiritual famine for the Word that goes unmet through much of the North American landscape. False teachers and despisers of God's Word abound. Beware.

These heretical teachers are not only deviating from the truth, but they are also *dividing the church.* Notice with me all the strong descriptions in 6:4-5. Words like "unhealthy craving for controversy," "quarrels about words," "produce envy," "dissension," "slander," and "evil suspicions," and "constant friction" dominate this part of the letter and echo 1:4-6. Arrogance has nurtured an unhealthy interest in controversies, resulting in a war of words that has led to fault finding, suspicion, and persistent friction in the church. All of these words paint a picture of spiritual sickness. I once served a congregation where this kind of spirit permeated the church. There were multiple "wannabe-leaders" who worked shrewdly and cunningly behind the scenes to control and manipulate. The first two years of ministry in that church were torturous and depleting.

Several times, I contemplated leaving. I just couldn't bring myself to hand off this ugly situation to another servant leader. I wanted to leave it better than I found it. God's Word, in passages like this very one, sustained me for the long haul.

Heretical teachers in Ephesus were also *drunk on money.* They were not interested in godliness, but in gold. Spiritual formation, a life shaped by the Holy Spirit, was not on their agendas. Paul showed his brilliance at this point. I can hear him advising Timothy with Scriptural clarity and Spirit-filled counsel. You can hear his questions to his young understudy. Does their teaching match Scripture? Does their teaching build up the church? Does their teaching really promote godliness? Beware of anyone who doesn't ace those three questions. Let's explore this idea more deeply. Our first caution is clear. Beware of heretical teachers. Here is the second caution.

Beware of greedy Christians (6:6-10). Paul returned at this point in the letter to what he has previously written in 4:8: "…godliness is of value in every way…" Some apparently thought that godliness was a means to financial gain (6:5). Real contentment, the kind grounded in a life intimately attached to Jesus, does not depend upon external life. That's the essence of the word "contentment" (autarkein). Contentment is based upon Christ's sufficiency, not self-sufficiency. True contentment cannot be found in money, but in Christ alone. Without overstating it, I would want to say loud and clear that money is highly addictive. It is not neutral for most of us. And it is only tamed through honoring God with it and submitting it to His authority and purpose. I never read this section of 1Timothy and not have Proverbs 30:7-9 come to mind:

> Two things I ask of you; deny them not to me before I die:
> Remove far from me falsehood and lying; give me neither
> poverty nor riches; feed me with the food that is needful for
> me, lest I be full and deny you and say, "Who is the LORD?" or
> lest I be poor and steal and profane the name of my God.

Some of you know there are somewhere in the vicinity of two thousand verses in the Bible that deal directly with the issue of money and possessions. The substantial size and concern of God is enough to invite us into deep reflection and caution when it comes to the seduction of money and greedy Christians. I have written of this elsewhere, but it is good to repeat myself now. I know the subtle and tempting nature of having possessions that possess me. I have a long history of hurt and anger with my earthly father. A dysfunctional upbringing, a divorced home, and an alcoholic father wounded my dad deeply. On top of that, he experienced hell on earth as a prisoner of war during WW2. He once asked to borrow five hundred dollars from me to put down on a house in Cincinnati, Ohio. He was relocating to a new ministry and did not have the necessary earnest money. I told him that I did not have that kind of money. I lied. There is no way I can make it look and sound any better than that. I deceived my own father. The Holy Spirit broke me. Before the day was over, I went to the local bank, retrieved the money, and gave it to my dad. Money cannot buy peace of mind. I so appreciate some words that I have tried to memorize. I don't know who originally penned them:

> "Money will buy a bed, but not sleep; books, but not brains; food, but not an appetite; a house but not a home; medicine but not health; luxuries but not culture; amusement but not happiness; a crucifix but not a savior."

Contentment is found in romancing the Divine, not in a love affair with the dollar. Beware. A third word of caution is in order.

Beware of personal compromise (6:11-16 and 6:20-21). I've always been intrigued by the fact that Paul doesn't call Timothy by name until the end of the letter (6:20). I'm not sure what to make of that decision, if anything. I do love the nickname Paul gives Timothy in 6:11 – "man of God." There is something beautiful and prophetic about that description. Man of God is a biblical image or metaphor that is steeped in Old Testament imagery. The term elevates a special relationship with

God. It was used of people like Moses, Samuel, David, Elijah, Elisha, and others. Timothy is called to be the exact opposite of heretical teachers that have infiltrated the life and witness of the church at Ephesus. He is to be tethered to God. Vigorous verbs are used to caution and to encourage Timothy toward authentic ministry and apprenticeship with Jesus. Flee (6:11), pursue (6:11), fight (6:12), take hold of (6:12), charge (6:17), and guard (6:20) are all imperatives. Timothy, as we will see more deeply in 2 Timothy, has been given a sacred trust. He has been "entrusted" (paratheke) with the Gospel of Jesus Christ. The word used is a banking term. It describes a legal transaction, a picture of money or valuables given to someone for sake-keeping. Timothy is called by Paul to be a steward of *the* faith. Don't miss the obvious. On three separate occasions in Paul's closing comments, he speaks of *the* faith and its importance (6:10, 12, 21).

This is the sacred trust of remembering, elevating, and passing along the essential importance of Jesus's life, death at the cross, burial in a borrowed tomb, and ultimate resurrection and victory over sin and death (1 Corinthians 15:1-3). The content of that story, the essence of God's grand meta-narrative is what Paul is passing along to Timothy. It has been passed on to us as a perpetual relay of truth (2 Timothy 2:2). So, another critical question is appropriate here. What are you doing as a servant leader to insure that the Gospel is not compromised? Watch out for the cunning way in which the enemy tries to start the downward compromise with personal decisions that seem so small. Think of your time alone with Jesus. Think of your Scripture-intake. Consider your personal rhythms and disciplines, your free-time, and especially your need for on-going grace. Perhaps that is why Paul concludes with, "Grace be with you" (6:21). A fourth and final word, perhaps an obvious one, is needed.

Beware of trusting things (6:17-19). I know it can sound like I'm repeating myself. But there is a subtle difference here. Notice with me all the "rich" talk in this little paragraph. On four occasions, Paul speaks of riches and wealth. It sounds like he is talking to poor Christians at this point, but I think he is actually addressing rich ones. There is a vital contrast between 6:6-10 and 6:17-19. In the first paragraph, it sounds like Paul is describing Christians who are struggling financially and want to become rich. That's why he offers the caution about the love of money. It is the root of all kinds of evil (6:10). However, in this second part Paul seems to caution Christians who have resources to avoid succumbing to false pride and false security. That kind of temptation can lead to forgetting God and forgetting the needs of others. The implication is clear. God is generous, and so we should be as well. A quarter of the world's population lives in abject poverty. That is, they do not know whether or not they will eat again. Many of them have never heard the Good News of Jesus or seen it at work.

The command language of 6:17 and 6:18 is a reminder to Timothy that we can only command if we have already obeyed. Watch out for placing your hope in wealth. It will disappoint. It will mislead. It will seduce. Generosity is the way of the Kingdom. Paul's words in 6:19 echo Jesus's words in the Sermon on the Mount found in Matthew 6:19-21:

> [19] *Do not lay up for yourselves **treasures** on earth, where moth and rust destroy and where thieves break in and steal,* [20] *but lay up for yourselves **treasures** in heaven, where neither moth nor rust destroys and where thieves do not break in and steal.* [21] *For where your **treasure** is, there your heart will be also.*

Treasure (thesaurus), in Paul's day, was found in gold, grain, and garments. Personal possessions and things can be taken from us. Moths can eat away at garments. Rust can tarnish and diminish what we hold dear. Thieves can dig into our safe places and rob us of our treasures. The clear way out, the wise way, is found in investing in Kingdom matters. Good deeds, generosity of resources, and a willingness to share what God has given us is the Jesus way (6:18).

I know a married couple who have modeled for me the kind of Kingdom investment this section of Scripture is describing. Instead of placing trust in *things*, my friends have chosen to place their trust in *the sovereign God*. Year after year, they have increased their giving by a percentage or two. Their ultimate objective, which both agreed upon, was to come to the place where they surrendered back to God and invested in His service half of their income. God deals with each of us individually as stewards of His possessions. Paul never tells Timothy to give away half of the treasures God has entrusted to his care. Rather, he carefully lays out a portrait of servant leadership that is saturated in the life of Jesus. So let that be our final word in 1 Timothy. Be aware of Jesus's heart and way and serve accordingly.

A Little Manual for Servant Leaders

CHAPTER 10
Shaping the Servant Leader's Character
2 Timothy 2:1-18

"Spiritual formation is the imparting of the character of Christ in the inmost self"
(Willard, Dallas. Averbeck, R., Bock, D., & Willard, D. (1999). **Biblical Theological Foundations for Spiritual Formation.** *(p. 18). Spiritual Formation Conference conducted at Trinity Evangelical Divinity School, Deerfield, IL).*

Servant leadership is ongoing character training. Our character is constantly being formed by the indwelling presence of the Holy Spirit as we cooperate with His purpose. But what exactly is character? Let's take another pause before hammering away at that question. Fifteen years have come and gone since Paul met, recruited, and mentored Timothy (Acts 16:1). Lots of time and travel has occurred between Lystra, Timothy's home town, and Ephesus, his current ministry assignment. Two significant missionary journeys have come and gone (2nd and 3rd – Acts 16:1-21:3), and Timothy has completed two previous ministries in Thessalonica and Corinth (1 Thessalonians 3:2 and 1 Corinthians 4:17). Paul has landed in a Roman prison, and his execution is imminent. There is lots of speculation on the exact date of Paul's death, but, regardless, he realizes the day of his departure from this life is close. Somewhere between 65 and 67 AD, he writes this final letter to his beloved partner in ministry. Perhaps a year or two have elapsed between the writing of his first letter and this one. Paul's preoccupation is with Timothy's character as it relates to the Gospel and his leadership. Timothy, of course, is way in over his head. Aren't we all? So, back to our question, what is character?

Originally, "character" (Greek – charakter) was an engraving tool. Later, the word was used to describe the impression the engraving tool made. When the writer to the Hebrews wanted to select a word that portrayed the relationship between God the Father and God the Son, he chose this very one. Jesus is the "exact imprint" of the Father (Hebrews 1:3). In other words, Jesus is the real or genuine image of God. He is uniquely distinctive from the Father but equal to the Father. Character becomes the way in which we describe someone's integrity. If, for example, we say of someone, "She has character," we mean she is genuine or authentic. A person of character is someone who can be trusted. I deeply appreciate the way Os Guinness defines our topic:

> "As traditionally understood, from the Hebrews and Greeks onward, character is the inner form that makes anyone or anything what it is – whether a person, a wine, or a historical period. Thus character is clearly distinct from such concepts as personality, image, reputation, or celebrity. It is the essential 'stuff' a person is made of, the inner reality and quality in which thoughts, speech, decision, behavior, and relations are rooted...So a person's character expresses most deeply what constitutes him or her as a unique individual" (1999, p. 12).

So, what shapes the character of a servant leader according to the Apostle Paul? Here is what he told Timothy:

1 *Paul, an apostle of Christ Jesus by the will of God according to the promise of the life that is in Christ Jesus,*

² *To Timothy, my beloved child:*

Grace, mercy, and peace from God the Father and Christ Jesus our Lord.

³ I thank God whom I serve, as did my ancestors, with a clear conscience, as I remember you constantly in my prayers night and day. ⁴ As I remember your tears, I long to see you, that I may be filled with joy. ⁵ I am reminded of your sincere faith, a faith that dwelt first in your grandmother Lois and your mother Eunice and now, I am sure, dwells in you as well. ⁶ For this reason I remind you to fan into flame the gift of God, which is in you through the laying on of my hands, ⁷ for God gave us a spirit not of fear but of power and love and self-control.

⁸ Therefore do not be ashamed of the testimony about our Lord, nor of me his prisoner, but share in suffering for the gospel by the power of God, ⁹ who saved us and called us to a holy calling, not because of our works but because of his own purpose and grace, which he gave us in Christ Jesus before the ages began, ¹⁰ and which now has been manifested through the appearing of our Savior Christ Jesus, who abolished death and brought life and immortality to light through the gospel, ¹¹ for which I was appointed a preacher and apostle and teacher, ¹² which is why I suffer as I do. But I am not ashamed, for I know whom I have believed, and I am convinced that he is able to guard until that Day what has been entrusted to me. ¹³ Follow the pattern of the sound words that you have heard from me, in the faith and love that are in Christ Jesus. ¹⁴ By the Holy Spirit who dwells within us, guard the good deposit entrusted to you.

¹⁵ You are aware that all who are in Asia turned away from me, among whom are Phygelus and Hermogenes. ¹⁶ May the Lord grant mercy to the household of Onesiphorus, for he often refreshed me and was not ashamed of my chains, ¹⁷ but when he arrived in Rome he searched for me earnestly and found me—¹⁸ may the Lord grant him to find mercy from the Lord on that Day!—and you well know all the service he rendered at Ephesus.

God is constantly molding the character of a servant leader. I hear Paul identifying five significant tools in the hands of God for character formation. Here's the first one – *calling* (1:1 and 1:9). God shapes the character of the servant leader through constant and persistent reminders of calling. Paul begins with a reminder to Timothy that he is a man on mission, "one who has been sent" by God (apostle), not by Paul's own design or initiative, but by "the will of God" (1:1). This man has an unswerving conviction that God has laid claim on his life. That's calling talk, not elitist talk. Everyone is called to follow Jesus. All are gifted in specific ways to work alongside the Father to accomplish His global mission. This is true of Paul, Timothy, you, and me. Some of us are called to specific locations and to certain leadership responsibilities, but all are called. God, through Jesus, has "saved us and called us" to this holy life (1:9). Paul never got over this point. Nine of his thirteen letters, depending upon authorship, begin in the same way this letter does. The Apostle reminds his readers about God's will, His command, His calling. God made all of this possible. Paul merely yielded and followed. This mentor to Timothy was not self-appointed. Do you believe this same God has appointed you to servant leadership? Do you have an inner conviction placed there by the Holy Spirit and confirmed in God's Word and affirmed by His church that He has called you? That calling can sustain you. It has encouraged me over and over again to stay the course.

I was a young man in military service when I heard the story of Dawson Trotman, founder of the Navigators. The Navigator mission is to know Christ and to make Him known. Dawson was living a life of deep discontentment and rebellion against God. Two older ladies in a Southern California church challenged him to begin memorizing Scripture. Dawson simply did it. Amazing! God's implanted Word began to take hold of his heart, and, ultimately, he realized that God was speaking directly to him and surrendered to our Savior's purpose and plan. Only heaven knows how many men and women were influenced for eternity. Dawson began to share his faith actively and grew to understand the importance of helping a new believer to grow in Christ. In ways beyond my understanding, because of Dawson's obedience to the calling of God, I'm here today as a Jesus-follower. Trotman lost his life trying to save a woman from losing her life in 1959. I was only six years old. I never met him, but his spiritual legacy is intertwined with mine. It was through Charlie Webb, a man working with a "Navigator ministry" on my Kansas base, that I came to yield my life to the Lordship of Jesus. The same God that called Paul called me, and He became my King of Kings and Commander-in-Chief. Calling is one of God's most loved character-shaping tools.

God also uses *home* to refine our character. Most of us do not come from perfect homes. Maybe none exist. Some, of course, are better than others. What we know about Timothy's is sketchy at best. His father was probably not a Christian. His mom was Jewish and a Jesus-follower, but his dad was Greek (Act 16:1). Timothy's primary influence, prior to Paul, was probably female. Both his mother and grandmother were used by God to deepen his faith in Christ. None of us ever stand alone. All of us have people in our journeys that are significant influencers and cheerleaders in our Jesus-following-life. Home remains one of the most character-shaping places long after we have left it. Whether our memories are negative, positive, or mixed, God can and does use that environment to His glory. Notice with me the references to home and family. Paul mentions his own legacy in 1:3 by speaking of his "ancestors." He does not forget his own physical and spiritual family tree. He also specifically identifies Timothy's grandmother Lois and mother, Eunice, as key influencers in this young apprentice's spiritual journey (1:5). Home is a significant instrument in God's divine tool box. There is in Paul a lasting confidence that God uses the home as a character-shaping place.

Do you ever wonder what you would be like if not for God's soul-carving of you through your home? Do you ever contemplate growing up in someone else's family? Be assured, God makes no mistakes. I grew up in a home that was migratory and dysfunctional. We moved eight times in my first seventeen years of life. Financial stress and family anger flavored my home experience. I longed for a genuine home and looked for it anywhere and everywhere. I often cried and ached over the mess that was my home life. For a long period of time, I tried to squelch it, to deny it, and even to throw it away. However, God wastes nothing. He is forever at work morphing us to look more and more like His Son. Home and all the "stuff" that comes with it is part of God's building material. So, what is God teaching you about your home life that He can use for His glory and His purpose?

God has a third character-molding tool. We'll call it *friendship.* On two separate occasions early in the letter, Paul hints at this vital ingredient (1:2, 1:4). The Apostle has a deep awareness that God uses friendship, especially Christian friends. Paul refers to Timothy as, "my beloved child" (contrasted with 1Timothy 1:2 – "my *true* child") and speaks of the intimate friendship that exists in the Triune God – "God the Father and Christ Jesus our Lord" and "by the Holy Spirit" (1:2, 1:14). Here, then, are two marvelous examples of friendship – one earthly and one heavenly. In an extraordinary confession, Paul remembers Timothy's tears at their last departure and announces, "I long to see you" (1:4). Only genuine friends talk like that. John Stott says, "After our parents it is our friends who influence us most, especially if they are also in some sense our teachers. And Timothy had in Paul an outstanding friend" (1973, p. 28). Spiritual friendship shapes our character.

Several years ago, while studying the Book of Proverbs, I noticed all the friendship talk. That study provided for me four critical questions that must be asked of every friend and friendship. First, *will this friend stand by me?* No one needs a fair weather friend. All of us require someone who will stick with us through thick and thin. Loyalty is the word. Proverbs 17:17 puts it like this, "A friend loves at all times, and a brother is born for adversity." Second, *will this friend tell me the truth?* No one can travel very far in the Jesus-following life without someone who walks along and speaks the truth in love. Christian friendship is not cheap, and it cannot be hurried. Proverbs 27:6 declares, "Faithful are the wounds of a friend; profuse are the kisses of an enemy." Third, *will this friend keep a confidence?* Close and honest communion is a prerequisite to real friendship. All of us long for a friend who can keep our secrets in the vault of his heart. Proverbs 17:9 warns, "Whoever covers an offense seeks love, but he who repeats a matter separates close friends." Fourth, and most importantly, *will this friend cause me to love God more?* An authentic friend compels me to do my best, especially in my relationship with God. Anyone who would intentionally lead me astray is not my faithful friend, but my spiritual enemy. Run. Proverbs 22:24-25 offers this wise caution: "Make no friendship with a man given to anger, nor go with a wrathful man, lest you learn his ways and entangle yourself in a snare." Sacred friendships make all the difference in our long journeys. A spiritual friend is one of God's greatest masterpieces in deepening and defining our characters.

God has a fourth tool often overlooked in our character development. Let's label this one ***giftedness.*** Paul speaks of this directly to Timothy: "I remind you to fan into flame the gift of God, which is in you through the laying on of my hands" (1:6). The tendency of fire is for it to go out. We must always watch over the fire of our hearts. Here, in this passage, Paul uses a fascinating word for Timothy's giftedness. He uses the word "charisma," or "grace thing." In other words, our giftedness is not dependent upon us. It comes from above, from the Father who delights in sharing His grace with His children. He shapes our gifts based on His will and mission and on our personality and passion. He decides. He offers. He shapes. Each gift mix is unique. The Scriptures speak of many different kinds of "grace things" – prophesying, serving, teaching, speaking, encouraging, contributing, leading, showing mercy, healing, miraculous powers, discerning, tongue speaking and interpreting, offering hospitality, etc. (Romans 12:3-8, 1 Corinthians 12:4-11, Ephesians 4:11-

13, and 1 Peter 4:10-11). The lists are not intended to be exhaustive, but representative of the varied ways God gifts each of us. These gifts are not earned. We do not work out the design on our own. We simply cooperate. We hone and refine what God has entrusted to our care. We "fan into flame" our giftedness (anazopureo). This language isn't found anywhere else in the New Testament. We have a holy responsibility. Admittedly, Paul does use two other words to describe these gifts that do not occur in 2 Timothy. He speaks of them as "pneumatikos" or "spiritual things" in 1 Corinthians and "domata" or "gifts" in Ephesians 4. All of the language assumes God as the source, but reminds us of our need to stoke the inner fire of our own hearts so that spiritual atrophy is avoided. I'm humbled.

We simply do not know what Timothy's gift mix was. Based on what we read in 1 and 2 Timothy, we can assume his giftedness included teaching, preaching, and sharing the Good News. Whatever they were, God had given Timothy a sacred trust. Timothy was a caretaker or steward of those gifts. As I get older, I want to honor God more and more through how I care for what He has entrusted to me – resources, possessions, time, health, and especially my giftedness. How about you? Our calling, regardless of how God has gifted us, is to apply them courageously and caringly to the ministry He has given us. No one is unimportant. No gift is unnecessary. God alone has graciously given us spirits of power, love, and self-discipline to accomplish what He intends (1:7). It will require some work, and some cooperating on our part.

The first time I preached was a miserable experience for me and for those listeners. I was to speak at the Broadway Christian Church, in Mattoon, Illinois, on a Sunday evening. The preacher gave me specific instructions. Preach for twenty minutes. I said everything I knew about the passage given to me in five minutes, so I simply repeated myself three more miserable times. Oh, how I prayed for Jesus to return! I learned that evening in an unforgettable way that God gave me some gifts, but I was responsible for honing them. This fourth tool is a sobering reminder that

God has gifted every apprentice of Jesus, and we must continually stoke the holy fire needed to work alongside Him. That is profoundly character-shaping.

Fifth, and finally, God uses *the Gospel* to form our characters (1:8-18). This particular tool gets most of Paul's emphasis and attention. Paul reminds Timothy of three crucial duties when it comes to the Gospel. Timothy is to actively share it (1:8a, 11), bravely suffer for it (1:8b & 12), and faithfully secure it in his heart and mind (1:13-14). We are called to that same Gospel commitment. We "entrust" because God has "entrusted" (1:12, 1:14). God acted first. He committed something to us, and so we, in turn, say "yes." Will we blow it? Of course we will. Will He remain faithful when we are faithless? Of course He will. The emphasis is upon God, but the Gospel does give us a holy responsibility. "Follow" (eche) and "guard" (phylasso) are the primary words here. They paint a picture of a soldier's allegiance and loyalty. An urgent attention and submission is assumed. Servant leaders have a "good deposit" given to them. Paul even offers a negative example of two people who failed to do what Paul is exhorting Timothy to do (1:15). These two deserters of the Gospel are Phygelus and Hermogenes. We are clueless about who they were and what exactly they did. Somehow, they lost their devotion to the Gospel. On the positive side, Onesiphorus is presented as someone who anchored himself to that same Gospel. He even showed up in that Roman prison and did everything he could to refresh and to renew Paul. The Holy Spirit is the one who makes all of this even possible (1:14). The life, death, burial, and resurrection of Jesus – this Good News – is the primary tool God uses to morph us into looking more and more like His Son. Are you, servant leader, cooperating with what God wants to do in and through you? Is your life more and more branded with the Gospel of Jesus Christ?

None of us ever gets beyond the Gospel. There is nothing more sophisticated or advanced than what Paul is attempting to speak into the heart of Timothy and to us. Not long ago, I was reading an article that Dr.

Tim Keller had written on his website. He called it "The Centrality of the Gospel" (2009, redeemercitytocity.com). His words get to the heart of the essential nature of the Gospel in our character development. Prayerfully consider them.

> "After the Gospel has regenerated us and we are converted, it is the instrument of all continual growth and spiritual progress...The Gospel is a living thing (cf. Romans 1:16), like a seed or a tree that brings more and more new life...The Gospel is not the minimum required doctrine necessary to enter the kingdom but the way we make all progress in the kingdom. We are not justified by the Gospel and then sanctified by obedience; rather the Gospel is *the way* we grow (Galatians 3:1-3) and are renewed (Colossians 1:6)...All our problems come from a failure to apply the Gospel...All of us to some degree live around the truth of the Gospel but do not 'get it.' So the key to continual and deeper spiritual renewal and revival is *continual rediscovery of the Gospel*...We must bring *everything* in line with the Gospel...The Gospel is the way that *anything* is renewed and transformed by Christ – whether a heart, a relationship, a church, or a community" (pp. 1-5).

God is constantly shaping the character of a servant leader through tools like calling, home, friendship, and giftedness, but none more powerfully than the Gospel. Servant leaders have been eternally marked by it.

CHAPTER 11
Finding Your Servant Leadership Metaphor
2 Timothy 2:1-13

"When we encounter an image in the Bible, therefore, we need to learn to ask two questions. (1) What is the literal picture? (2) What does this image evoke? Answering the first question will insure that we have allowed the Bible to speak to our 'right brain' – that part of us that responds to the concrete realities that the Bible records. Answering the second question will lead to an awareness of connotations, associations and significance. If either of these levels of response is missing, our experience of the Bible is impoverished"
(Ryken, Leland, Wilhoit, James C., Longman III, Tremper. (1998). Eds.
Dictionary of Biblical Imagery. *(p. xiv). Downers Grove: IVP).*

I delight in a good metaphor. For quite some time, I thought of motorcycle riding as a perfect picture of life's journey. I even framed up a personal mission statement that I used for a while that went like this: "I will ride the Holiness Highway with joy and invite as many as I can to come along with me." I know; it's a bit clunky and corny, but it was heartfelt. Ultimately, I have gravitated toward the use of "soldier" as my chosen metaphor. It fits me. I won't bore you with the details.

Scripture embraces the use of images and metaphors. God, Himself, is called a rock, shield, sword, fire, refuge, and other assorted images. Jesus refers to Himself as bread, light, way, door, gate, shepherd, vine, water, and other metaphors. Even Christians are not exempted from having those same metaphors and images applied to them – salt, light, epistles, living stones, holy priesthood, chosen people, aliens, strangers, and other word pictures. The Bible describes itself as a fire, a hammer, a sword, a lamp, etc. You get the idea. Metaphors and images abound. When Paul was attempting to explain to Timothy what it looked like to be a faithful servant leader, he chose multiple metaphors. Four significant ones are found in the following passage:

> **2** *You then, my child, be strengthened by the grace that is in Christ Jesus, ² and what you have heard from me in the presence of many witnesses entrust to faithful men who will be able to teach others also.³ Share in suffering as a good **soldier** of Christ Jesus. ⁴ No soldier gets entangled in civilian pursuits, since his aim is to please the one who enlisted him. ⁵ An **athlete** is not crowned unless he competes according to the rules. ⁶ It is the hard-working **farmer** who ought to have the first share of the crops. ⁷ Think over what I say, for the Lord will give you understanding in everything.*
>
> *⁸ Remember Jesus Christ, risen from the dead, the offspring of David, as preached in my gospel, ⁹ for which I am suffering, bound with chains as a **criminal**. But the word of God is not bound! ¹⁰ Therefore I endure everything for the sake of the elect, that they also may obtain the salvation that is in Christ Jesus with eternal glory. ¹¹ The saying is trustworthy, for:*
>
> *If we have died with him, we will also live with him;*
>
> *¹² if we endure, we will also reign with him;*
>
> *if we deny him, he also will deny us;*
>
> *¹³ if we are faithless, he remains faithful—*
>
> *For he cannot deny himself.*

"Think over" (noeo – 2:7) is the focusing word phrase. It simply means to reflect, perceive, or ponder something until you understand it. In this case, the reference is to the metaphors Paul employed. He opens this section of Scripture with a reminder to Timothy to "be strong in the grace that is in Christ Jesus" and to be a part of a perpetual relay of truth intentionally that includes Paul, Timothy, "reliable men," and "others." Four specific exchanges of the Gospel baton are presented (2:1-2). All of this grace talk and relay imagery unfolds for us these four concrete metaphors worthy of our attention as servant leaders.

First, **servant leadership looks like a good soldier** (2:3). The picture here is one of obeying and serving. I'm convinced from my own study that Paul was an admirer of the Roman army. He may not have always appreciated their methods, but he was drawn to their discipline. Soldiers were posted all over the Empire, and someone as well-traveled as Paul would have encountered them everywhere. This, of course, is not the only place in Scripture where he mentions them directly or reminds the reader of soldiers indirectly. Consider the following:

*"Who serves as a **soldier** at his own expense?"* (1 Corinthians 9:7)

*"...By truthful speech, and the power of God; with the **weapons** of righteousness for the right hand and for the left..."*
(2 Corinthians 6:7).

*"For though we walk in the flesh, we are not **waging war** according to the flesh. For the **weapons** of our **warfare** are not of the flesh but have divine power to destroy strongholds"*
(2 Corinthians 10:3-4).

"Finally, be strong in the Lord and in the strength of his might.
*[11] Put on the **whole armor** of God, that you may be able to stand against the schemes of the devil. [12] For we do not wrestle against flesh and blood, but against the rulers, against the authorities, against the cosmic powers over this present darkness, against the spiritual forces of evil in the heavenly places. [13] Therefore take up the **whole armor** of God, that you may be able to withstand in the evil day, and having done all, to stand firm. [14] Stand therefore, having fastened on the belt of truth, and having put on the breastplate of righteousness, [15] and, as shoes for your feet, having put*

on the readiness given by the gospel of peace. ¹⁶ *In all circumstances take up the shield of faith, with which you can extinguish all the flaming darts of the evil one;* ¹⁷ *and take the helmet of salvation, and the sword of the Spirit, which is the word of God,* ¹⁸ *praying at all times in the Spirit, with all prayer and supplication"* (Ephesians 6:10-18).

*"I have thought it necessary to send to you Epaphroditus my brother and fellow worker and **fellow soldier**..."* (Philippians 2:25).

*"Paul, a prisoner for Christ Jesus, and Timothy our brother, to Philemon our beloved fellow worker and Apphia our sister and Archippus our **fellow soldier**, and the church in your house: Grace to you and peace from God our Father and the Lord Jesus Christ"* (Philemon 1-2).

Paul seems to have a clear assumption of focused allegiance when he inserts soldier imagery into his writing. Dr. Walter Liefeld eloquently describes the power of Paul's metaphor:

"By Paul's time the Roman Empire had long since secured its dominance, but to maintain the borders was a continuing task. The military forces were everywhere, and rapid troop movements were made possible by the famous Roman road system. Soldiers were especially concentrated at the far-flung borders, where insurrections were especially likely. This meant extensive training. There could be no weakening of resolve, skill, or strength. Daily discipline was enforced; diversions could not be tolerated. Because of the extensive distribution of the troops, Paul's image of the soldier's devotion was immediately recognizable and impressive" (1999, pp. 247-248).

The Roman soldier modeled a life of difficulty, not ease. All Jesus-followers are soldiers on active duty, no exemptions and no exceptions. Paul reminds Timothy that a soldier must "share in suffering" (sunkakopatheo) or endure in hardship. The invitation is clear. All Jesus-followers are invited into a life of "shared suffering." It is the same word

Finding Your Servant Leadership Metaphor

Paul used in 2 Timothy 1:8. Devotion to duty and the desire not to disappoint the commanding officer shapes what Paul wanted to speak into the life of Timothy and us. Roman soldiers were always training. Some observers have noted that these disciplined men appeared to be born with weapons in their hands. They lived an exceptionally structured life. Each one drilled constantly to march, jump, run, swim, fight, and survive. Don't overlook the obvious as it relates to your life of servant leadership. Watch out for compromise and distraction. Detachment from trivial pursuits is at the core of the Jesus-following soldier's duty. The imperatives are obvious. Keep the regiment of your spiritual training. Hone your spiritual disciplines. Carry your spiritual weapons everywhere you go. Soldiers stay focused. The mark of a good soldier, as they say, is what it takes to stop him. Servant leadership looks like that.

Second, ***servant leadership looks like an honest athlete*** (2:5). Paul's second metaphor is all about training correctly and competing fairly, no short cuts, no cheating. Think back to 1Timothy 4:7-8 and the invitation to a life of godly training. Paul embraced pictures of athletes who competed according to the rules (1 Corinthians 9:24-27). John Stott says it so succinctly: "No rules, no wreath" (1973, p. 55). Rule-keeping may sound unattractive to our twenty-first century ears, but no one can become the servant leader God desires that does not submit to an ordered way of life. Paul is not speaking of keeping the Law. Christ alone saves, not the Law. What he means when he speaks of the athlete who "competes according to the rules" (nominos) is someone who is marked with integrity in following the prescribed requirements. It is also the same word he used back in 1Timothy 1:8: "Now we know that the law is good if one uses it *lawfully*." Paul never spells out for Timothy what those rules might be for the servant leader. Maybe Paul had witnessed the Isthmian Games held near Corinth. We talked about this previously. Maybe he saw the implications for the servant leader as he viewed athletes running, wrestling, and boxing according to prearranged rules. Donald Guthrie has assisted my thinking here:

"In the Olympic games there were strict rules which had to be obeyed…Each athlete for these Olympics had to state on oath that he had fulfilled the necessary ten months' training before he was permitted to enter into the contest. Any athlete who had not subjected himself to the necessary discipline would have no chance of winning and would in fact lower the standard of the Games. There were severe penalties imposed on any who infringed the rules" (1990, p. 153).

Whatever Paul had in mind with this metaphor he meant for Timothy to be a minister and do ministry in a way that won the prize. Again, Paul was not speaking of earning salvation, but intentionally finishing with excellence what Timothy had started. The wreath imagery here was something coveted by ancient athletes. This treasured prize, woven together from a palm branch or celery stock and placed on the winner's head, resembled modern Olympians having a gold medal placed around their necks. Amazing! We are not talking about a victor's crown crafted from solid gold. The notion of striving for that kind of prize is humbling when I consider the eternal reward of being in God's presence without sin, pain, and brokenness.

It fascinates me that some of the early Christians thought of themselves as "athletes of God." William Harmless, in a majestic work called *Desert Christians: An Introduction to the Literature of Early Monasticism* (2004), assists us in grasping the significance of the athletic metaphor. Harmless is writing about John Cassian (360 to 435 AD), a monk influenced by two of my spiritual heroes, John Chrysostom and Evagrius Ponticus. In Cassian's *Institutes*, the monk is described as an Olympic athlete. Harmless offers this insight:

"Just as Olympic athletes train and subject their bodies to fierce discipline to achieve mastery and freedom of action, so monks discipline their bodies to cease being 'slaves of fleshly desire.' Just as young athletes must move up the ladder of competition to qualify for the Olympics, so the young monk progresses from bodily disciplines to interior ones: 'Victory in the contests is never wanting to the athlete of Christ as he dwells in the flesh, but the stronger he grows through successive triumphs, the more demanding the series of struggles that waits him.' And just as Olympic athletes keep their gaze fixed on the ultimate goal, the laurel crown (the ancient equivalent of the gold medal), so the monk keeps his gaze fixed and 'does not run in uncertainty because, in looking upon the heavenly Jerusalem, he is clear as to where his swift and undeviating heart should be directed'" (p. 385).

Wise servant leaders meditate regularly on this imagery of the athlete.

Third, *servant leadership looks like a hardworking farmer* (2:6). Jesus always seemed to draw on this metaphor as He taught large crowds and a small huddle of apprentices. He spoke often of plowing, sowing, tending, and harvesting (Matthew 13:3ff and Luke 8:5ff). "A farmer went out to sow his seed" was the way in which our Savior would introduce a Kingdom story that involved indiscriminate seed scattering that seemed careless, fragile, vulnerable, and earth shattering (Mark 4:1ff). This metaphor has a long and illustrious career. Adam, the Bible says, was left in the Garden of Eden "to work it and keep it" (Genesis 2:15). The prophet Amos was a farmer called by the Lord to do a different kind of farming (Amos 7:14-15). The specific emphasis here in 2 Timothy 2:6 is that of hard work. The vital piece in understanding this word picture is the costly labor involved in growing and eventually harvesting a crop. There is no glamour in this, no large crowds that would generate applause and recognition. One farmer toiling with persistence eventually experiences deep satisfaction.

My life has been deeply blessed through the writings of Ray Stedman, long time pastor of the Peninsula Bible Church in Palo Alto, California. Ray died in 1992, but his teaching continues to outlast him. In a beautiful reflection on the Pastoral Letters, Stedman reminds us all of the way of the hardworking farmer:

"There are too many Christians who think that the Christian life is focused totally on them. It's all about what God can do for them, not what they should do for God. They have a sense of spiritual entitlement. They think they should be able to pray for a big house with a Mercedes in the garage, and a life of ease, devoid of any major problems. A number of preachers encourage this kind of self-centered Christianity. Those who adopt this attitude of Christian entitlement have a weak faith that is easily shattered…You won't find this kind of Christianity in the Bible. Salvation is a free gift, but it isn't a free ride…So Paul warns us in this passage against assumption that we are entitled to a life of ease. The Christian life takes work…Like a farmer, we might have to rise up early and work in expectation of a harvest" (2009, pp. 207-208).

Simply put – farmers work hard. This deserves some time and attention in the life of the faithful servant leader.

Most Bible students and commentators do not spend any time exploring the implications of Paul's fourth metaphor. Perhaps I am simply wasting time here, but I'll risk it. ***Servant leadership looks like a chained criminal*** (2:9). Of course, my suggestion for this fourth metaphor can appear silly. Can there even be a good "criminal?" My mind immediately races to Joseph and Jeremiah in the Old Testament (Genesis 39:20ff and Jeremiah 37:4ff) and to Peter and Paul in the New Testament (Acts 12:4ff, 16:23ff, 24:27, Ephesians 3:1, 4:1, and 2Timothy 1:8). The term "criminal" (kakourgos) was reserved for those who committed heinous crimes against Rome. We don't know the specific reasons why Paul chose this term for himself. A criminal was literally one who did "wrong" or "evil." Revolutionaries or insurrectionists, like the two hung on each side of our Lord at Golgotha, were labeled with this term (Luke 23:32, 33, 39). The vivid contrast Paul chose here was between his circumstance and the Word of God. Paul might be chained, but the Scriptures were not. Paul might be confined, but the Word was not. Paul might be executed by

Emperor Nero, but God's Word could not be stopped. The entire picture here is one of hardship and suffering. It absolutely fits the overall portrait Paul wanted to paint for Timothy. The Jesus-following life is not easy.

C.K. Barrett, respected New Testament Scholar (1917-2011), offers a superb summary:

> "The main point of this small paragraph (vv. 3-7) as a whole is to exhort Timothy to take his share of hardship; and the metaphors, when duly pondered, suggest that beyond warfare is victory, beyond athletic effort a prize, and beyond agricultural labor a crop. In the same way, Timothy's share of hardship will be followed by reward" (1963, p. 102).

I would humbly add, beyond imprisonment is ultimate release. Give these images some time and attention. Just as a soldier eventually needs leave, an athlete renewal, a farmer rest, and a criminal justice, so the servant leader needs silence and solitude. Reflect. Think. Create some space for meditation. Find your metaphor.

Whatever Paul meant by all this metaphor talk, surely he intended to encourage and comfort Timothy with these words. At the close of this section of Scripture, Paul elevated the example of Jesus (2:8), himself (2:9), and the entire Christian experience ("we" in 2:10-13). Perhaps scholars are correct when they suggest that these final verses composed some kind of early Christian hymn. The symmetry is astounding. Soldier, athlete, and farmer set alongside Jesus, Paul chained as a criminal, and the 24-7 cross-bearing-life of the Jesus-follower. At every turn, Paul emphasized the cost of discipleship. The power of a metaphor is its ability to instill perseverance and stamina. Find yours. Absorb all the meaning out of it you can. After all, servant leadership is never easy, but our Savior always remains faithful.

A Little Manual for Servant Leaders

CHAPTER 12

The Servant Leader's Long Obedience
2 Timothy 2:14-26

"The essential thing in heaven and earth is…that there should be long obedience in the same direction…the long run… something which has made life worth living"
(Nietzsche, Friedrich. (1907). **Beyond Good and Evil.** *(pp. 106-109, Section 188). Translated by Helen Zimmern. London).*

Somewhere in my early fifties, I began a concentrated effort to reclaim my body. You understand, right? My six-foot, two-inch frame had begun to sag. Sorry for that mental picture. I, like so many, had not exercised properly, eaten correctly, or rested intentionally. I simply decided one morning to do something about it. I got up and started walking, eventually running – maybe the words plodding and pounding are more accurate, always under the cover of darkness. No one wants to see a middle-aged guy huffing and puffing through the neighborhood, close to cardiac arrest, dragging along a large belly. One block turned into one mile. One mile turned into two miles. Eventually, a 5K race was completed. And that led to a half-marathon and, ultimately, to a full marathon. Some of the credit should be given to my oldest daughter, Lindsey, the health advocate (nut!) and some to a friend who encouraged me to do more heart-related exercising (Chuck Sackett – still my friend). I had lifted weights for years but had failed to keep my own weight off and to do any kind of cardio training. Almost ten years have come and gone. Weight control will always be a battle for me. I will never have the sculptured look some desire. I'm really ok with that. My mind, though, has been resolved. I want to continue the stewardship of my body. A long obedience is required.

Surely, at this point in reading the book, you have discerned that servant leadership, whatever it entails, includes a long obedience. Because Paul was Timothy's greatest encourager, he selected three more metaphors to assist his younger partner in ministry. These three are worker, vessel (vessels), and servant. We will unpack them in this chapter. However, before we explore these rich and meaningful images, let's take another pause and remind ourselves of the historical and literary context. Paul's choice of metaphors is not haphazard. He harbors great concern for Timothy and the church he pastors. The First Christian Church at Ephesus needed constant reminder to stay the course. Word wars, quarreling about words, had begun (logomacheo – 2:14). This is the only occasion in the New Testament where this verb occurs. The noun, ironically, is found in 1Timothy 6:4. Some sort of theological wrangling and hairsplitting was prevalent. The tricks of Satan abounded. The enemy's strategy to divide and conquer needed to be recognized and defeated. Remember that false teachers had infiltrated the Ephesian church. Scripture quarreling was dividing the congregation.

No one ever wins in verbal combat. I know husbands and wives who think they got the best of their spouses or politicians who think they defeated their opponents with slick and polished retort. But if we could step back for a moment and carefully weigh the arguments, most of the time we would concur that no one wins the war of words, especially as it relates to the Jesus-following life. Please know I'm not speaking here of theological debate. There is a legitimate place for apologetics and biblical discussion. What I'm particularly trying to describe here is the needless arguing and wrangling over words and positions that only alienate faith-based people even further. Word wars, then and now, can easily sabotage the servant leader's faithful journey. Ray Stedman was absolutely correct when he wrote the following:

> "I have seen Christians battle one another over such matters as the proper mode of baptism, the proper interpretation of Bible prophecy, styles of worship music, and on and on. Is it right to split the church over such matters? Or should we be more concerned to show love for one another, whatever our differences? Today, one word that divides many churches is *inerrancy*. This is a good word. It means that the Scriptures were given to us by God through the Bible writers without scientific, historical, or theological error. This is a good doctrine, and I believe it. But people in the church sometimes get so caught up defending the Bible that they forget to practice the essence of Christianity, which is love. They forget that the best way to defend Scripture is to proclaim it. That's Paul's counsel to Timothy: Avoid word battles. Share the truth of the Gospel, and let God's Word defend itself" (2009, p. 214).

With eloquence and directness, Paul wrote the following to Timothy and to us. These words are a timeless reminder to all servant leaders that how we handle the Scriptures not only interprets their meaning for others, but reveals whether that same Word has shaped our own life and words.

> [14] *Remind them of these things, and charge them before God not to quarrel about words, which does no good, but only ruins the hearers.* [15] *Do your best to present yourself to God as one approved, a* **worker** *who has no need to be ashamed, rightly handling the word of truth.* [16] *But avoid irreverent babble, for it will lead people into more and more ungodliness,* [17] *and their talk will spread like gangrene. Among them are Hymenaeus and Philetus,*

[18] who have swerved from the truth, saying that the resurrection has already happened. They are upsetting the faith of some. [19] But God's firm foundation stands, bearing this seal: "The Lord knows those who are his," and, "Let everyone who names the name of the Lord depart from iniquity."

*[20] Now in a great house there are not only **vessels** of gold and silver but also of wood and clay, some for honorable use, some for dishonorable. [21] Therefore, if anyone cleanses himself from what is dishonorable, he will be a **vessel** for honorable use, set apart as holy, useful to the master of the house, ready for every good work.*

*[22] So flee youthful passions and pursue righteousness, faith, love, and peace, along with those who call on the Lord from a pure heart. [23] Have nothing to do with foolish, ignorant controversies; you know that they breed quarrels. [24] And the Lord's **servant** must not be quarrelsome but kind to everyone, able to teach, patiently enduring evil, [25] correcting his opponents with gentleness. God may perhaps grant them repentance leading to a knowledge of the truth, [26] and they may come to their senses and escape from the snare of the devil, after being captured by him to do his will.*

Let's return to our starting premise. ***Servant leadership is a long obedience.*** The first metaphor Paul inserted into this section of his letter to Timothy is ***worker*** (ergates – 2:15). Good workmen or laborers endure. Paul instructed Timothy, "do your best" (skoudaso). That's the mark of a quality workman. He or she literally makes haste or are zealous and diligent about how they handle Scripture. A bad workman was to be avoided. A lousy spiritual workman was someone who delighted in controversy, who loved to argue over the finer points of Scripture. Paul indicated that this kind of workman "ruins" (katastrophe – 2:14) or brings about a catastrophe when it comes to the life and witness of the local church. The ideal worker "rightly handling the word of truth" (orthotomeo – 2:15). Literally, the word phrase means "to cut rightly." If that is the primary ingredient that identifies the best kind of worker, then what does that term, "rightly handling the word of truth," mean? There are four possible answers.

First, Paul might have in mind *a farmer* who had the ability to make straight rows for his crops. Think back to 2 Timothy 2:6. Growing up in central Illinois has given me a first-hand look at farmers who take the time to plant their corn and soybeans carefully. Another possible picture is that of *a mason* or bricklayer. A good mason takes the time to use a plumb-line to be certain that the brick or block work is straight and will stand the test of time. Nothing shoddy is acceptable. Years ago, while a seminary student and assistant basketball coach at Lincoln Christian University, I noticed the outside wall of the men's locker room was unfinished. I walked by it day after day. It simply got to me. I couldn't stand it. I asked Lynn Laughlin, then the head basketball coach and athletic director, if I could take on the task of finishing it. I got some expert advice and launched into the project. What should have taken only a few hours to complete took an entire day, and I wasn't finished until late that night. I even used the lights from my pickup truck to help with the finishing touches. Anyone who knows anything about bricklaying would readily recognize that some incompetent amateur finished the project. I have a long way to go in "rightly handling" mason work.

The third possibility is that Paul had in mind *a butcher* or meat-cutter. I spent part of my formative years growing up in Heyworth, Illinois, a little town ten miles south of Bloomington/Normal. There was, in those days, a small mom and pop grocery store that my mother would send me to periodically. My task was to pick up a loaf of bread and some baloney. I would tell the owner how much meat my mom wanted, and he would cut it. He did something that I never understood until I was older. After my order was completed, he would stand back from the meat scale, fold his arms, and pronounce the exact weight of my baloney and give me the price. He always did it the same way. I now understand what I did not comprehend then. Apparently, there were all kinds of disreputable butchers who liked leaning on the scale and raising the weight and price. Meat-cutters who "rightly handle" their task do so with complete integrity.

The fourth possibility, and the most likely one, is that of a road builder. In Paul's day, the Roman army expertly built thousands of miles of road. A person might average 30 to 50 miles a day if able to travel by horseback or chariot. Paul used that very road system to share the Good News of Jesus Christ. Even today, if you go to places like ancient Philippi (modern Greece), you can see the expertise of these past road builders. They knew what they were doing. Often laying down several layers of sand, concrete-like material, and perfectly formed and smoothed rocks, these builders offered a remarkable means of transportation for military, government, and commercial use. Like today, repair work was constant. Laborers were needed. A worker who could skillfully lay out a straight road that would last for centuries was someone who "rightly handled" his trade.

Don't miss the essential point here. A good worker of Scripture is one who not only "cuts Scripture correctly," but has the ability to stay on the road of good interpretation and not wander off on tangents ("swerved from the truth" – 2:18). "Irreverent babble" (2:16) is another indicator of someone who has slipped into a war of words and missed staying on task. Good workmen get to the point, speak directly, and, as we sometimes say, "Don't beat around the bush." Some never get to the essential point. Apparently two such men were Hymenaeus and Philetus (2:17). Hymenaeus was mentioned back in 1 Timothy 1:20. The core issue was misinterpreting the resurrection of Jesus Christ (2:18). It seems that these two false teachers were declaring that there was no future resurrection. We are uncertain of the specifics. Maybe this issue parallels the one found in the church at Thessalonica where some false teachers were claiming that the coming of Jesus had already taken place (2 Thessalonians 2:1-3). Paul wanted Timothy to know that God's Word still stood firm like a solid foundation (2:19). False teaching was upsetting and frustrating, but God's truth was unshakeable and still standing the test of time. God's real people, His genuine children are anchored firmly in their attachment to Jesus and His finished work. A long obedience is needed. A good worker is well aware of that reality.

Several years ago, I was invited to speak at a large men's gathering in a beautiful northeastern Ohio camp setting. The magnificent fall colors added to the occasion. A question and answer time was arranged after each teaching time, and it soon became clear to me that some had intentionally come to that quiet place of study and retreat in order to argue and to divide. Several times I was tempted, nearly lured, to fall into the trap of splitting theological hairs. But then, and now, I was reminded of what a good worker looks like and how he handles himself and the Word. I constantly rehearse in my own mind the significant truth of this section – *servant leadership requires a long obedience with Scripture.*

?The second metaphor Paul placed in the heart and mind of Timothy was that of a *vessel* or instrument (skeuos in 2:20-21). I once had a student who thought that Paul was writing about trumpets or drums. That student ended up writing a very fine paper on Paul's use of musical instruments to explain the life of a servant leader. I hated bursting his bubble and reminding him of the importance of a good word study. So, let me state the sometimes-not-always-understood truth. The imagery here is something very different from harps and cymbals. The metaphor is drawn from the first century home. Once again, Paul described a contrast (2:20). On one side was a picture of ordinary, everyday ***kitchenware*** – pots, pans, and dishes. On the other side is a picture of fine and ***expensive pottery***, something suitable for special guests. Perhaps Paul was even contrasting a bronze jar ("honorable") from a clay one ("dishonorable"). Maybe he was suggesting that Timothy and others like him were special instruments, while these false teachers were common and disposable vessels. The language intrigues me.

Dr. Luke, in his second volume, the book of Acts, drew on this metaphor to describe Paul's special calling from God on the Damascus

Road. Ananias, an apprentice of Jesus, was told to go to a house on Straight Street owned by someone named Judas, and there he would find a man struck blind, Saul of Tarsus. Ananias initially resisted the commission. After all, Saul's reputation (soon to be Paul) had preceded him. God made His perspective abundantly clear to Ananias. "Go!" God said, "He is a chosen *instrument*..." (Acts 9:15). Additionally, when Paul wanted to describe for the combative Corinthian church what his ministry was really like and who they really were, he drew on this very same metaphor: "But we have this treasure in *jars of clay* to show that this all-surpassing power belongs to God and not to us" (2 Corinthians 4:7).

Typically, a jar of clay or a household pot was cheap, disposable, and replaceable. Cracked pots were strewn all over the Roman Empire (I know there is a joke in there somewhere). Granted, some of these instruments were expensive and made of bronze. Somewhere around 6000 BC, people began to shape and to mold instruments for use in everyday life. Twenty one times in the New Testament, various writers use this term. I say all of that so that we won't miss what Paul is attempting to describe through the use of this imagery. Behind all of this instrument-talk is a strong theme of service. Instruments are to be ready for use anytime, anywhere, however, wherever, and whenever needed. Clean and ready for use is the essential idea. No one wants to come into someone's house and to be given a dirty plate to eat from or a filthy glass from which to drink. There are, according to Paul, certain things that all servant leaders are to flee (2:22). Escape is the imperative. On the other hand, there are certain goals that all servant leaders are to pursue. Run after is the command. Both verbs – flee and pursue – are imperatives. Run from sinful selfishness and run toward spiritual service just like 1Timothy 6:11. Be an instrument ready for use. Is that clear enough? ***Servant leadership is a long obedience in service.***

We now come to Paul's third and final metaphor in this section of Scripture – *servant* (2:24). "Wait a minute," you might be saying, "I thought we already talked about that." Well, we have and we haven't. How's that for double-talk? Remember that this discussion actually represents our seventh metaphor in the larger literary context of 2 Timothy 2 (soldier, athlete, farmer, criminal, worker, vessel, and servant). The shift of metaphor is clear – from vessel ready for use in a house to one of a servant in that same house. Paul described this place of service with two very strong words (2:23). The first one is "controversies" (zeteis), and the other one is "quarrels" (machas). I would remind you that part of what the servant leader is instructed to pursue is "love and peace" (2:22). The word for "controversies" shows up three times in these Pastoral Letters (1Timothy 6:4, 2 Timothy 2:23, and Titus 3:9). Apparently, it was a problem in both Ephesus and Crete. Some false teachers took delight in arguing over petty things and miniscule issues, ranging from myths to endless genealogies (remember 1Timothy 1:4). "Quarrels" describes what we have been talking about throughout this chapter – a battle of bravado (2:14, 2:23, and 2:24)! Some people can't resist using words and the Word to beat up other Jesus-followers.

The word for servant here (doulos) is the most common one in the New Testament (100 plus times). It paints a portrait of a slave without rights. Whatever we think of ourselves in terms of servant leadership, perhaps it is wise to recall this metaphor. We are not as great or significant as we might think. There are five other words for "servant" that Paul could have drawn on at this point in the letter. We'll talk about those later in the book. For now, it is good to note that he used this same word picture in Titus 1:1 to describe his ministry. Paul never incorporated this metaphor in a negative manner. He thought of himself and Timothy as humble servants in the house of God. Here's the kicker. In the midst of all of this arguing and quarreling, Paul called on Timothy to be kind and gentle. He spoke of a servant leader as someone who "gently" instructed those in his care. I recall some words that I read years ago. William Barclay, that well known Scottish New Testament scholar from the twentieth century, made this crystal clear to me:

"The Christian leader must be *kindly* to all; even when he has to criticize and point out a fault, it must be done with the gentleness which never seeks to hurt...There may be greater sins than touchiness, but there is none which does greater damage in the Christian Church. He must discipline his opponents in *gentleness*; his hand like the hand of a surgeon, unerring to find the diseased spot, yet never for a moment causing unnecessary pain. He must love men (and women), not batter them, into submission to the truth" (1977, p. 181).

One of the pastoral principles I seek to live by each day is, "do no harm." I have failed on occasion miserably. But I continue to strive for what Paul described for Timothy in this part of his letter – to be a gentle expositor of the Word. The hope here is for the arguing and quarreling person to come to repentance, to accept the truth, and to escape from the devil (2:25-26). I have, on occasion, spoken of the home in which I was raised. My father's simmering anger permeated every part of my upbringing. Like a volcano, he could explode without notice. It amazed me how gentle he could seem toward those in the church and even those who had not yet met Jesus and then come home, in the place where kindness and gentleness were most needed, and unleash on us a fire storm of poisonous words like lava and gas escaping from a gigantic eruption. Servant leadership, whatever it entails, calls for our very best. It is a 24-7 commitment. Scripture will not let us pick and choose the places where we conduct ourselves as good workers, ready vessels, and humble servants. *Servant leadership is a long obedience through squabbles*, but it is also a long obedience through everyday life.

CHAPTER 13

What Wise Servant Leaders Know
2 Timothy 3:1-9

"These are the numbers of the men armed for battle who came to David at Hebron to turn Saul's kingdom over to him, as the Lord had said…men of Issachar, who understood the times and knew what Israel should do…"
(1 Chronicles 12:23 & 32).

There is nothing quite like knowing what needs to be done when it needs to be done. One of the most influential people to enter my life was a man who owned and operated a tire and television shop in Marshall, Illinois. His name was Dan L. Harper, and his store was called Harper Tire. I've talked about his impact on my life in other writings and sermons. He did for me what spiritual directors and life coaches do for others. He helped me to think and to live as a God-honoring man. He treated work as an act of worship. Dan was not an overtly outspoken Jesus-follower. His faith became more vocal as cancer ate away at his body, but it was during a nine month on-the-job-training experience when God used this man to prepare me for the rest of my life. I, of course, was unaware. Very few people make that kind of significant contribution.

I worked for Dan changing truck, tractor, and car tires from December 1971 through August, 1972. When work slowed down, I would clean the shop or run errands for him. Now and then, he would send me out alone to handle a semi-trailer flat on Highway 40 or dispatch me to a farmer with a ruptured tractor tire out in some distant field in Clark County. The only way that I was capable of handling those jobs on my own was that he mentored me at the shop. He would explain, demonstrate, ask me questions, and then let me do the work. Correction and encouragement was built into the process. We always debriefed when I got back, usually over a cold coke. I felt, for the first time in my life, what it was like to know how to do something and to do it well. At his bedside, before Dan died from a brutal battle with prostate cancer, I thanked him for his rich investment and prayed with him. I still have moments when I'm tackling some issue or thinking through some situation, and I will see his face and hear his clear voice of instruction. I am eternally indebted to Dan.

I say all of that because of the way in which Paul made a similar investment in the life of Timothy. We come to a portion of this letter where Paul takes on an earnest tone about the challenges and difficulties Timothy faced. The old apostle wanted his young disciple to understand the times and to know what to do. Paul's words are abundantly clear:

> **3** *But understand this, that in the last days there will come times of difficulty.* [2] *For people will be lovers of self, lovers of money, proud, arrogant, abusive, disobedient to their parents, ungrateful, unholy,* [3] *heartless, unappeasable, slanderous, without self-control, brutal, not loving good,* [4] *treacherous, reckless, swollen with conceit, lovers of pleasure rather than lovers of God,* [5] *having the appearance of godliness, but denying its power. Avoid such people.* [6] *For among them are those who creep into households and capture weak women, burdened with sins and led astray by various passions,* [7] *always learning and never able to arrive at a knowledge of the truth.* [8] *Just as Jannes and Jambres opposed*

Moses, so these men also oppose the truth, men corrupted in mind and disqualified regarding the faith. ⁹ *But they will not get very far, for their folly will be plain to all, as was that of those two men.*

Here, then, is our focusing question. What do wise servant leaders know?

They know these are the last days, and these days are stressful (3:1). Notice with me two significant phrases – "the last days" and "times of difficulty." Let's start with the last one. "Times of difficulty" (chalepos) describes something hard to bear, something dangerous and difficult. In the ancient Greek culture, the word was used to portray a ferocious animal or a raging storm out on the sea. This particular word is only used two times in the entire New Testament, here, of course, and in Matthew 8:28. Matthew uses the word to describe two demon-possessed men who lived in a cemetery. These twin towers of evil were so *violent* (chalepos) that "no one could pass that way." Only Jesus was strong enough to exorcise those demons and to save the day. Place all of this language into Paul's situation. He had been arrested, was chained in prison, and was, for the most part, alone (4:9-11). Whoever these false teachers were that had wiggled their way into the church at Ephesus, they were not minor frustrations like a paper cut or a hang nail. These people were extremely dangerous. Timothy needed to understand this, and so must we. False teachers do not readily identify themselves. No one approaches a Jesus-follower and says, "Hi, I'm a deceptive and dangerous teacher. Can I have a few minutes of your time?" Spiritual alertness is required.

The initial phrase Paul used – "the last days" – really sets the tone for the entire section of Scripture we are studying. So much misunderstanding has occurred over this phrase. Don't get tripped up here. The last days are not something out on our future horizons. They are here now. They have actually been here since the birth of our Lord and Savior. We are living in the last days. Two significant Bible passages, Acts 2:14-

21 and Hebrews 1:1-2, make this abundantly clear. When Jesus arrived, we began the journey into the final days. Remember Peter's insightful statement, "But do not overlook this one fact, beloved, that with the Lord one day is as a thousand years, and a thousand years as one day" (2 Peter 3:8). The times are demanding. As we have already noted, they are abundantly dangerous. The enemy, like a hungry lion, prowls around looking for someone to devour (1 Peter 5:8). Seduction marks this age. With each passing moment, the Second Coming of Jesus draws closer. Wise servant leaders are not blown away by "in the last days there will come times of difficulty." They simply recognize it and respond in a Jesus-honoring way. What else do they know?

They know these are the last days, and these days are sin-filled (3:2-7). Paul wanted Timothy to grasp the times. Nineteen different sin-filled examples are incorporated by Paul. Count them if you want. They can be grouped into four categories. First, there are misguided lovers: lovers of self, money, pleasure, and not God (3:2 and 3:4). When love of God is not right, nothing is right. Second, there are self-absorbed lovers: they are proud, arrogant, and abusive (3:2). These people have an exaggerated view of themselves and a diminished view of others. Third, there are sub-par lovers: they are disobedient, ungrateful, unholy, heartless, and unappeasable, (3:2-3).

In the Greek New Testament, all five words begin with a prefix, the first letter of the Greek alphabet – the letter "alpha" – which implies something negative or not present. In our English language, we often attach the prefix "dis" or "un," as in words like disobedient and words like ungrateful, unholy, and unappeasable. You can see that meaning in our text. All of these words imply a breakdown in the family unit. Fourth and finally, there are self-destructive lovers: they are "slanderous, without self-control, brutal, not loving good, treacherous, reckless, and swollen with conceit" (3:3-4). These seven words or phrases help to identify people that we are to avoid.

Like I said earlier, I grew up in small town, USA. People went to the local post office to get their mail. It was not delivered. Everyone had an assigned box, and you simply retrieved your mail when you had the time. Typically, I was sent to pick it up when my father couldn't. George Maris, a faithful member at the church my dad served, was the postmaster. My memories are positive of his kindness and helpfulness. I do recall, though, how the post office walls were lined with "Most Wanted" posters. Pictures and descriptions of people you wanted to avoid were everywhere. It was frightening stuff for a little boy. In some ways, these nineteen vices paint a picture of "Most Wanted" false teachers and evil influencers who had already tricked some of the people in Ephesus and were actively recruiting others (3:6). These were religious people who failed to have a personal relationship with Jesus. Perhaps they even sang, gave, listened, prayed, participated in the Lord's Supper, and carried on like any other disciple of Jesus. Shocking! They were sly and sneaky. Whoever these women were that had come under the influence of false teachers, let's not rush to condemn them. Paul called them "weak-women" (gynaikaria). He literally meant "little women." It is a term of ridicule and contempt. Men are just as capable of being silly or "little." Caution is required. None of us are so far along in this Jesus-following life that we can boast of our spiritual maturity. Again, wise servant leaders grasp the brokenness of the world and how easily sin slips into the life of the church. One final piece of understanding is present in this passage.

Wise servant leaders know these are the last days, and these days are seductive (3:8-9). I wish I could tell you something insightful about Jannes and Jambres, but I can't. This is the third set of terrible twins Paul has inserted in the letter (Phygelus and Hermogenes in 1:15 and Hymenaeus and Philetus in 2:17). Jewish tradition suggests that Jannes and Jambres were sorcerers or evil magicians in Moses' day. Apparently, they had given themselves over to the dark side, but they are never mentioned in the Old Testament. Perhaps they were false teachers that Moses opposed and, like them, Timothy must now oppose his own form of Jannes and Jambres in the church at Ephesus. Paul was confident that these infiltrators of evil would not get away with it. Some might be seduced, but, in the end, God would be triumphant.

I confess that sometimes I grow disheartened. It feels like Jannes and Jambres are winning the day. It is especially true if I have overextended myself and not maintained a proper stewardship of my body and soul. Timothy might have been susceptible to that very thing (1 Timothy 5:23). I need to hear 2 Timothy 3:9 over and over again: "But they will not get very far, for their folly will be plain to all." Hallelujah! My hope is revived. Perseverance is called for, and I must invest myself to knowing the Word and handling it with the utmost care and accuracy. And, more than anything, I must live it out in the real world in front of real people. This entire section reminds me of what Jesus said of His church: "...And the gates of hell shall not prevail against it" (Matthew 16:18). Servant leadership is tethered to that grand truth.

For generations, the Moken people have subsisted off the west coast of Thailand in the Andaman Sea. The Thai call them "Chao Lay" or "people of the sea." Some have referred to the Moken as "sea gypsies." Their origin is uncertain. Scholars suggest they migrated from China over 4,000 years ago. Except for the monsoon seasons, they live entirely on their boats. I recall, back in December of 2004, an Indian Ocean tsunami brought incredible destruction and heart wrenching loss of life. It was the Moken elders who saw the signs, understood them, and knew what to do. They saved thousands of people and were able to carry on their chosen way of life. In powerful ways, I am reminded of the need for wise servant leaders in the church, like Paul, who understand the times and know what to do.

CHAPTER 14

What Kingdom-Driven Servant Leaders Really Look Like
2 Timothy 3:10-4:5

"What, then, is our basic need? If it is not a reinterpretation of Christianity intellectually and socially (though both of these, as we have seen, are included), what is it? It is a rediscovery of Christianity as a vital relationship to a living Christ" (Stewart, James S. (1978). **A Faith to Proclaim.** *(p. 143). Baker Book House).*

"Be different." How many times have we heard those words? Christians are infamous for trying to shrink the grand and magnificent story of God's grace through Jesus into some kind of portable and manageable size. Bumper sticker slogans abounded when I was a child. People would say, "Be in the world, not of the world." "Stand up and stand out." "Don't let the world squeeze you into its mold." That one is a little tougher to reduce to bumper sticker size, but I understand the attempt. Some today say things like, "Walk the talk and talk the Walk." "Live 24/7" or "Be a 365 Disciple." The truth of the matter is that it is not easy to follow Jesus faithfully. We look for help anywhere and everywhere, even succumbing to television preachers with charisma and questionable teachings. There are enormous pressures generated by our culture to conform to the ways of the world. We hunger for help. There is urgency to our faith.

It is that very urgency that caused Paul to take great pains to define for Timothy what a kingdom-driven servant leader really looked like. His words are compelling:

> [10] ***You, however***, *have followed my teaching, my conduct, my aim in life, my faith, my patience, my love, my steadfastness,* [11] *my persecutions and sufferings that happened to me at Antioch, at Iconium, and at Lystra—which persecutions I endured; yet from them all the Lord rescued me.* [12] *Indeed, all who desire to live a godly life in Christ Jesus will be persecuted,* [13] *while evil people and impostors will go on from bad to worse, deceiving and being deceived.* [14] ***But as for you***, *continue in what you have learned and have firmly believed, knowing from whom you learned it* [15] *and how from childhood you have been acquainted with the sacred writings, which are able to make you wise for salvation through faith in Christ Jesus.* [16] *All Scripture is breathed out by God and profitable for teaching, for reproof, for correction, and for training in righteousness,* [17] *that the man of God may be complete, equipped for every good work.*
>
> 4 *I charge you in the presence of God and of Christ Jesus, who is to judge the living and the dead, and by his appearing and his kingdom:* [2] *preach the word; be ready in season and out of season; reprove, rebuke, and exhort, with complete patience and teaching.* [3] *For the time is coming when people will not endure sound teaching, but having itching ears they will accumulate for themselves teachers to suit their own passions,* [4] *and will turn away from listening to the truth and wander off into myths.* [5] ***As for you***, *always be sober-minded, endure suffering, do the work of an evangelist, fulfill your ministry.*

Whatever is involved in the kingdom-driven servant leader's life, it is fundamentally not about him or her. Paul used a grammatical marker or conjunction in this passage to chisel away any notion that any of us are at the center of the universe. Three separate times, Paul used the phrase "You, however," "But as for you," and "As for you" (su de – 3:10, 14, and 4:5). The New International Version closely parallels the ESV and translates that conjunction this way: "You, however," "But as for you," and "But you." Each occasion offers a clue to my question: What does a purpose driven servant leader really look like?

First, *a kingdom-driven servant leader looks like someone who has thoroughly investigated the cross life* (3:10-13). Paul took Timothy back to their initial meeting and subsequent life together (Acts 16:1ff). The Apostle's claim is that his young disciple "*followed*" everything (paraleolutheo). Paul used a very unique word. It meant that Timothy had made extensive effort to know about Paul's teaching and life. Timothy had traced it out, investigated it carefully, and diligently checked all the facts. Paul even backtracked further in describing experiences of persecution in Antioch, Iconium, and Lystra (Acts 13-14). The jealousy, hatred, and stoning that Paul endured were common knowledge to Timothy. He was fully aware of all that Paul had faced in the Name of Christ. There was no "name it – claim it" religious jargon in Paul's testimony. Please notice there is not an ounce of health, wealth, and prosperity theology in these verses. Timothy had heard and seen firsthand that the Jesus-following life included a cross. Anyone intentionally moving toward life with God would and will encounter stiff opposition. "You, however, *have followed*" are Paul's words to Timothy.

Dr. Luke drew on this same word in his Gospel introduction to Theophilus. He claimed, "It seemed good to me also, *having followed* all things closely…" (Luke 1:3). Paul and Luke recognized the value of close examination. They literally "walked in someone else's steps." They encountered the truth of Jesus, accepted that truth, walked in that truth, and shared that truth with all who would listen. When I was young, it seemed that our winter storms were measured in feet rather than inches. I know that exaggeration is a possibility here. Regardless, I liked being the first one out of the house, heading off to school. My sisters would want me to mark out a path in the drifts so that they wouldn't get snow in their boots. I would attempt to take larger than life steps in order to keep them from having an easy time drudging through the snow. Shame on me. Paul's reminder to Timothy was that his "exact steps" were not exaggerated. They included suffering, persecution, and a cross. No true Jesus follower gets out of this. All kingdom-driven servant leaders "follow this closely" and are reminded that Jesus is at the center of the universe and not them.

Second, ***kingdom-driven servant leaders look like someone who passionately remains faithful to Scripture*** (3:14-4:4). Are you getting tired of this? Paul came back to this theme again and again in his correspondence with Timothy. "***Continue***" (meno) is the vital word here: "But as for you, continue." Paul wanted Timothy intimately "attached" to the Hebrew Scriptures. The word Paul used is the very same one Jesus did in the Jerusalem upper room on the night He was betrayed. Our Lord told those Twelve, "***Abide*** in me and I in you" (John 15:4). The kingdom-driven servant leader stays in the Word. She abides in the Scriptures. He avoids chasing fads. She is always steering away from gimmicks. He detours from all slick programs. She anchors herself in God's truth. Notice with me that Paul indirectly reminded Timothy of the investment that Lois and Eunice, grandmother and mother, had made in his life (3:14-15 – "a faith that dwelt first in your grandmother Lois and your mother Eunice and now, I am sure dwells in you as well" – and back to 1:5).

Perhaps one of the most beautiful and striking parts of the entire letter are the words found in 3:16-17. Paul exhorted Timothy to feed deeply on the Scriptures. Remember that, in the historical context, Paul was talking about the Hebrew Scriptures, what we call the Old Testament. But what was true of the Old Testament is true of the New Testament. The Word encourages a lifelong commitment to devouring its content. It is, by definition, "breathed-out by God" (Theopneustos). It wasn't dead, and God had to breathe life into it. Rather, Scriptures' origin was and is found in God's heart. He exhaled it. His Word is divinely given. So, why is the Bible so vital to the purpose-driven servant leader? Five brief answers will suffice.

First, ***Scripture always tells the truth***. Paul told Timothy that Scripture was profitable or useful for "teaching" (didaskaliov). Doctrine is revealed here: who the Triune God is; what He's done in Christ; why He matters; what He has on His heart; what He is doing right now, how His Spirit is at work, how we can know Him, what His longing for His church is, and all of that and more is implied here. The Bible is God preaching to us. He is the Supreme Teacher. Every congregation must become a Bible college. Other books are helpful, but none exceed the power of the Word to tell us what is right. The essential characteristic about us is what we believe God is like. Only the Scriptures can reveal that mega truth.

Second, ***Scripture always exposes lies***. Paul told Timothy that Scripture was useful for "reproof" (elegmon). This particular word is only used here in the New Testament. Lots of other synonyms are found in its pages, but this specific word implies that God's Word has the ability to illuminate our errors, mistakes, and sin. Don't forget the place where Timothy has been called to serve. Ephesus was steeped in spiritual darkness. The Bible brings the clearest message about what is not right in any and every culture.

Third, ***Scripture always straightens out messes***. Paul told Timothy that Scripture was useful for "correction" (epanorthosin). The Bible can change our behavior. Dr. Howard Hendricks was famous for reminding students, "Dusty Bibles lead to dirty lives." He was right. Only the Word has the Divine ability to show us how to get right with God, others, ourselves, and creation. It alone, by and through the Holy Spirit, transforms our life. Churches can be cleaned up and set right when one single person takes the initiative regularly and lovingly to preach the Word. Other books can be helpful, but none cleans up a person and a church like God's Book.

Fourth, ***Scripture always coaches godly living***. Paul told Timothy that Scripture was useful for "training" (paideia). It alone instructs us like a loving mother or father and leads us through all the necessary childhood training. Someone said, "If your Bible is falling apart, the chances are, you probably aren't." No other book has the ability to show us how to stay right with God. It is our spiritual coach.

Fifth, ***Scripture always grows mature people***. Paul told Timothy that Scripture alone can "complete" and equip the man and woman of God for every good work. Think of all the colossal challenges that Timothy faced. There were immature people in the church and lost people outside the church. False teachers were infiltrating everywhere. Religious pluralism saturated the city. Materialism and hedonism was wrecking the affluent city of Ephesus. What chance did this young servant leader have? Timothy had no hope apart from God's Word being living and active, sharper than any two-edged sword (Hebrews 4:12). Let me offer two suggestions. First, if, in this season of your life, you find Scripture dry and dull (no one ever wants to admit this), get on your knees and ask the Spirit to blow a new wind of refreshment on your heart. Second, find a different translation or paraphrase and see how that difference might bring a new season of Scripture-intake. Some have discovered that the habit of listening to Scripture read aloud brings about a renewed hunger for the Word. Several free online resources are available.

I recall a story I heard and have retold on several occasions about Dr. Clive Calver, past president of World Relief. He was visiting an African village in the Sudan when he saw about 250 people gathered under the shade of a tree. He had been to Africa enough to know what that meant – a worship service was taking place. He asked them what they were doing. Someone responded, "We're worshiping Jesus." Dr. Calver asked, "You're worshiping Jesus?" "Yes," they said, "Do you know Jesus?" Dr. Calver replied, "Yes, I know Jesus." The Africans responded, "We heard there is a book." "Yes, there is a book," Dr. Calver assured them. The Africans inquired with great curiosity, "Have you seen this book?" "Yes," he said, "I have several copies of the book back home." The 250 worshippers were astonished! Then Dr. Calver said, "Look, the church in America brought you seeds to plant, so you can grow food, and your children won't die." The Africans said, "Oh, that's nice. Please tell the people in America, thanks for the seeds. But could we have the book first?" Could we have the book first? There is the lifeblood of the servant leader who lives on purpose. Ground everything in Scripture. Let's return to our original question: What does a kingdom-driven servant leader look like?

Third and finally, *a kingdom-driven servant leader looks like someone who intentionally stays focused in every aspect of ministry* (4:5). Don't forget that "su de" marker – "But you." Whatever Paul was intending Timothy to grasp here, this is fundamentally not about you and me; rather, it is about cooperating with God's intent to grow a healthy church. Paul piled up four commands on top of each other. All four verbs are aorist, active, imperatives (be, endure, do, and fulfill). There's nothing overly technical here, simply a reminder that Paul put emphasis on what he said. His instructions to Timothy went like this (my translation): stay self-controlled, hug your pain, keep sharing God's story, and honor your vows. There is hope for Ephesus and mighty hope for us. Bottom line – nurture your sense of urgency.

When I was a small boy, maybe seven or eight years old, I began to spend time at my grandparents' farm, my mother's home. My grandfather died when I was only 16, so grandma stayed on the farm and continued the way of life she desired for decades. She raised a garden, served her church, and loved people. Grandma Beaty was known far and wide for being one of the finest cooks around. She would butcher her own chickens and prepare a meal fit for royalty. On one particular occasion, she asked me if I wanted to help her. I foolishly agreed. I had never seen chickens butchered, and when Grandma grabbed that first chicken, placed its head under her foot and yanked, well – let's just say I came of age. That chicken bounced around the coop like microwave popcorn. Blood was spurting everywhere, other chickens were running for their lives, and I joined the chaos by shouting at the top of my lungs, "Grandma that chicken is alive!" It was then and there she became my first real spiritual director. "No," she said, "That chicken is dead, but doesn't know it." People live that way and so do churches, detached from their heads, hurrying and scurrying. Without Christ as the head, they bounce around, attempting to convince anyone watching that they are alive. But the harsh truth is evident. Kingdom-driven servant leaders know the difference. They embrace the cross, devour the Scriptures, and saturate their ministries with the living presence of Jesus Christ and, more than anything, remain attached to "the head of the body, the church" (Colossians 1:18).

CHAPTER 15
When Servant Leaders Must Step Up
2 Timothy 4:6-22

"As you embark on your quest to shape the future, remember that in the wake of your leadership is the next crop of next generation leaders. They are easy to spot: They will remind you of you when you were their age. They will be the ones asking all the questions. They will be the influencers. In some cases, they will be the troublemakers. But most importantly, they are your responsibility"
(Stanley, Andy. (2003). **Next Generation Leaders.** *(pp. 161-162). Multnomah Publishers).*

Can servant leadership and hesitation coexist? In a variety of ways I've been asked that question repeatedly. I've even asked it of myself. I may very well be one of the most reluctant servant leaders you will meet. I'm not sure I was always like that. My mother delights in telling a story from my childhood. According to her, and she is a truth-teller, I convinced the other kids on Sullivan Street to strip down to their birthday suits and to skinny dip in the neighbors front yard that had become a warm swimming pool due to a heavy summer rain. Maybe I'm more of a troublemaker than a leader. What I've certainly discovered about myself over the years is this: My biological family life, some hard knocks in the church, and a greater understanding of my own giftedness, personality, and calling have honed leadership hesitation. Like a lot of you, I will lead when there is a leadership vacuum, but I'm better in the second seat. The issue becomes much larger when I pause and consider the next generation. Who among us is intentionally passing the leadership torch to future servant leaders? Even beyond that critical concern, when should next generation servant leaders step up? Paul had some very insightful instruction to offer Timothy. Here's what he said:

> [6] *For I am already being poured out as a drink offering, and the time of my departure has come.* [7] *I have fought the good fight, I have finished the race, I have kept the faith.* [8] *Henceforth there is laid up for me the crown of righteousness, which the Lord, the righteous judge, will award to me on that Day, and not only to me but also to all who have loved his appearing.*
>
> [9] *Do your best to come to me soon.* [10] *For Demas, in love with this present world, has deserted me and gone to Thessalonica. Crescens has gone to Galatia, Titus to Dalmatia.* [11] *Luke alone is with me. Get Mark and bring him with you, for he is very useful to me for ministry.* [12] *Tychicus I have sent to Ephesus.* [13] *When you come, bring the cloak that I left with Carpus at Troas, also the books, and above all the parchments.* [14] *Alexander the coppersmith did me great harm; the Lord will repay him according to his deeds.* [15] *Beware of him yourself, for he strongly opposed our message.* [16] *At my first defense no one came to stand by me, but all deserted me. May it not be charged against them!* [17] *But the Lord stood by me and strengthened me, so that through me the message might be fully proclaimed and all the Gentiles might hear it. So I was rescued from the lion's mouth.* [18] *The Lord will rescue me from every evil deed and bring me safely into his heavenly kingdom. To him be the glory forever and ever. Amen.*
>
> [19] *Greet Prisca and Aquila, and the household of Onesiphorus.* [20] *Erastus remained at Corinth, and I left Trophimus, who was ill, at Miletus.* [21] *Do your best to come before winter. Eubulus sends*

greetings to you, as do Pudens and Linus and Claudia and all the brothers.

²² *The Lord be with your spirit. Grace be with you.*

I was a very young servant leader graduating from Bible College and heading off to seminary. I was already serving a small church about fifteen miles south of Lincoln, Illinois. I was struggling with trying to ascertain where I fit in the larger Kingdom of God. I wondered if I was primarily called to be a pastor-preacher in a local church or whether God was equipping me to enter into a life of preparing and equipping ministry students. One evening, while wrestling ardently in prayer, I found myself knocking on the door of Professor Charles Mills. I mentioned him in a previous chapter. Mr. Mills greeted me warmly but knew something weighed heavily on my heart, mostly due to the fact that I was crying. He got me something to drink, and we sat in his living room, and, together, we explored my calling into servant leadership. He mostly listened, and I mostly blubbered. In the end, he offered me one of the finest pieces of advice I have ever received. He simply said, "Stay where you are. Be a servant there. God will direct you accordingly. You are carrying a burden that is not yours to carry." Mr. Mills was right. As some of you know, God did clearly direct me. I kept one foot in the church and one foot in ministry education. That very kind and wise man helped me to see that now was the time to serve, now was the time to step up. Now was the time simply to open myself to the purpose and plan of God. That's what I want to talk about in this chapter.

Let's come back to my question: When should servant leaders step up? ***Younger servant leaders should step up when seasoned servant leaders will need to be replaced*** (4:6-8). Duh! Amazingly, I have watched the obvious go unnoticed. Capable, intelligent, and highly gifted younger servant leaders have remained sidelined while older leaders burn out and give up. Sometimes the problem rests with older leaders not inviting and encouraging younger servant leaders to enter the good fight. Regardless, please notice with me that Paul made it abundantly clear to Timothy not to delay in his service. Paul called himself a "drink offering" (4:6 – spendomai). The language, of course, is drawn from the Old Testament sacrificial system. Think Numbers 15:1-12 and 28:7. Fermented wine was the drink offering to be poured out at the base of the altar. It was to be a daily occurrence. Ironically, it was also the smallest offering. Of all the images to select, Paul chose this one to describe his life and ministry. Every single day, he thought of himself in terms of wine being emptied at the altar of God. Beautiful. Humbling. There is one other place in the writings of Paul where he employed the same word picture. To the much loved church at Philippi, he wrote, "Even if I am to be poured out as a *drink offering* upon the sacrificial offering of your faith, I am glad and rejoice with you all" (2:17).

For at least a dozen years, my office at Lincoln Christian University was located just down the hall from Dr. Marion Henderson's. "Doc" had been teaching fifty years by the time I became his neighbor. He would often drop by and catch up or offer a word of affirmation. Now and then, he would hand me a book from his library as a gift and express that he was passing something along to me for future ministry. Dr. Henderson, I never could bring myself to call him Marion, faithfully coached and encouraged me to step up and to be the servant leader God had called me to be. He is dead now, and I thank God in heaven for "Doc's" Paul-like reminder.

Paul incorporated a second coaching metaphor that was intended to prompt Timothy toward faithful service. He wrote, "The time of my *departure* has come" (4:6 - analuseos). We don't exactly know what Paul had in mind when he used this image. The reference is either to a ship that has untied and is sailing away or a soldier that has taken down his tent, is breaking camp, and heading off to another battle. Paul might even have in mind the picture of a prisoner who has been unchained in order to walk "the green mile" to his execution. The metaphor, regardless of the specifics, describes Paul taking one last journey. He simply knew his days were numbered. What he wanted was for Timothy to embrace that same reality. In one of the most gripping descriptions of departure ever written, Paul stacked three perfect tense verbs on top of one another: *I have fought* (agonizmai from agonizomai, literally "I have agonized the good agony"), *I have finished* (teteleka from teleo), and *I have kept* (tetapaka from tereo – 4:7). Paul had signed, sealed, and delivered all that had been entrusted to his care. His fight was good. His race had concluded. The Gospel was intact. He anticipated his crown, and now Timothy must step into the gap.

The small towns I was raised in had volunteer fire departments. Constant readiness was the prerequisite. The siren would sound, and men came from all over that community to face whatever emergency was at hand. That picture of vigilance and preparedness has preached to me over the years of the urgency of readiness. This seems like a good place to pause again and to think together about the importance of mentors and good mentoring. Now and then, someone will ask me, "How do I find a good mentor?" I typically pause long enough to list a few suggestions. Let me do that here. 1). Pray. Bathe the desire for spiritual coaching in persistent prayer. 2). Don't overlook the "dead guys," that is the great devotional writers of the past. Our "Paul" doesn't have to be living. Sometimes the just-right-spiritual-coach walks into our lives through the reading of some devotional classic. We discover someone who speaks our heart language. 3). Put the emphasis on character development, not gimmicks. Watch for those who are already practicing a life of character. 4). Ask questions of seasoned leaders. What would I want to know if I had a divine encounter with a seasoned servant leader? Come up with a set of questions. Keep them close by. 5). Watch for open doors of service. As we earn our serving stripes, we will often encounter surprising and momentary mentors who can speak into our lives briefly, but powerfully. 6). Ask those leaders who naturally intersect with our lives to evaluate our competence and readiness for service. 7). Reflect deeply on this vital question: What am I doing right now to step into the shoes of those in front of me?

Years ago, I was asked by the elder team of a church my family and I were attending to spend two weeks with a missionary family in deep need of prayer and pastoral attention. I agreed and made the long flight to England. The couple had poured themselves into that community and church. The spiritual soil was hard. Some disciples had been made, but the work had been enormously depleting. They cried. I listened. They grieved. I prayed. Somewhere in that two week conversation, we were invited to join an elderly couple for dinner at their countryside cottage. It was a picture-book setting. Beautiful flowers lined the Hobbit-like house. The Grass was as green as a St. Patrick's Day Parade. There was quite a contrast between that lovely setting and the arid inner world of that missionary couple. We were given a tour of the cottage and grounds, blessed with some tea, and ultimately set down to a delightful meal and holy conversation. Somewhere during that enchanted evening, I was struck by the portrait of a seasoned servant leader concluding his journey and the colossal need for a younger servant leader to step up.

Here's a second occasion when younger servant leaders should step up: ***when current servant leaders feel alone and isolated*** (4:9-13 and 4:19-22). There is little doubt in my mind that Paul was feeling this way as he awaited his execution. He longed for Timothy. He missed his friendship and fellowship. Paul was clear about the urgency of his situation (4:9&21). His friends are gone (4:9-13); Alexander the metalworker has hurt and opposed him (4:14-15), and Paul has been alone in his first defense in front of the Roman courts (4:16-18). Let's trace these three issues.

Demas, a past valued partner in ministry (Colossians 4:14 and Philemon 24) has "*deserted*" (enkataleipen) Paul. This is very strong language. Notice that the same word occurs in 4:16 as Paul described his first defense. He felt abandoned or forsaken. This was the exact description of Jesus' experience in Matthew 27:46 and Mark 15:34 as He endured the pain of the cross: "My God, My God, why have you *forsaken* me." Jesus knew His Bible. These words prayed on the cross are actually drawn from Psalm 22:1. No other words would do in our Savior's hour of greatest need. Remarkable! Demas's flight to Thessalonica smells of compromise and betrayal. We don't know the circumstances. Eugene Peterson in *The Message* translates the verse this way: "Demas, chasing fads, went off to Thessalonica and left me here." I've been to that seaside city, and it is enticing. Perhaps Demas simply grew tired of ministry. Perhaps he wanted to sit on the beach and sip sweet tea. Regardless, Paul needed him and Demas had abandoned his post.

The other friends mentioned in 4:9-13 are apparently away on ministry assignments. Crescens was serving in Galatia, located in Central Asia Minor (modern day Turkey). Titus was at work in Dalmatia, along the eastern shore of the Adriatic Sea (modern day Croatia, Bosnia, and Herzegovina, Serbia, etc.). Tychicus was ministering in Ephesus, apparently with Timothy (again, located in modern day Turkey). Carpus was sharing the Good News of Jesus in Troas, a Greek city where Paul had left his coat (now located near Bozcaada, Turkey). Only Luke was visiting Paul in prison, and the apostle felt acute loneliness (monos). No doubt other believers were seeking access to Paul, but Luke remained the constant encourager. I love that thought. What a loyal M.D. Here was a physician not merely of the body, but of the soul (Colossians 4:14). Sometimes we simply need other servant leaders surrounding us. Amazingly, Paul even asked for John Mark. We assume reconciliation had occurred somewhere and somehow (Colossians 4:10, Philemon 24, and 1 Peter 5:13). You may recall the story of John Mark abandoning Paul and Barnabas on their first missionary trip (see Acts 13:13). We don't know why this young disciple went home. Malaria, disagreement, mountain terrain, fear of falling, homesickness, or some other issue caused Mark to return to Jerusalem. When Barnabas, his cousin, wanted to take Mark on the second missionary tour, Paul absolutely refused. A very heated conversation ensued between these two pillars of the faith. The result was that Barnabas took Mark and headed off to Cyprus, and Paul chose Silas and left for Syria and Cilicia in order to strengthen the churches (Acts 15:38-39). Now, years later, Paul wanted Mark at his side.

Loneliness stalks the servant leader. It is as relentless as a hungry pack of hyenas. None of us gets very far in servant leadership without great companions at our side. I went through a very dark season in ministry. Criticism and exhaustion took their toll. One Sunday evening, after preaching, I simply fell apart. We ended up at the home of one of my elders. This gracious and godly man reached into his billfold and gave me gas money and said, "Get out of the area code. Let me know where you are and get some rest." So, my wife and I, along with our children, headed to Arkansas. We spent several weeks with my in-laws. I wasn't sure I could return to that ministry. Fortunately for me, several of those good servant leaders in that church mailed me a picture of them, along with a very encouraging note, imploring us to return. Thank God we did. Some of the most fruit bearing times took place in the next few years. Everyone needs a group of servant leaders to step up when he or she is feeling alone and isolated.

There is a very meaningful side note sometimes overlooked by Bible readers. Notice with me that, in the midst of all Paul's lonely-talk, he asked Timothy for three specific items. First, he's old and cold; therefore, he wanted his "cloak" (phailones – 4:13). Paul wanted the heavy outer garment commonly crafted with a single opening for the head. Think of a poncho. Second, his mind needed stimulation; therefore, he asked Timothy to bring his "books" (biblia). Scholars debate what Paul meant, but more than likely he was referring to general reading books, perhaps some of his favorites, or maybe the documentation for his Roman citizenship. Timothy would know what he meant. Third, his soul was in need of replenishment; therefore, Paul asked for the parchments, "above all the parchments" (membranas). As with so much of this letter, there is extensive debate about what Paul really meant. Some argue that Paul was asking for his own letters. Others conjecture that he was asking for some kind of handmade leather bag that contained a book or two. Remember that Paul was a leather maker (tent-maker) by trade (Acts 18:3). I like to think Paul was asking for his own copy of Scripture, the LXX, the Greek translation of the Hebrew Bible. If there was one book that would renew his inner life, it was Scripture. Perhaps the two words, scrolls and parchments, are simply referring to the same thing. We simply don't know. Regardless, the words of Charles Sprugeon seem particularly appropriate:

> "Even an apostle must read. Some of our very ultra-Calvinistic brethren think that a minister who reads books and studies his sermon must be a very deplorable specimen of a preacher. A man who comes up into the pulpit, professes to take his text on the spot, and talks any quantity of nonsense, is the idol of many. If he will speak without premeditation, or pretend to do so, and never produce what they call a dish of dead men's brains – oh! That is the preacher. How rebuked are they by the apostle! He is inspired, and yet he wants books! He has been preaching at least for thirty years, and yet he wants books! He had seen the Lord, and yet he wants books! He had had a wider experience than most men, and yet he wants books! He had been caught up into the third heaven, and had heard things, which it was unlawful for a man to utter, yet he wants books! He had written the major part of the New Testament, and yet he wants books! The apostle says to Timothy and so he says to every preacher, 'Give thyself unto reading.' The man who never reads will never be read; he who never quotes will never be quoted. He who will not use the thoughts of other men's brains, proves that he has no brains of his own. Brethren, what is true of ministers is true of all our people. You need to read." (1863, http://www.spurgeon.org/sermons/0542.htm).

There is one other time, according to Paul, when younger servant leaders need to step up: ***when godly leaders are opposed by ungodly peo-***

ple (4:14-18). This paragraph fascinates me. Who was Alexander, and what made him so harmful to Paul and the Gospel? Who were these Roman officials, other than Nero, who seemed so determined to rid the earth of Paul? Why does the enemy take such delight in nurturing opposition to the Gospel? These and other questions may remain only partially answered. Paul described Alexander in this manner – "*(he)* did me great harm" (endeiknymi – 4:14). We don't know what that harm looked like. So much is hidden beneath the biblical text. It might mean that Alexander was one of the state's witnesses against Paul at his first defense. The verb used above can have a legal connotation to it, that is, Alexander "informed or spoke against" Paul. Regardless, the apostle was not pursuing some kind of vendetta or measure of revenge. He entrusted the whole matter to God. The ever wise and alert Paul does warn Timothy to keep his distance from Alexander. Paul seemed to recognize God's hand in all of this. He, with great maturity, saw an opportunity to share the Gospel in the political center of the known world. The church desperately needs servant leaders who are ever alert to the open doors God creates for the advancement of His message and plan.

Alexander is described as a "coppersmith" or metalworker (chalkeus). Apparently, he made objects from copper (vases, utensils, idols, and other bronze articles). Perhaps he even worked in one of the local copper mines. Some Bible students have suggested that this is the same Alexander mentioned in 1Timothy 1:20 or the man identified with the Ephesus riot in Acts 19:33. Since Alexander was a very common name, there is no evidence of that connection. The opposition that occurred in the Roman courts may very well mean that Paul was not granted a defense lawyer, but had to present his own case. Some have noted that this section, especially 2 Timothy 4:16-18, has the feel of Paul's Gethsemane. It is doubtful that the reference to being "rescued from the lion's mouth" referred to the Roman Coliseum, but rather described a divine rescue from clear and present danger. Paul, after all, was a Roman citizen and could not be punished in that manner. There was a localized opposition to the Jesus Way in Rome mostly due to the accusation that Christians were atheists, that is, they did not accept the Emperor as Savior, nor the other gods and goddesses that saturated the Roman culture. In the midst of this spiritual war, Paul did not ask to be exempted, but instead prayed for strength in the battle. What a marvelous model for all servant leaders undergoing intense spiritual opposition. God uses all opposition to shape and mold the servant leader's heart and mind to look like His. Praise His Name!

I cherish the final verses of this letter. Paul took the time to rehearse for Timothy significant partnerships in ministry. The faithful wife and husband team of Priscilla and Aquila are greeted. Paul first met them in Corinth (Acts 18:1-3). Like him, they were leather workers or tentmakers and passionate about the advancement of the Gospel. They had been serving in Ephesus (Acts 18:19), and one of the churches was meeting in their house (1 Corinthians 16:19). Eventually, they had migrated to Rome and planted another church in their home (Romans 16:3-4). This old and long friendship was a source of great comfort to the apostle. Paul also said hello to the household of Onesiphorus (note the connection with 1:16-18). The generic greeting might mean that Onesiphorus was dead, but Paul had maintained his love and appreciation for the family. Erastus was greeted and was more than likely the same Erastus mentioned as a city official in Corinth (Romans 16:23). On a very personal note, I have actually seen an inscription located in ancient Corinth with the name of Erastus carved into the stone. It is also worthy to note there is an Erastus mentioned in Acts 19:22 as a traveling buddy of Timothy's. Perhaps these two references were of the same person. Paul made a very brief acknowledgment of Trophimus who had been left behind in Miletus due to illness. Maybe this was the same Trophimus who accompanied Paul to Jerusalem in Acts 20:1-6. The apostle then linked together a greeting from four of Paul's Roman companions: Eubulus, Pudens, Linus, and

Claudia. The first three were brothers in Christ, and the last was a sister in the Lord. Others are mentioned with a generic "and all the brothers" (4:21). There is something deeply comforting about these references. It was, I think, a reminder to Timothy that Paul's imminent death would not stop the advancement of the Gospel. Others were ready to step up and continue the eternal work.

The enemy is ever cunning and persistent. He takes great delight in thwarting any reception to the Good News of Jesus. "Evil attack" or literally as the ESV translates it "every evil deed" was and is Satan's game plan (4:18). Paul never seemed to lose sight of the fact that his enemies were not flesh and blood, but spiritual forces (Ephesians 6:12). This primary realization shaped every part of Paul's ministry. He never seemed to get suckered into fighting with others. Granted, the Corinthians tested him greatly (2 Corinthians 10-13), but his focus remained the same. N.T. Wright's observation seems accurate to me:

> "The picture we get, as we take leave of this intimate and personal letter, is of a man facing serious trouble and likely death, beset with problems and anxieties, but who nevertheless remains determined to bring every single aspect of his life into the orbit of the Gospel itself, the royal proclamation of Jesus as Lord. He lives in the present world, Caesar's world, as already a cheerful citizen of the world to come, Jesus' world. He longs to see Timothy working hard and effectively for Jesus as he himself has done. And, as we listen in to his end of the conversation, we are left in no doubt as to what kind of advice he would give us today" (2004, pp. 134-135).

Guard the Gospel. Share Jesus anywhere and everywhere. Strategize the good strategy. Stay the course. Paul invited Timothy and, now, through those same Scriptures invites others to step up against waves of ungodliness.

For some time, I have been drawn to the moving story of the Cambridge Seven. Somewhere in my listening and reading of missionary biographies, I came across a barely noticeable reference to these men and their families. I don't remember a beginning date, but a tiny fragment and one small footnote have led me on a long journey. Even though, as a professor and preacher, I have researched and written other pieces, I have found myself never too far away from this remarkable group of nineteenth-century Christians. This missionary dream team did not suddenly appear in China. If you saw their story placed on a historical timeline, it might be logical to come to that conclusion. Some might prefer telling the story that way – seven men made a conscious decision based on the preaching of D.L. Moody to work alongside Hudson Taylor in order to advance the Gospel of Jesus Christ in 1885. However, long before 1885, those seven – Montague Beauchamp, William Cassels, Dixon Hoste, Arthur and Cecil Polhill-Turner, Stanley Smith, and C.T. Studd, were prayed for, hoped for, and ultimately called for by God to step up as servant leaders. Our God has not changed.

A Little Manual for Servant Leaders

CHAPTER 16
The Servant Leader's Dance with God
Titus 1:1-4

"We must not be led to believe that the Disciplines are for spiritual giants...Far from it...The Disciplines are best exercised in the midst of our normal daily activities...Neither should we think of the Spiritual Disciplines as some dull drudgery aimed at exterminating laughter from the face of the earth. Joy is the keynote of all the Disciplines...When one's inner spirit is set free from all that holds it down, that can hardly be described as dull drudgery. Singing, dancing, even shouting characterize the Disciplines of the spiritual life"
(Foster, Richard. (1978). **Celebration of Discipline.** *(pp. 1-2). Harper and Row).*

I've never been very good at dancing. I'm not lacking in the desire department, but I simply never got the special ability or training to do it well. I still dance, mind you, and it's not pretty. Here's a case in point: third grade, Mrs. Yates' class, and some kind of special evening event was going on at the Heyworth grade school. Our beloved teacher decided to create a dance contest. The music chosen was Chubby Checker's 1960 smash hit, *The Twist*. We danced our little hearts out. In the end, it came down to Jimmy Funk and me. Jimmy won. I only got that far in the contest because I danced passionately like someone who had tropical fire-ants in his shorts. Please don't dwell on that too long. The two words I want you to embrace are dancing and passion.

In our exploration of the Pastoral Letters, we've landed in an epistle called Titus, Paul's letter to a servant leader assigned to ministry on the Mediterranean Island of Crete. Though the words never occur in the opening paragraph, I still hear, see, and encounter a passionate dance between God, Paul, and Titus. Paul wrote the following:

> **1** *Paul, a servant of God and an apostle of Jesus Christ, for the sake of the faith of God's elect and their knowledge of the truth, which accords with godliness,* **2** *in hope of eternal life, which God, who never lies, promised before the ages began* **3** *and at the proper time manifested in his word through the preaching with which I have been entrusted by the command of God our Savior;* **4** *To Titus, my true child in a common faith: Grace and peace from God the Father and Christ Jesus our Savior.*

The apostle likely wrote this letter sometime between the writing of 1Timothy and 2 Timothy, though some historians suggest that Titus was written first. A number of scholars are persuaded that Paul wrote to Titus after his first arrest and subsequent release (Acts 28) and before his second arrest in Troas and return to prison, perhaps around 67 AD. One of the early Church Fathers, Clement of Rome, tells us of seven imprisonments Paul endured! Admittedly, there is some uncertainty about where the apostle was located, but, likely, he wrote the letter from somewhere in the region of Macedonia or the city of Ephesus. We don't directly know how the church was first planted in Crete. Again, some Bible students are convinced that Paul and Titus made their way to the island while on the proposed mission trip to Spain (Romans 15:24-28). I say all of that so that we can have some kind of framework for understanding what Paul was attempting to say to his trusted and loyal ministry partner in Crete. There is one last helpful reminder before we dig into these first four verses of Titus. Ray Stedman offers a good and concise recap of the three letters:

"All three of the pastoral letters of Paul, the two letters to Timothy and the letter to Titus, demonstrate similar themes and intent on the part of Paul. In all three letters, Paul instructs Timothy and Titus in four basic issues: appointing leaders (elders) in the church; teaching those leaders to guard the faith; teaching the congregation sound doctrine; and remaining on guard against false teachers. Paul told Timothy to carry out these four tasks in Ephesus; he charged Titus to do the same in Crete" (2009, p. 290).

Let me raise four questions in light of Paul's initial greeting.

First, what do we know about Crete? Crete is the largest island in the eastern Mediterranean Sea, approximately ninety miles off the southeast coast of Greece. It is 156 miles long and ranges from seven to thirty-five miles wide. Crete is peppered with mountainous terrain, fertile valleys, and probably first inhabited by Philistine mariners. The landscape, in Paul's day, was dotted with gigantic palaces and beautiful architectural design. Wealth abounded. Mercenary soldiers retired there. The Roman army even recruited skilled fighters from this scenic island. Apparently, there was a large Jewish population that called Crete home as well. On the Day of Pentecost, described in Acts 2, some islanders showed up for the annual feast in Jerusalem and ended up hearing the Good News of Jesus (Acts 2:11). In addition, Dr. Luke tells us that Paul and his traveling companions sailed along the shoreline of this island on their way to Rome. There might have been a brief stopover at Fair Havens, Crete, and perhaps Paul shared the Good News with someone there (Acts 27:8). We don't know for sure. We do know that Paul warned those in charge of the journey that danger was imminent due to winter weather, but the centurion, a soldier named Julius, along with the pilot and owner of the ship, decided to shuck Paul's advice and to sail on, hoping to stop at Phoenix on the southwestern side of Crete. Of course, Paul was right, and the ship was blown out to sea. Eventually, the boat struck a sandbar, ran aground, and finally broke into pieces from the pounding surf at Malta (Acts 27:41).

There is one solitary fact about this island worth noting. It contained a group of house churches that desperately needed biblical instruction, doctrinal correction, healthy elders, and a servant leader who could "straighten out what was left unfinished and appoint elders in every town" (Titus 1:5). Titus was the man for the job. Crete was infamous for its arrogance, greed, and combative spirit. Ben Witherington offers this insight:

> "Cretans believed that they were the original Greeks, having emerged from the earth itself. Cretans even claimed that the Olympian gods were in fact men and women of Crete elevated to the status of deities because of the benefactions that they did for humankind. It is not surprising, then, that they also believed that their island was the birthplace of most of the gods, particularly Zeus, who also was thought to be buried there. This allowed Cretans even to claim that worship of the gods began on Crete" (2006, p. 87).

Paul's quote from Epimenides (600-500 BC), a Cretan poet-prophet, painted a challenging picture for Titus. Paul's exact words were, "One of the Cretans, a prophet of their own, said, 'Cretans are always liars, evil beasts, lazy gluttons.'" (Titus 1:12). We'll talk more about this later and its impact on the work Paul has entrusted to Titus.

Every servant leader must ask this kind of question: What do I know about my Crete? I asked it of the small farming community and church I served. It was my holy practice to make "house calls" on Saturday morning. I would simply walk from house to house, trying not to make a nuisance of myself. Lots of conversations took place in driveways or front lawns. Some folks always invited me in. The unincorporated village of Lake Fork, Illinois, and the surrounding area was my Crete. I don't mean anything disrespectful by that. It was simply my divine assignment. Those weekly house calls filled with cups of coffee, small talk about the weather, sports, and farming helped me gather the vital information needed for genuine ministry. I listened more than talked. I laughed, cried, and prayed with people. I grew to accept the incessant cigarette smoke and to love those people. Without sounding too melodramatic, they taught me far more than I ever taught them. They made me into a pastor. Crete will do that to a person. Servant leaders never stop asking, "Who are these people that God has placed in my life? How can I help them become the disciples that God is shaping them to be?" My primary task is simply to be present in my Crete.

Second, what do we know about Titus? Amazingly, this apprentice to Jesus is never mentioned in the book of Acts. Because of Paul's letter to the Galatians, we know Titus was a Gentile, Greek by birth (Galatians 2:3), that came to saving faith in Jesus through the ministry of Paul. The specifics are unknown. We do know that Titus was the chief organizer, under the supervision of Paul, of the significant cross-cultural benevolence offering taken up for the Jewish Christians in Jerusalem. His part is highlighted ten different times through 2 Corinthians (2:13, 7:6, 7:13, 7:14, 8:6, 8:16, 8:17, 8:23, 12:18^{2x}). Perhaps there is no better answer to our question than Paul's statement in 2 Corinthians 8:23: "As for Titus, he is my partner and fellow worker..." Whatever Paul meant by the above statement, Titus seemed to have a knack for doing the right thing at the right time in the right way. He was Paul's troubleshooter. He was a Christian diplomat loved by the apostle. In our opening text, he was called by Paul, "my true child" (1:4). This was the very same language used of Timothy (1Timothy 1:2). Titus was the perfect portrait of a shepherd-pastor and such a vital part of Paul's life and ministry that he was asked to join Paul in Nicopolis (a city located along the northwest coast of Greece) where Paul planned to winter (Titus 3:12). Eusebius, Bishop of Caesarea and church historian (260 to 340 AD), tells us that Titus eventually returned to Crete after meeting with Paul in Nicopolis, becoming the first bishop there and ultimately serving in that location until the day he died. Whoever Titus was, he was a Jesus-follower faithful to the very end. Every servant leader can benefit from Titus' persevering example.

Third, what do we know about Paul from this letter? Notice with me that Paul thought of himself as a "servant" (1:1 - doulos). As we have already observed earlier, this was his favorite term for describing himself. He could have chosen a variety of other "servant" words to get his point across. Ponder for a moment the possibilities. He could have used the word "deacon" (diakonos). It shows up some twenty-nine times in the New Testament and is even used of Jesus on one occasion (Romans 15:8). The word literally means, "one who waits on tables." Paul might have chosen the little-used word for a common household servant (oiketes). It only shows up four times in the New Testament (Luke 16:13, Acts 10:7, Romans 14:4, and 1 Peter 2:18). He could have selected the term for a slave that helped row a ship (huperetes – twenty times in the N.T.). The "under-rower" imagery would fit so much of Paul's slant on servant leadership. Since the Jerusalem temple was such a significant place in his life, he might have incorporated the word for temple servant into his writing (leitourgos). Though the noun does not occur in the New Testament, the verb associated with temple service (latreuo) is used widely, even in 2 Timothy 1:3, where Paul said, "I thank God, whom I *serve...*" Finally, the apostle might have handpicked "therapon" – someone who served with dignity like Moses (Hebrews 3:5 – only occurrence in the N.T.). Instead, Paul came back to his old standby. Interestingly, he never used this term negatively (doulos).

Paul also incorporated into his thinking the word "apostle" (1:1 – apostolos). Literally, Paul was "one who was sent." Just as Jesus was sent on mission, so was this man (Hebrews 3:1). His life objective was defined in these opening words. In a very layered, opening single sentence, (1:1-4) Paul described his credentials for lifelong ministry:

"He is an apostle on behalf of the Christian faith and the truth that leads to godliness and the hope of eternal life. Paul was chosen to be an apostle in order to take the gospel to those who were chosen (God's elect) to receive the hope of eternal life. To know that God has chosen us even before we chose Him should fill our hearts with awe, gratitude, and love for Him" (2009, p. 291).

The apostle's goal is to build up faith and knowledge of God. His firm hope is in God's unbreakable promise. This man believed, down to his apostolic toes, that he had been entrusted with a sacred mission. The two magnificent words he used to bless Titus – "grace and peace" – were the very words he had discovered in his own life. No servant leader gets very far in the Jesus-following life without immeasurable amounts of His grace and peace. It would be a good spiritual exercise to pause for a few minutes and simply to recount God's ample supply of grace and peace in your life, the kind of grace and peace that goes beyond your salvation, but always points back to it.

My very first ministry experience located me in the small community of Ashland, Illinois, just west of Springfield. I was called a youth minister, but I was a far cry from anything that resembled someone gifted for youth work or ready for the holy mantle of vocational ministry. At the time, the church was experiencing a great deal of inner conflict and mission confusion. The two enemy tactics often seem to go hand and hand. One defining Sunday morning, I was making my way from teaching a high-school Sunday school class to preaching in the adult worship service. It was what we called in those days "youth Sunday." I walked directly into a full blown verbal war between the preacher's wife and one of the elders. These were typically good and loving people. On this day, though, ugly words were exchanged. Each went into the auditorium and prepared for worship. I was completely undone. Shell-shocked might be a closer description. I couldn't focus, couldn't worship, couldn't share in the Lord's Supper, and couldn't offer much of a sermon that day. I noticed throughout my brief two-year ministry that many carried on their lives as if there was nothing unhealthy about that church. I didn't know it at the time, but I had stumbled into Titus' Crete. What's it like to serve in a place like that? One final question might help us.

Fourth, what do we know about God from this letter? At minimum, we know that God mightily and miraculously brings people together. Paul and Titus are Exhibit A. God orchestrated Paul, servant and apostle, to divinely meet Titus, this man's true son in the faith, somewhere and somehow. Beyond that, God is crazy, absolutely head over heels crazy, with providing the necessary ingredients for a healthy life and ministry – knowledge, faith, hope, grace, peace, and more than anything – a Savior. This God is the world's premier promise-keeper. Paul said God does not lie but has a promise He has kept before the beginning of time (1:2). The echo of Numbers 23:19 can be heard loud and clear, ironically offered from Balaam's oracle: "God is not a man, that He should lie; nor a son of man, that He should change His mind. Does He speak and then not act? Does He promise and not fulfill?" The singular promise Paul described over and over is, was, and forever will be, centered in the person of Jesus Christ.

Notice with me that Paul used the word "Savior" twice in this opening greeting (1:3 and 1:4). He applied it to God the Father and to God the Son. In Paul's day, the term used, "soter," was attached to pagan gods, kings, doctors, and philosophers, but especially to ancient city-state leaders. Ultimately, it became the defining term for Rome's emperors. The word literally meant "one who preserves" or "one who delivers." Paul saturated the letter with it. As mentioned, he used "Savior" twice in this opening, but he also strategically placed it into the letter on four other occasions (2:10, 2:13, 3:4, and 3:6). Just in the nick of time, God brought His Word to light through Paul. If I've said it once, I have said it a thousand times: God is seldom early, but He is never late. Paul wanted Titus not only to know, but completely to embrace the timing of God. Catch the incredible chronological contrast between "before the ages began" (1:2) and "at the proper time" (1:3). God's message, the Good News found in Jesus, was perfectly timed – not a second early and not a minute late.

So, what does it take to serve in Crete? We need a servant leader who knows how to do what has been asked. We have that in Titus. We need a servant leader who knows how to get out of the way and to stay in the Way. We have that in Paul. We need a servant leader who knows how to come to the rescue at just the right time. We have that abundantly in God. Please, young servant leader, seasoned elder, experienced pastor, don't forget that Crete is everywhere. We still need servant leaders who know how to do what is asked. We still need servant leaders who know how to get out of the way and to stay in the Way. We still have a Savior who knows how to come to the rescue at just the right time. There is ample reason to celebrate, plenty of cause to dance, and lots of encouragement to worship.

I told you at the beginning of this chapter that I've never been good at dancing. It has not stopped me from trying. My wife and I, now and then, while fixing supper together, will turn toward each other and begin to dance. Music is not required. The movement of two hearts intertwined by mutual love and respect, shaped by lots of time together and a life full of soul-shaping experiences provides all the necessary lyrics, melody, and instruments. And so it is with God. He is calling, encouraging, and pleading with us to join Him in a dance. Not just anywhere, but especially in Crete. Amen.

A Little Manual for Servant Leaders

CHAPTER 17
Standing Tall as a Servant Leader
Titus 1:5-16

"One of the most important things I have learned along the way is having the courage to stand by my convictions – those things that I know are right, those guiding principles that I know to stick with. Sometimes that means standing out from the crowd or not being popular, but sometimes that's the only responsible place to be. It doesn't necessarily make the days any easier, but at least I feel like I'm still heading in the right direction when the day is over and the next one is on its way"
(Dungy, Tony (2009). **Uncommon.** *(pp. 29-30).Tyndale).*

Servant leadership comes in all shapes and sizes. I'm confident that is not surprising to you. There is no singular profile where one size fits all. Our unique giftedness and personality help form a one-of-a-kind servant leadership life. God is not an assembly line God. Each of us has been customized to partner with Him in His grand purpose and plan. There probably is no better insight into the incomparable way God has made us than how we approach the common and ordinary opportunities He brings into our paths each and every day. The seemingly small things like the manner in which we take out the trash, greet people in the workplace, open doors for others, clean up messes, and all kinds of other

Jesus-like actions reveal much about our servant hearts. So often, servant leadership's apparent big side is seen through our willingness to confront another brother or sister in Christ, introduce someone to Jesus, listen attentively to someone seeking spiritual direction, or pray intently for a person in need. All of these and more give some indication of our comprehension of the servant side of leadership. However, labeling things big or small can violate the very essence of what it means to be a servant leader. All tasks are to be done in the name of Jesus as an offering to God. In other words, we are called to "stand tall" in any and every circumstance that divinely intersects our lives. Servant leadership, at some point, inevitably involves a Crete-like challenge. At some juncture, every servant leader is tempted to say, "You can take that job (large or small) and shove it." Sorry about the crassness of that statement. Here's how Paul described it to Titus:

> [5] *This is why I left you in Crete, so that you might put what remained into order, and appoint elders in every town as I directed you—* [6] *if anyone is above reproach, the husband of one wife, and his children are believers and not open to the charge of debauchery or insubordination.* [7] *For an overseer, as God's steward, must be above reproach. He must not be arrogant or quick-tempered or a drunkard or violent or greedy for gain,* [8] *but hospitable, a lover of good, self-controlled, upright, holy, and disciplined.* [9] *He must hold firm to the trustworthy word as taught, so that he may be able to give instruction in sound doctrine and also to rebuke those who contradict it.*
>
> [10] *For there are many who are insubordinate, empty talkers and deceivers, especially those of the circumcision party.* [11] *They must be silenced, since they are upsetting whole families by teaching for shameful gain what they ought not to teach.* [12] *One of the Cretans, a prophet of their own, said, "Cretans are always liars, evil beasts, lazy gluttons."* [13] *This testimony is true. Therefore rebuke them sharply, that they may be sound in the faith,* [14] *not devoting themselves to Jewish myths and the com-*

mands of people who turn away from the truth. ¹⁵ *To the pure, all things are pure, but to the defiled and unbelieving, nothing is pure; but both their minds and their consciences are defiled.* ¹⁶ *They profess to know God, but they deny him by their works. They are detestable, disobedient, unfit for any good work.*

I'm going to flip this passage upside down. I'd like to look at 1:10-16 first and then come back to where Paul started in 1:5-9. I specifically want you to notice Titus' work conditions in Crete. Ten telling descriptions are revealed. The initial introduction to this extensive portrait of evil, 1:10-11, runs non-stop as a single sentence in the Greek New Testament.

- "insubordinate" (1:10 anypotaktoi) – Paul is describing wild or rebellious people. He is painting a picture of a wild animal that needs muzzling.
- "empty talkers"(1:10 mataiologoi – same as 1Timothy 1:6) – The apostle is simply identifying people whose words were empty or contained no lasting value.
- "deceivers" – (1:10 phrenapatai) These are people who have turned from the truth of the Gospel and are tricking others into a similar counterfeit life.
- "for shameful gain" – (1:11) These false teachers are motivated by money, not ministry in the name of Jesus. They were "teaching things they ought not to teach" (didaskontes ha me dei – which parallels 1Timothy 1:4 and "heterodidaskalein" or teaching heresy). This section of Scripture also parallels 1Timothy 6:3ff.
- "liars" – (1:12 pseustai) They don't have the ability to speak the truth. This is the same word found in 1Timothy 1:10.
- "evil beasts" – (1:12 kaka tharia) The picture here is stunning. Pau, in quoting Epimenides, is describing a wild animal, a beast, or even a snake that has a wicked or hurtful intention.
- "lazy gluttons" – (1:12 gasteres argai) In an almost comical word picture, Paul is suggesting through Epimenides that Cretans were "slow stomachs" or "bellies," as the old King James Bible put it.

It may seem odd to our contemporary ears, but the idea is that Titus was ministering in and among people who tended toward being greedy, overindulgent pleasure seekers.

- "detestable" (1:16 bdeluktos) – These false teachers profess to know God, but deny him by the manner in which they live. The word portrays the idea of someone who lives a sacrilegious life.
- "disobedient" (1:16 apeithes) – This is the same word used in 2 Timothy 3:2 and later in Titus 3:3. These people were, ironically, unwilling to be taught. They could not be persuaded to believe and to live in a way that honored Christ.
- "unfit" (1:16 adokimos) – Once again, this word parallels what Paul said in 2 Timothy 3:8 of Jannes and Jambres and men like them who oppose the truth. They are unfit or can't stand the test for servant leadership. The word actually is drawn from the world of the metalworker. When a particular metal cannot withstand the refining fire and necessary shaping required, it is discarded. So it is with these false teachers who could not pass the test for "doing anything good."

These ten descriptions represent a thought-provoking and disturbing picture of Titus' working conditions. The false teachers described are a constant, relentless, and God-dishonoring presence in Crete. I especially want you to pause for a moment and to reflect on Paul's incorporation of the Epimenides quote. Here's the background. A long standing debate ensued as to whether Crete actually housed the grave of Zeus. Accusations flew back and forth between Crete and Greece. Name calling and counter claims abounded. Ben Witherington makes it all very clear:

> "So the point in part is that Cretans, including Cretan teachers, are apt to make false claims about God, and therefore Christians should be wary of their teaching...Lest we think that the claim about Cretans being liars is just rhetoric about one particular matter, we should note that there was in Greek antiquity a verb *kretizo,* which literally means 'to Cretanize,' but the force of which connoted 'to lie or cheat.' Some Greeks even

ranked the Cretans as one of the three most brutish people on earth, the other two groups being Cappadocians and Cicilians. Even Epimenides joked about his own people that the absence of wild beasts on the island was filled by the human inhabitants" (2006, pp. 123-124)!

Servant leaders cannot escape Crete. Paul has made it perfectly plain that Titus was to stay in Crete in order to accomplish two fundamental tasks. First, straighten out what was left unfinished. Second, cultivate and appoint shepherd leaders. Paul couldn't have used the Epimendes quote as a way for Titus to avoid ministering in Crete. If *every Cretan* was irredeemable – a liar, evil brute, and lazy glutton – than how could shepherd leaders be appointed? Why remain in Crete if making disciples was impossible? You get the point, right? Overstatement or exaggeration, as a means of communicating a general truth, is not uncommon in our day. All servant leaders face their own Crete-like circumstances. God's willingness and ability to accomplish His purposes are unstoppable. Our task is to take a vow of stability and to serve until God, by His Spirit, releases us. This brings us then to Titus 1:5-9.

Paul seemed to identify three places or locations particularly where Titus needed to stand tall. First, Paul instructed Titus to **stand tall in the home** (1:5-7). The most significant word incorporated in this counsel was the term "above reproach" (anenkletos – a synonym to 1Timothy 3:2 where Paul told Timothy that elders were to be "above reproach" – anepilempton). "Above reproach" or blameless describes a servant leader who is beyond accusation, anyone would believe. Because we have spent a great deal of time discussing shepherd-elder leadership in 1Timothy 3, I won't explore it again here. Suffice it to say that much of what Paul told Timothy, he also told Titus. All of the "husband of but one wife, a man whose children believe," talk is domestic in nature. The reference was and is to the home life of the shepherd servant leader. Consider this. What do you want in a home? The difficulty of Crete grows smaller and smaller when the home becomes stronger and stronger. Give this your very best attention.

I have been richly blessed by observing and experiencing homes where the husband stood tall by loving his wife as Jesus does the church and where the wife stood tall by yielding to her husband's leadership. Their mutual submission to one another shaped and formed a beautiful, peaceful, and edifying place. What followed were children who honored and obeyed their parents. No home, of course, is perfect. Sin infiltrates every part of reality. Remember my earlier observation. Crete is everywhere.

Second, Paul instructed Titus to **stand tall in the heart** (1:7). Five interior concerns or heart matters appear all prefaced with the word "not." The shepherd servant leaders were *not* to be overbearing, quick tempered, drunk, violent, or in pursuit of dishonest gain. If we were to put this into very contemporary language, we could say: *"don't* be self-willed, nurse a grudge, get intoxicated, punch someone, or pursue the dollar." Servant leaders have experienced spiritual heart surgery and continue to be under the Great Physician's care. Servant leaders not only understand King David's prayer, but incorporate his prayer in their everyday lives, "Create in me a clean heart, O God" (Psalm 51:10). Of the five heart ailments mentioned by Paul, which one could potentially wreck your life? Why? Take a holy pause and give this some prayerful thought.

Third, Paul advised Titus to **stand tall in holy habits** (1:8). The apostle highlighted three significant spiritual exercises. They are, *the habit of the open door* – "be hospitable" (think 1Timothy 3:2 and the power of loving strangers); *the habit of the healthy heart* – "lover" of all that is good, self-controlled (same as Titus 2:2), upright, holy, and disciplined (consider all the ways that a life marked with holy habits can draw people to Jesus); and *the habit of the Christian mind* – that is he or she is able not only to model sound doctrine and thinking Christianly, but also to correct any divergence from the Gospel. Crete is not transformed by some great scheme, new fad, or slick program. Crete transformation requires cooperation with the Holy Spirit. If we pull together Titus 1:5-9, the message is crystal clear – prioritize the home, watch the heart, and cultivate the mind for Christ. Crete can become good and fruitful soil for the Good News of Jesus Christ.

Most of us who have the slightest bit of humility recognize how good we are at giving advice and not taking it. When our children were small, 1 they often tried all kinds of tricks and schemes to keep me in their bedrooms one more minute. "Daddy, would you tell us another story?" "Can I have one more drink?" "Let's pray some more." Each question or statement was intended to delay the inevitable bedtime. The biggest delay tactic was this one: "Daddy, I'm scared of the dark. Would you check under the bed one more time?" "Daddy, have you ever been afraid?" It would have been easy for me to blow off their child-like concerns. As much as I recognized their cunning strategies, the last question always caused me to pause. They knew they had it made at that point, but I didn't care. Wise parents pick their battles carefully. I wanted the kids to know they had a father who understood them. Their dad was a guy who had experienced all the stuff of this world they were now experiencing, including being afraid.

It seems to me that Paul took on a father-like understanding in this section of Titus. He knew Crete was a tough place. He knew Crete demanded the very best from Titus. He knew Crete transformation would require a holy persistence and determination. But more than anything, this apostle knew that real change doesn't start with some well-planned strategies or grandiose plans, but with a simple prayer, "Lord, change me." Crete gets whittled down to manageable size when we stand tall in our own lives

A Little Manual for Servant Leaders

CHAPTER 18
Saying What You Mean as a Servant Leader
Titus 2:1-15

"After a leader receives and owns a vision, the next challenge is to communicate it to others. What good is a vision unless a leader can help others to see it? But how? How does a leader best communicate a vision? By embodying it. By personifying it. By living it out (Hybels, Bill. (2002). **Courageous Leadership.** *(p. 38). Zondervan).*

Servant leaders say what they mean, and they mean what they say, no hidden agenda, no double talk. My mind tends to race toward thinking of my third grade teacher, Mrs. Yates. I've mentioned her previously. She was a remarkable woman, fair yet firm, gracious but not a push over, attractive without being narcissistic, especially alert to the grace of God without becoming a religious Bible thumper. There she was faithfully at work in a small central Illinois grade school, dispensing the Gospel without violating the constitutional boundaries between church and state. She was as rare as a North American jaguar. When she spoke, we listened. I've often looked back at her impact on my life and have marveled at her exceptional ability to communicate a God-shaped vision for each of her students. She was an extraordinary teacher who meant what she said and said what she meant. So it was with Paul's instruction to Titus. We have come to a section of the letter where the apostle used repetition to explain what he meant. The reader will notice there is some parallel to 1 Timothy 5:

> **2** *But as for you, teach what accords with sound doctrine.* [2] *Older men are to be sober-minded, dignified, self-controlled, sound in faith, in love, and in steadfastness.* [3] *Older women likewise are to be reverent in behavior, not slanderers or slaves to much wine. They are to teach what is good,* [4] *and so train the young women to love their husbands and children,* [5] *to be self-controlled, pure, working at home, kind, and submissive to their own husbands, that the word of God may not be reviled.* [6] *Likewise, urge the younger men to be self-controlled.* [7] *Show yourself in all respects to be a model of good works, and in your teaching show integrity, dignity,* [8] *and sound speech that cannot be condemned, so that an opponent may be put to shame, having nothing evil to say about us.* [9] *Bondservants are to be submissive to their own masters in everything; they are to be well-pleasing, not argumentative,* [10] *not pilfering, but showing all good faith, so that in everything they may adorn the doctrine of God our Savior.*
>
> [11] *For the grace of God has appeared, bringing salvation for all people,* [12] *training us to renounce ungodliness and worldly passions, and to live self-controlled, upright, and godly lives in the present age,* [13] *waiting for our blessed hope, the appearing of the glory of our great God and Savior Jesus Christ,* [14] *who gave himself for us to redeem us from all lawlessness and to purify for himself a people for his own possession who are zealous for good works.*
>
> [15] *Declare these things; exhort and rebuke with all authority. Let no one disregard you.*

Let's start our conversation by observing all the repetition. First, notice the four occurrences of "self-control" talk (sophroneo/sophronizo – in 2:2, 5, 6, 12). The New American Standard translation inserts the word "sensible." The King James Bible translates it with four different words: temperate, discreet, sober-minded, and soberly. Paul chose a word that described a person who showed proper conduct, was in his right mind, or gave evidence of mastering his own life. Also repeated, though not always clearly translated, are six separate occurrences of "purpose statements" (2:4, 5, 8, 10, 12, 14). The ESV uses words like "so," "that," "so that," and "to" while the NIV translators use words like "then," "so that," and "to" to communicate the idea. It is easier to spot in the Greek New Testament where the word "hina" marks out each of the six purpose statements. Along with the "so that" statements are five references to family talk (2:2, 3, 4, 6, 9). Paul included older men, older women, younger women, young men, slaves, and masters in the conversation. Finally, and most importantly, there is a teaching emphasis throughout the chapter. Notice with me all the words that are inserted: "teach," "sound doctrine," "teaching," and "teaches" (2:1, 2:2, 2:3, 2:7, 2:9, 2:10, 2:12, and 2:15). Ten different references are included. Paul was not simply talking about the *content* of what was taught, though that was included, but he was reminding Timothy of the urgency in living out the Gospel, something we could call *conduct*. In light of that emphasis, what was Paul saying to Timothy? Or to put it into a more contemporary question: ***What are servant leaders saying that they really mean?***

At the heart of that question was Paul's centering thought in 2:11-12. Let's start there and work our way outward. First, then, ***servant leaders are saying "no" to anything that dishonors Jesus.*** What they preach, they practice. Literally, Paul said, "Grace schools us…" It trains us step by step. It is our tutor or mentor. Grace instructs us like a good coach to steer away from anything that would compromise or embarrass the Gospel. Now, look with me, at how Paul sought to apply that fundamental teaching in this passage. Older men are to be "sober-minded" (nephalious – see 1Timothy 3:2), "dignified" (semnous – see 1Timothy 3:8), and "self-controlled" (sophronas – see 1Timothy 3:2 and the other uses in this section of Titus). I'm really drawn to this triangle of holy living (also mentioned in 1Timothy 6:11-12, 2 Timothy 3:10, and 1 Thessalonians 1:3). These older men were to be instructed to say no to anything that would cause excess and harm in light of the Gospel with food, work, play, dress, and so on.

Older women were to be "reverent in behavior, not slanderers or slaves to much wine" (2:3). I'm particularly drawn to the "not slanderers" piece (me diabolous – 1Timothy 3:11). These women were to say no to gossip, to attacking another person's reputation. Notice with me how Paul included the careful monitoring of wine consumption in this instruction. Too much drink can lead to too much destructive talk. For whatever reason, Cretan older women were possibly prone to being addicted (doulo), held captive, even enslaved to alcohol. Grace, rightly understood invited a rejection of that kind of unhealthy dependency.

Slaves were given specific spiritual direction not to steal (2:10). There was to be no inconsistent witness to their masters. Grace was to teach slaves (employees in our day) to say no to anything that might display disrespect to those they served, not an easy path. Freedom in Christ requires submission to authority. What a paradoxical life we have been called to live. Whatever the Christian life includes, it cannot, however, be defined entirely by a set of "nos." Grace is always sensitive to how, when, where, and why we live out the Jesus-following life. The old adage, "don't drink, don't smoke, and don't chew, and whatever you do, don't go with the girls that do," can't possibly be the defining mission statement for a disciple of Jesus. So, "yes" is needed, but "yes" to what?

Servant leaders are saying "yes" to everything that honors Jesus. Come back to the centering passage with me. Paul said that grace not only teaches us to say "no" to ungodliness and worldly passions, but to live life in a way that is marked by self-control and godliness. Again, notice with me how Paul applied that "yes" piece to this section of Titus. Older men were to say yes to anything that deepened their faith, enlarged their love, and developed their spiritual endurance (2:2). If a Fig Newton, time with friends, and some chocolate raspberry mocha help you do that, then say "yes" to all those things. Older women were invited to say yes to anything that helped them teach and train younger women to love their families and to manage their homes in Jesus' Name (2:3-5). Younger women and younger men needed models that positively affirmed the goodness of the Gospel. Paul knew how vital this was. Elsewhere, he said, "For all the promises of God find their Yes in Him" (2 Corinthians 1:20). I cannot express strongly enough to any and all servant leaders how vitally important all of this is. The "yes" Paul referenced is the centrality of the Gospel. The Good News of Jesus is not the minimum required doctrine of the disciple, but it is the essence and on-going fuel to love God and neighbor. Even slaves and masters were to embrace the message of Jesus in a way that made the Savior attractive to any and all.

I want to grow more and more into the "yes" of Christ. Attention to my wife and family, especially a new generation of grandchildren, are worthy of Jesus's "yes." My regular time of devotion and worship, what I refer to as my "tent of meeting" has Christ's affirmation written all over it. Spiritual reading, physical exercise, laughter, good food, journal keeping, the practice of other holy habits, encouragement to other disciples, attention to those who don't know Jesus, and so many other every day experiences are part of Christ's oceanic "yes." Please notice with me that manner in which Paul elevated Jesus as "God our Savior." The phrase is used twice in this part of Titus (2:10 and 2:13). God the Father is our "Soter," and God the Son is as well. The word for savior describes a divine rescue. As noted earlier in Titus 1:3-4, the word was used of false gods, kings, doctors, and philosophers in the ancient Greek culture. But Paul reclaimed the word and attached it to our Lord where it rightfully belonged. I more than recognize that there are people who claim to be Christians and who deny that Jesus is God in flesh. They hold to a heresy that views Jesus as created by God. An honest and careful study of significant passages like John 1, Colossians 1, all of Hebrews, and other Scriptures reminds us of the supremacy of Jesus. All of these speak to Jesus as completely and totally sufficient. He alone is full of grace. Grace lines up our motives. It keeps us alert to the presence of God. Oh, praise His Name. There is one final word on the lips of servant leaders that needs underscoring.

Servant leaders are saying, "Mission matters." Throughout Titus 2, Paul hammered away at the purposes of God. Older women had a mission, a purpose bigger than they could imagine. They were called to live in a Jesus-honoring way *so that* they could "train the younger women to love their husbands and children" (2:4). Younger women were to imitate that pattern *so that* "the word of God may not be reviled" (2:5). Timothy was to live in a way that younger men were captured by the person of Christ *so that* those who opposed his ministry would be put to shame (2:8). Christ-following slaves were to live a submissive and yielding life *so that* the teaching about "God our Savior" would be attractive to any and all (2:10). Grace, wrapped up in the mission of God, never stops teaching. According to the wise apostle, grace coaches all of us *so that* we can learn to say "no" to ungodliness and *so that* we can be redeemed (2:12 and 2:14).

?This section of Scripture concludes with another reminder to teach (2:15). Actually, the word that was used by Paul was the Greek word "lalei" for talk. Here it is translated "teach" (2:1) and "declare" (2:15). So, this paragraph is shaped by every day, ordinary, common talk that focuses on Jesus. Titus, like Timothy, was reminded to, "not let anyone despise" him. The connotation was that no one was to attempt "to go around" Titus or to "look down on" him (see 1Timothy 4:1). The primary way that defense happens is through the servant leader's saturation in trustworthy speech, soaked in the person of Christ.

Years ago, I read the story of Dr. Boris Kornfield, a Jewish surgeon, who was arrested without trial, accused of anti-Soviet propaganda and ultimately placed in Russia's infamous Gulag. He landed in his very own Crete. Another prisoner eventually shared the Good News of Jesus with Dr. Kornfield. The doctor's life was forever changed. He became a living demonstration of Kingdom salt and light (Matthew 5:13-16). This twentieth century Dr. Luke was constantly caring for other prisoners and sharing with them the saving story of Jesus Christ, the very story he had heard and believed. One day, he was called on to save the life of a sadistic prison guard. Boris Kornfield said, "Yes." He had already said "no" to bitterness and revenge. Tragically, Dr. Kornfield was brutally murdered by another prisoner, but not before he had witnessed Christ's love to one more inmate suffering from cancer. The cancer-ridden prisoner was none other than Aleksandr (Alexander) Solzhenitsyn (December 11, 1918 – August 3, 2008). This now-famous writer and dissident who ultimately won the 1970 Nobel Prize in Literature and was deported from his home country in 1974 became an apprentice of Jesus. That's the way of grace. It never gives up. It, like genuine servant leaders, says what it means and means what it says. Grace's "no" is freeing, and grace's "yes" is eternal.

A Little Manual for Servant Leaders

CHAPTER 19

The "Doing Good" Reminder of Servant Leadership
Titus 3:1-8

"I frequently ask spiritual leaders what they are doing that they see God doing. Learning to see God, to hear Him, is the real object of prayer...For example, each member of the staff at one church was instructed to go to a coffee shop, sit on a park bench, or stand in a mall parking lot and pray a simple prayer: 'Lord, help me see what You see'...They began to see broken families, homeless people, at-risk children, stressed teenagers – all people they were not engaging with their church ministry. Gripped by the heart of God, they gained an urgency to address what they saw"
(McNeal, Reggie. (2009). **Missional Renaissance.** *(p.70). Jossey-Bass).*

Here's a colossal question. How do servant leaders impact culture for Christ? So much conversation has focused on that question over the years. Richard Niebuhr wrote a now famous work sixty-plus years ago (1951) entitled *Christ and Culture.* In that book, Niebuhr presented several ways that Jesus-followers could impact culture for Christ. Suffice it to say that some people choose a course of action that positions them against culture in a combative posture. The chief means of impacting culture is through constantly challenging culture and rubbing up against it like holy sandpaper. Others select a path that leads them to step away from culture, to attempt to avoid its seductions by isolation. The danger, of course, is that it can cause those who select that course of action to be viewed as irrelevant. Still others look for some kind of middle ground and choose a path that can lead to compromise. Regardless of where you land in that discussion, it is vital to recognize that Paul counseled Titus in a direction that would impact Crete for Christ.

Before we hear the apostle's words to his trusted partner in ministry, let me remind you of something John Stott observed in his reflection on Titus. This nifty analysis has proven helpful to me. Stott suggests that there are three major themes or movements in the letter. First, Titus 1:5-16 reveals "doctrine and duty in the church," or the importance of good teaching and living in the Body of Christ. Second, Titus 2:1-15 discloses "doctrine and duty in the home," or the importance of good teaching and living in the family. Third, Titus 3:1-11 unfolds "doctrine and duty in the world," or the importance of good teaching and living in the culture (1996, p. 167). This fundamental view is at the heart of Servant Leadership 101. Our willingness to mesh together good teaching and Christ-like living is at the core of cultural impact. What we will define in this chapter as "doing good" constructs the needed bridge between Jesus-followers and those who do not yet know Him. My wife once posted a plaque in our house that was entitled "Rules of the Home." Our family was encouraged to read it regularly. The statements on the plaque went like this: "Rule 1: Mom is right. Rule 2: If Mom is wrong refer to Rule 1." It is so easy to lose sight of the basics. When it comes to the life and the witness of local churches and the vitality and ministry of servant leaders, consistent reminders are needed. Bad memories lead to bad messes. Here, then, is Paul's "doing good" reminder to Titus:

> **3** *Remind them to be submissive to rulers and authorities, to be obedient, to be ready for every good work, ² to speak evil of no one, to avoid quarreling, to be gentle, and to show perfect courtesy toward all people. ³ For we ourselves were once foolish, disobedient, led astray, slaves to various passions and pleasures,*

passing our days in malice and envy, hated by others and hating one another. ⁴ *But when the goodness and loving kindness of God our Savior appeared,* ⁵ *he saved us, not because of works done by us in righteousness, but according to his own mercy, by the washing of regeneration and renewal of the Holy Spirit,* ⁶ *whom he poured out on us richly through Jesus Christ our Savior,* ⁷ *so that being justified by his grace we might become heirs according to the hope of eternal life.* ⁸ *The saying is trustworthy, and I want you to insist on these things, so that those who have believed in God may be careful to devote themselves to good works. These things are excellent and profitable for people.*

Servant leaders do not mind repeating themselves. So, what were the basics that Paul was reminding Titus to repeat? First, **remind people that their public lives becomes their pulpit** (3:1-2). "Remind" (hupominaske), or more accurately, "keep on reminding" was foundational to raising up genuine apprentices to Jesus. This is the same word our Lord used in His farewell speech to the Twelve in that Jerusalem Upper-Room. He said, "But the Helper, the Holy Spirit, whom the Father will send in my name, He will teach you all things and will *bring to your remembrance* all that I have said to you" (John 14:26). Once again, we see the importance of this crucial reminding business through the ministry of the Holy Spirit in the life of the church. It is the very same thing Paul instructed Timothy to do: "*Remind* them of these things" (2 Timothy 2:14). Notice with me that the reminders were shaped by six infinitive phrases or applications all prefaced with the word "to" – be subject, obedient, ready to do whatever is good, slander no one, be peaceable and considerate, and show true humility. All six reminders look and sound like Jesus. People of all stripes – government leaders and people in general – were to be respected. Perhaps all six applications could be summarized under the heading of Christian civility. Paul wanted Titus never to forget that "doing good" in the Name of Jesus was a foundational kingdom principle. The "submissive" (hupatasso) theme permeates this section (2:5, 9, 3:1). In other words, our workplace can become the primary launching pad for our witness of Jesus.

Surprisingly, it was not Scripture or seminary that taught me this necessary discipleship basic. I learned this through the constant reminder and example of Dan Harper, the man I spoke of earlier in this book. Over and over, he modeled for me the power of "doing good" in the workplace. Dan was not an evangelist by gifting or calling, but he was passionate about giving God excellence in what he did. After being diagnosed with cancer, he became even more intentional about viewing his public life as his pulpit. I once watched with interest as Dan attempted to build a work bench in the tire shop. There was always a need to organize tools. He just could not accept doing anything that was half-hearted or done with mediocrity. I was shocked and quietly laughed as he tore the work bench off the wall when he realized it was not up to his standards. Forty-plus years later, I still recall the impact that had on my life. How I approach my public work attracts or detracts from the cause of Christ. Questions begin to surface in my heart. Do I regularly pray for those in positions of authority? Do I truly listen (obey – peitharcheo) to those over me? Am I constantly ready to do whatever is good? Do my words reveal that I refuse to speak ill of others? Do those with whom my life naturally intersects encounter the peace and kindness of Jesus? Am I combative? More than anything, is my life marked with the gentleness and humility of Christ? The genuine witness to Jesus is never pretentious, pushy, or presumptuous. I ache for others to hear the message of Jesus in and through my public workplace.

Perhaps you recall the children's song, "This little light of mine, I'm going to let it shine. This little light of mine, I'm going to let it shine, let it shine, let it shine, let it shine." Several other lines followed: "Won't let Satan blow it out, I'm going to let it shine" or "Shine until Jesus comes, I'm going to let it shine." The chorus was based on Jesus's reminder to all kingdom people, "You are the light of the world...let your light shine before men, that they may *see your good deeds* and praise your Father in heaven" (Matthew 5:14-16). Our public life is truly made of the stuff that others see. What they see (and hear) makes all the difference.

Paul offered another reminder to Titus. Second, ***remind people that their stories become their songs*** (3:3-5a). The six previous applications Paul instructed Titus to pass along to others on the Island of Crete now were contrasted with seven ugly realities from the past. At one time, the Cretans were foolish, disobedient, deceived, enslaved, living in malice, living in envy, hating others, and being hated in return. Their ability to see the world as God does was veiled by the enemy (2 Corinthians 4:3-4). The Cretans were blinded to God's truth. Therefore, they rejected God's thoughts and His ways. What a mess! Because of Jesus's divine rescue everything, and I mean everything, had changed. "He *saved*" (esosen from sozo) is the main verb. Everything else revolves around it. The finished work of Jesus is the centering thought here. Only the kindness and love of God made this possible. Our story is much like the story of God's creation (Genesis 1:1-2). He took what was "without form" and "void," while we were still living in "darkness," and He did for us what we could not do for ourselves (Ephesians 2:1-10). Servant leaders never get over this "before Christ" and now "in Christ" story. He saved us. He is the source and ground of our salvation. God, in Christ, began the process of putting everything back together that was shattered by sin, including those of us who respond to His free gift. Our response is one of faith in the completed work of Jesus. Of course, we are still projects under construction. We are a "new creation" (2 Corinthians 5:17), but God will keep His promise and continue the necessary renovation and renewal (Philippians 1:6). That narrative, God's story intertwined with our story, becomes the song we sing. We don't forget it. Titus, as has been noted, found himself in a tough spot. Crete permeates our time and place. We must remember and always remind.

Third, ***remind people that their salvation becomes their service*** (3:5b-8). This part of Paul's letter to Titus overwhelms me. I simply want to pause, to get on my knees, and to worship (and I did). I can hardly type the words because my heart is so moved by Paul's reminder. Paul instructed Titus to teach continually that God declared us right. That's justification. God "justified" us by His grace (3:7). He also counseled Titus to teach continually that God makes us right. That's sanctification. The necessary regeneration and on-going renewal was and is carried out by the Holy Spirit. These two mighty works of the Spirit cannot be separated. This entire section feels and looks like a theological mountaintop. As noted above, the *source and ground* of our salvation is here – "our Savior appeared" and "He saved us." The *means* of that same salvation is here – "according to His own mercy." The *goal* of our salvation is here – "so that being justified by His grace we might become heirs..." The *evidence* of that same salvation is also here – "devote themselves to good works." Please don't overlook the obvious. Paul instructed Titus to "*insist on these things*" (3:8). What a magnificent picture of "regeneration" (3:5 - palingenesia). The spiritual movement is from death to life and from old to new. This is the only place in Scripture where this particular word is used in this specific fashion.

Jesus does incorporate the same word into the conversation with His confused disciples at their lack of understanding the nature of the kingdom. Our Savior had been talking with a man befuddled over what was involved in eternal life. When we combine the various parallel passages, we discover that this seeker who came to Jesus with a question ("Teacher, what good deed must I do to have eternal life?") was "a man" (Matthew 19:16 and Mark 10:17), "a ruler" (Luke 18:18), "young" (Matthew 19:22), and "had great possessions" (Matthew 19:22, Mark 10:22, and Luke 18:23). This seeker rejected Jesus's invitation. Jesus ultimately said to His bewildered apprentices, "I tell you the truth, at the *renewal* of all things, when the Son of Man sits on His glorious throne, you who have followed me will also sit on twelve thrones, judging the twelve tribes of Israel" (Matthew 19:28). At the Second Coming of Christ, everything and everyone will find their rightful places. In the meantime, our incredible salvation should lead us to our humble service, not because we have to, but because we want to. "We are," as my wise mentor and Old Testament Professor S. Edward Tesh was fond of saying, "Blessed to be a blessing." "Doing good" is the measure of the kingdom man and woman who has embraced the message of salvation. That kind of "good" shapes this paragraph (3:1 and 3:8). Notice with me how "good," even "good works," saturates the entire letter (1:8, 1:16, 2:3, 2:7, 2:14, 3:1, 3:8, and 3:14). Yes, God will be glorified in all of this, but Paul was far more down to earth here. His evangelist's and servant leader's heart was ever preoccupied with the lost world around him. Our public life is our pulpit. Our story is our song. Our salvation is our service. Servant leaders are in the reminding business.

A Little Manual for Servant Leaders

CHAPTER 20
Dying Daily as a Servant Leader
Titus 3:9-15

"He is no fool who gives up what he cannot keep to gain that which he cannot lose"
(Elliot, Jim. (1958). **Shadow of the Almighty,** *(p.108). Harper and Row).*

Servant leaders die daily. Some literally perish in the Name of Jesus in various parts of the world resistant to the Gospel. Still others come to recognize the paradoxical truths that we find by losing, we save by spending, and we live by dying (Mark 8:31-38). Denial or spiritually dying daily must become a regular part of the servant leader's life (Matthew 16:24, Mark 8:34, and Luke 9:23). Dying daily is actually a freeing experience. It reminds us that we do not have to spend so much energy getting our way. So, what does it mean to die daily? Here are Paul's final words to Titus:

> **3** *But avoid foolish controversies, genealogies, dissensions, and quarrels about the law, for they are unprofitable and worthless.* [10] *As for a person who stirs up division, after warning him once and then twice, have nothing more to do with him,* [11] *knowing that such a person is warped and sinful; he is self-condemned.*

> [12] *When I send Artemas or Tychicus to you, do your best to come to me at Nicopolis, for I have decided to spend the winter there.* [13] *Do your best to speed Zenas the lawyer and Apollos on their way; see that they lack nothing.* [14] *And let our people learn to devote themselves to good works, so as to help cases of urgent need, and not be unfruitful.*
>
> [15] *All who are with me send greetings to you. Greet those who love us in the faith.*
>
> *Grace be with you all.*

The last words of Paul to Titus echo with profound clarity – die to self. How? First, **die to winning silly Bible arguments** (3:9). A servant leader refuses to be sucked into foolish debates about Scripture. In Titus' case, these were Old Testament passages that were particularly marked with divisive opinions. Paul marked out four significant scenarios for Titus: controversies, genealogies, dissensions, and quarrels. Controversies (zetesis) were the same issue that Paul addressed with Timothy (1 Timothy 6:4 and 2 Timothy 2:23). The root word, zeteo, was a common word that described someone's seeking, searching, or asking questions. Many of us know that some people take special delight in raising questions that tear at the very fabric of unity that God has given us in Christ. We don't know the specifics here, but Paul recognized the foolish (moras) or moron-like manner of some who always seek, search, and raise questions, but never listen for Biblical answers. Genealogies (genealogias) were those records that Jews used to trace their family trees. Again, Paul doesn't explain the specifics, but we know that whatever was divisive in Crete was also divisive in Ephesus (1 Timothy 1:4). Often, these genealogies were interwoven with stories and tales of heroic acts. Some people love to "one-up" others. Exaggeration and bragging can cause such harm in the Christian community. Dissensions and quarrels (eris and machas) describe a contentious spirit and a fighting attitude (1 Timothy 6:4 and 2 Timothy 2:23). It is fascinating to watch Paul handle these issues. His past life, before Christ, would have been marked with these very words, but, under the Lordship of Jesus, he readily recognized a more excellent way (1 Corinthians 13).

Notice with me that Paul described controversies, genealogies, dissensions, and quarrels as unprofitable (anopheles) and worthless (mataios). This kind of divisiveness was void of one ounce of goodness and lacked any positive result. Paul counseled Titus to avoid or shun all of this. In all my years of ministry, I have never seen anyone led to Jesus or deepened in their faith through a condescending argument of any kind. There is nothing wrong with debate or discussion, but the problem enters when those prone to argument are not teachable. Constant combat is exhausting. It depletes the Body of Christ. I recall something I think Charles Spurgeon said: "Have one blind eye and one deaf ear" when it comes to Bible arguments.

Genuine servant leaders are like lion tamers. If a lion is in our presence, we don't need a reminder that the king of beasts is all-powerful. We recognize that the lion has strength we do not. No one in their right mind strolls up to a lion and begins to caress it like a family pet or, worse yet, to mistreat it. What is true of a lion is true of Scripture. Like the lion tamer, I simply bring it into the room, and everyone else finds their proper places. All we have to do is to present it. I am not required to defend it or to argue against every criticism that is heaped upon it. Yes, there is a place for apologetics, but that's not what Paul appeared to be addressing with Titus.

I once found myself surrounded by several men who believed that the act of baptism by immersion saved us. They believed that the dunking of a person in water was vital to the saving act. Their position was clear. The person being immersed was saved as he or she came up out of the water. According to them, and they had a long list, salvation didn't happen when one repented, didn't happen at one's confession of faith, didn't happen when one prayed, didn't happen when the person was going into the water, and didn't happen when the individual was waiting to be brought up out of the water. Salvation, from their viewpoint, occurred in the exact moment the person was raised from the watery grave. They wanted me to support their conclusion. How could I? Scripture doesn't teach that. What Scripture does teach is that we are saved by grace through faith in the finished work of Jesus Christ. They pressed and pressed and pressed some more. I tried looking for mutual ground by saying that baptism is a faith response. It is the norm in the New Testament for expressing faith in Christ. They wanted none of it. So, I simply walked away from the fruitless conversation. Servant leaders die daily to winning silly Bible arguments.

Second, ***die daily to getting along with everyone*** (3:10-11). One of the most difficult ministry assignments for a servant leader is to confront another brother or sister in Christ. Paul advised Titus to warn a divisive person once and, if that didn't work, warn them a second time. If that dual confrontation failed, then Titus was instructed to have nothing to do with that person. This section of Scripture sounds a lot like Jesus in Matthew 18:15-20. The Matthew text is specifically addressing the issue of a brother or sister who has sinned against another brother or sister. Remember this is a pre-Pentecost statement, even though the word for church, "ekklesia," (called out ones) occurs twice in 18:17. Jesus instructed His disciples to follow a four-fold practice. First, go to the offender privately. The conversation should be between the two of you only. Second, if that fails, take one or two others along with you. Third, if that also fails, then tell the church. Fourth, if the person is unwilling to listen even to the church, then that person is to be treated as an outsider. These are very strong words.

I'm quite sure you are weary of hearing this, but, once again, we don't know enough of the particulars in Crete to grasp what Paul had in mind. Whatever the circumstances, this does sound like some form of excommunication. Most of us want to live at peace with others. Most of us desire to love and to be loved. However, now and then we meet a person who simply refuses to live in harmony with other believers. The person I am attempting to describe perceives his work and his way as always right. I met a woman years ago in one of the churches I served. She was a strong Bible teacher. She doubted that I had the leadership gifts or teaching expertise to lead a congregation. She was chronically divisive. She spoke ill of me, spread false rumors about my life and ministry, and I confronted her privately. She denied that she was the source of the allegations. Her attempt to oust me or to undermine my work persisted. I returned to her home. This time, I took one of the church leaders. Ultimately, while attempting to follow Matthew 18 and Titus 3, in a very heated moment, she asked us to leave her house. She, along with her husband, never returned to the church. I longed to reconcile, but her unwillingness to repent was evident. Truth be told, the church thrived without them. Servant leaders die daily to getting along with everyone.

Third, ***die daily to many of our own needs*** (3:12-15). Paul asked three specific things of Titus: do your best to come to me at Nicopolis, to see that Zenas and Apollos have everything they need, and to teach the Cretans the basic work ethic of providing for daily necessities and not living unproductive lives. A replacement dispatched by Paul was on the way. Artemas or Tychicus, both capable brothers in Christ, would arrive and make Titus's departure for the west coast of Greece a possibility. Paul had a need that Titus could meet. He wanted his friend and brother at his side. Apparently, Zenas, who we know nothing about, and Apollos, who we know something about (see Acts 18:24-28 and 1 Corinthians 3:1-23) were on some kind of mission and needed support. Paul wanted Titus to make sure that nothing was lacking in their care. Another need was presented. Paul also desired Titus to teach "with all authority" (note 2:15). All believers on Crete were to give evidence that they were genuine Jesus-followers and had been taught to live a life marked by good works. Titus was to meet that need as well.

I wish with all my heart that we knew something of Titus's personal needs. What was it like for him in this difficult place of ministry?

What were his needs? Did he ever voice them to Paul? Was he ever tempted to walk away? Regretfully, we know very little of this troubleshooter for Christ. What we do know of him is really seen through the larger lens of Crete. Perhaps there was no more challenging place to serve in the Name of Jesus than on that Mediterranean island. It says a great deal about Titus that he took a vow of stability and served until Paul requested his presence. Church tradition tells us that he did do all that Paul asked of him and ultimately returned to Crete and devoted his life to serving the Gospel in that challenging place. Perhaps you find yourself in a similar spot. May I remind you that Crete is a temporary, transient, and teachable place? Servant leaders don't forget. Our labor in the Lord is not in vain (1 Corinthians 15:58). Those same servant leaders die daily to many of their own needs.

One of the finest servant leaders I have ever been privileged to know was Ken Broady. Ken was a humble servant, gentle of spirit, strong of body, and passionate about following Jesus. His wife, June, mirrored a Christ-likeness that blessed all who knew her. They have both passed away and are now waiting in the presence of Jesus for the final resurrection. A tragedy of colossal size entered their world when their beloved son took his own life. A dysfunctional second marriage and the kind of confusion that only comes from Satan prompted their son to end his life. The funeral, of course, was showered with great heartache and the kind of grief that only parents who lose a child can understand. I can still see Ken sobbing over the closed casket of his son.

Many of us traveled by car caravan to the family plot near the Wabash River for the final committal service. The second wife was unaware that a suicide note had been left and described with some detail how ugly the marriage had been and some of the abuse she had heaped upon Ken and June's son. The wife presented herself as loving and affectionate, but those of us who saw the note knew better. God was at work. He always is. I had closed the graveside service in prayer when I noticed she had made her way toward Ken. She was clearly distraught and was asking him to forgive her for what she had done. In this man's most vulnerable moment, I watched him put his arms around that woman and share with her the Good News of Jesus Christ. He offered her forgiveness in Jesus' Name. Those of us standing there witnessed one of the most holy moments a person can see on this side of heaven. I don't know what happened to Ken's daughter-in-law after that. I only know what happened to me. I saw a living example of what dying daily looked like. Servant leaders embrace this paradoxical, self-denying life.

A Little Manual for Servant Leaders

CONCLUSION

"When we meet Christ personally, I think we will all be prompted to say, 'Jesus Christ, thanks for fulfilling your ministry. Thanks for not bailing out on the way to the cross. Because you endured, you purchased my pardon, you transformed my life, you protected my family, you sustained my church, you changed my world, and you sealed my eternal destiny.' Hopefully all of us leaders will also be able to add, 'And Jesus, because of your example and with your help, I finished my ministry too'"
(Hybels, Bill (2002). **Courageous Leadership.** *(p. 252). Zondervan).*

Two servant leaders, Timothy and Titus, quite different from one another, received timely help from their friend and mentor, Paul. Timothy, in the first letter addressed to him, seemed to wrestle deeply with where exactly his leadership fit into God's plan and the need of the church in Ephesus. It remains an appropriate question: Where does real servant leadership belong? Titus, on the other hand, appeared to need special instruction on what precisely servant leaders do. Like the first question, this one is still appropriate. What do servant leaders do when faced with places like Crete? Finally, just before his death, Paul wrote a second letter to Timothy, his much-loved son in the faith. That letter acknowledged the fact that ministry is messy, and servant leadership is tough. The question behind this last letter might be framed up in this way: What kind of servant leader is needed in order to safe-guard the Gospel?

Paul, throughout the writing of all three letters, masterfully weaves into the conversation with Timothy and Titus a singular phrase. I have saved it for these concluding thoughts. Five separate occasions Paul inserts this line: "The saying is trustworthy" and sometimes includes "deserving of full acceptance:"

- "***The saying is trustworthy*** and ***deserving of full acceptance***, that Christ Jesus came into the world to save sinners, of whom I am the foremost" (1Timothy 1:15).
- "***The saying is trustworthy***: If anyone aspires to the office of overseer, he desires a noble task" (1Timothy 3:1).
- "***The saying is trustworthy*** and ***deserving of full acceptance***. For to this end we toil and strive, because we have our hope set on the living God, who is the Savior of all people, especially of those who believe" (1Timothy 4:9-10).
- "***The saying is trustworthy***: If we have died with Him, we will also live with Him; if we endure, we will also reign with Him. If we deny Him; He will also deny us; if we are faithless, He remains faithful, for He cannot deny Himself" (2 Timothy 2:11-13).
- "But when the goodness and loving kindness of God our Savior appeared, He saved us, not because of works done by us in righteousness, but according to His own mercy, by the washing of regeneration and renewal of the Holy Spirit, whom He poured out on us richly through Jesus Christ our Savior, so that being justified by His grace we might become heirs according to the hope of eternal life. ***The saying is trustworthy***..." (Titus 3:4-8).

It is good and right to remember that these five trustworthy sayings are expressions that are not found anywhere else in Scripture. Bible students have argued and debated these pastoral sayings for years. Regardless of where we land in terms of application, these statements were intended to prompt Timothy and Titus to remember what really mattered in terms of Christian truth. As to why there are three in 1Timothy and only one each in the other two letters, we can only speculate. It seems to me that the false teaching crisis in Ephesus was so great that Paul placed mega emphasis on Gospel teaching that was accurate and authoritative. These five sayings sound like a caring dad's farewell speech to a son or daughter leaving home for the last time or a loving mom's final counsel to a child heading off to school. The essence of what Paul was saying is timeless and intended to encourage all servant leaders. Perhaps the best way to think of them is in terms of the Gospel. Keep these prominent in all that you are and in all that you do.

- The Gospel is true.
- The Gospel can be trusted.
- The Gospel is universal and intended for everyone.
- The Gospel is universal, but it requires a personal response of faith in Christ.
- The Gospel is at the center of servant leadership.
- The Gospel is not designed to be theoretical, but personal.
- The Gospel does not make things easier, but will empower us to live a long obedience.

I pray that you have caught something of the size and significance of the Gospel, especially as it relates specifically to servant leadership.

So, what happened to these three servant leaders: Paul, Timothy, and Titus? Church history suggests the following. After his initial release from prison and a subsequent mission trip, perhaps to Spain, Paul was re-arrested and ultimately beheaded in Rome in 68 AD. Timothy, on the other hand, lived to be 80 years old. He died as Bishop of Ephesus during one of the Roman pagan holidays. Tradition says that Timothy was beaten to death while attempting to stop a pagan procession of idols. Titus continued a very long and faithful ministry on the island of Crete. He became the Archbishop and died from natural causes as a very old man.

John Bowling, in his engaging book, *Grace-full Leadership* (2000), tells the true story of an office building on the outskirts of London experiencing severe structural problems. Apparently, unexplainable cracks were appearing from one floor to the next. Initially, no one seemed to be alarmed, but, eventually, experts were called in and scoured the building in search of some kind of answer. When that didn't work, the original architect was summoned, and he began the long and tedious process. Ultimately, his careful investigation led him to the lowest level in the subbasement. There, he discovered that one entire supporting wall was missing. Unbeknownst to anyone, a worker had for years been removing one brick at a time from the building. Over time, he had gathered enough bricks to build a small garage! He was sure no one would notice (pp. 133-134).

Servant leaders must be ever prayerfully vigilant in keeping a firm Gospel foundation. For us it means we secure the Gospel personally, to stick to it faithfully, to study it diligently, to share it openly, and to be willing to suffer for it bravely. Let this be our finest hour. If Jesus tarries, may they say of this generation, they fought the good fight, finished the race, and kept the faith.

DISCUSSION GUIDE

for

A Little Manual for Servant Leaders:
A Study of 1 and 2 Timothy and Titus

*By J.K. Jones Jr.
And Jim Probst*

Study Guide

CHAPTER 1
Watching Out for Self-Appointed Leaders

---

¹ Paul, an apostle of Christ Jesus by command of God our Savior and of Christ Jesus our hope,

² To Timothy, my true child in the faith:

Grace, mercy, and peace from God the Father and Christ Jesus our Lord.

³ As I urged you when I was going to Macedonia, remain at Ephesus so that you may charge certain persons not to teach any different doctrine, ⁴ nor to devote themselves to myths and endless genealogies, which promote speculations rather than the stewardship from God that is by faith. ⁵ The aim of our charge is love that issues from a pure heart and a good conscience and a sincere faith. ⁶ Certain persons, by swerving from these, have wandered away into vain discussion, ⁷ desiring to be teachers of the law, without understanding either what they are saying or the things about which they make confident assertions.

⁸ Now we know that the law is good, if one uses it lawfully, ⁹ understanding this, that the law is not laid down for the just but for the lawless and disobedient, for the ungodly and sinners, for the unholy and profane, for those who strike their fathers and mothers, for murderers, ¹⁰ the sexually immoral, men who practice homosexuality, enslavers, liars, perjurers, and whatever else is contrary to sound doctrine, ¹¹ in accordance with the gospel of the glory of the blessed God with which I have been entrusted. (1 Timothy 1:1-11, ESV)

At a GLANCE

In this chapter, we addressed three specific profiles of self-appointed leaders:

1. *They are more interested in what is different than what is Divine (1 Timothy 1:3-4a).*
2. *They are more interested in trivia than transformation (1 Timothy 1:4b-7).*
3. *They are more interested in having their way than in living the Way (1 Timothy 1:8-11).*

GAUGE Your Response:

Have you ever encountered such leadership? In your more honest moments, do you recognize any of these tendencies in yourself?

The conclusion of this chapter leaves us with the following questions:

1. Do I believe there are biblical standards?

2. Do I believe Scripture, rightly taught, changes people?

3. Am I willing to submit to God's grand purpose for my life?

Discuss these questions with your group / trusted friend. Additionally, look for ways to demonstrate leadership that is "Savior-appointed" rather than "self-appointed."

Study Guide

CHAPTER 2
What a Servant Leader Should Never Forget

---

[12] I thank him who has given me strength, Christ Jesus our Lord, because he judged me faithful, appointing me to his service, [13] though formerly I was a blasphemer, persecutor, and insolent opponent. But I received mercy because I had acted ignorantly in unbelief, [14] and the grace of our Lord overflowed for me with the faith and love that are in Christ Jesus. [15] The saying is trustworthy and deserving of full acceptance, that Christ Jesus came into the world to save sinners, of whom I am the foremost. [16] But I received mercy for this reason, that in me, as the foremost, Jesus Christ might display his perfect patience as an example to those who were to believe in him for eternal life. [17] To the King of the ages, immortal, invisible, the only God, be honor and glory forever and ever. Amen. [18] This charge I entrust to you, Timothy, my child, in accordance with the prophecies previously made about you, that by them you may wage the good warfare, [19] holding faith and a good conscience. By rejecting this, some have made shipwreck of their faith, [20] among whom are Hymenaeus and Alexander, whom I have handed over to Satan that they may learn not to blaspheme. (1 Timothy 1:12-20, ESV)

At a GLANCE

In this chapter, we addressed two "mega truths":

1. *The grace of God is absolutely marvelous. It changes everything (1:12-17).*
2. *The Jesus-following journey is really dangerous. It requires alertness (1:18-20).*

In his challenge to Timothy, Paul reminds him of two weapons that were available to fight this good fight.

1. Faith (1:19)
2. A good conscience (1:19)

> These weapons are critical for our success and repeated three times in this first letter (1:5, 1:19, and 3:9). Without them, we risk rejecting the faith and "shipwrecking" others' faith (1:19-20).

GAUGE Your Response

The two "mega truths" of this text should mark our lives. As you discuss these truths with a group or a trusted friend,

1. Explain the way in which His grace has "changed everything" for you.

2. How have you been "alert" in "danger"?

Paul's stated, "Christ Jesus came into the world to save sinners, of whom I am the foremost"(1 Timothy 1:15b). Can you relate to this statement? Explain.

Paul notes in verse 19 that, "some have made shipwreck of their faith". How did he handle this? Have you had similar experiences? How did you respond?

Study Guide

CHAPTER 3
The Servant Leader's Highest Priority

---

¹ First of all, then, I urge that supplications, prayers, intercessions, and thanksgivings be made for all people, ² for kings and all who are in high positions, that we may lead a peaceful and quiet life, godly and dignified in every way. ³ This is good, and it is pleasing in the sight of God our Savior, ⁴ who desires all people to be saved and to come to the knowledge of the truth. ⁵ For there is one God, and there is one mediator between God and men, the man Christ Jesus, ⁶ who gave himself as a ransom for all, which is the testimony given at the proper time. ⁷ For this I was appointed a preacher and an apostle (I am telling the truth, I am not lying), a teacher of the Gentiles in faith and truth.

⁸ I desire then that in every place the men should pray, lifting holy hands without anger or quarreling; ⁹ likewise also that women should adorn themselves in respectable apparel, with modesty and self-control, not with braided hair and gold or pearls or costly attire, ¹⁰ but with what is proper for women who profess godliness—with good works. ¹¹ Let a woman learn quietly with all submissiveness. ¹² I do not permit a woman to teach or to exercise authority over a man; rather, she is to remain quiet. ¹³ For Adam was formed first, then Eve; ¹⁴ and Adam was not deceived, but the woman was deceived and became a transgressor. ¹⁵ Yet she will be saved through childbearing—if they continue in faith and love and holiness, with self-control. (1 Timothy 2:1-15, ESV)

At a GLANCE

In this chapter, we considered the "highest priority" of the servant leader. This priority of worship can be expressed in two fundamental ways:

1. Prayer is essential to our lives of worship as servant leaders (1 Timothy 2:1-7).
2. Praise is essential to our lives of worship as servant leaders (1 Timothy 2:8-15).

> Two potent phrases came to the surface in this chapter that leave a lasting impression and call for further consideration.
>
> 1. "Worship is the greenhouse for intimacy with God. It provides the just-right-conditions for knowing God and making Him known."
> 2. "Paul wanted Timothy to see the vastness of worship, as if peering into the Grand Canyon, not a pot hole."

GAUGE Your Response

In verse one of this text, Paul writes, "I urge that supplications, prayers, intercessions, and thanksgivings be made for all people."

1. In what way have you been "urged" toward intimacy with Christ? How was it received?

2. Who are you intentionally "urging" toward this kind of intimacy? How is this happening?

As we conclude this chapter, let's finish where we began! "The servant leader's highest priority is not **telling** others what to do. Nor is the highest priority of the servant leader **knowing** what to do. The servant leader's highest priority, bar none, is **intimacy** with God, the vibrant worship of Him day by day." Take a moment to discuss your current level of intimacy with God.

Study Guide

CHAPTER 4
What Does a Servant Leader Look Like?

---

¹· *The saying is trustworthy: If anyone aspires to the office of overseer, he desires a noble task.* ² *Therefore an overseer must be above reproach, the husband of one wife, sober-minded, self-controlled, respectable, hospitable, able to teach,* ³ *not a drunkard, not violent but gentle, not quarrelsome, not a lover of money.* ⁴ *He must manage his own household well, with all dignity keeping his children submissive,* ⁵ *for if someone does not know how to manage his own household, how will he care for God's church?* ⁶ *He must not be a recent convert, or he may become puffed up with conceit and fall into the condemnation of the devil.* ⁷ *Moreover, he must be well thought of by outsiders, so that he may not fall into disgrace, into a snare of the devil.*

⁸ *Deacons likewise must be dignified, not double-tongued, not addicted to much wine, not greedy for dishonest gain.* ⁹ *They must hold the mystery of the faith with a clear conscience.* ¹⁰ *And let them also be tested first; then let them serve as deacons if they prove themselves blameless.* ¹¹ *Their wives likewise must be dignified, not slanderers, but sober-minded, faithful in all things.* ¹² *Let deacons each be the husband of one wife, managing their children and their own households well.* ¹³ *For those who serve well as deacons gain a good standing for themselves and also great confidence in the faith that is in Christ Jesus.* (1 Timothy 3:1-13, ESV)

At a GLANCE

There are two distinctive functions for servant leaders in this passage (shepherd-servants fulfilling large oversight as seen in 3:1-7 and practical-servants completing specific tasks as seen in 3:8-15).

Notice that there are three shepherding terms in the New Testament:

1 *Overseer (episkopos)-originally describing someone in charge or who led city government.*
2. *Elder (presbuteros)-an older, seasoned, and spiritually mature leader.*

3. Pastor / Shepherd (poimen)-caring for God's people like a shepherd with his sheep.

A variety of traits are listed for those in leadership:
- Positive and negative traits for shepherding leaders
- Positive and negative traits for serving leaders
- Positive and negative traits for female servant leaders

These traits are intended to help the church find the right people for the right places of service, not to be reduced to a "check list."

GAUGE Your Response

1. In what ways have these shepherding terms and traits helped you to understand church leadership?

2. Are there any "traits" that require some accountability as you "aspire" to new or continued leadership roles?

3. What additional concepts require further study and reflection?

Discuss these questions with your group / trusted friend. Additionally, pray for greater harmony between the life you live and the leadership characteristics conveyed in this passage.

Study Guide

CHAPTER 5
Servant Leadership Paradoxes

---

14 I hope to come to you soon, but I am writing these things to you so that, 15 if I delay, you may know how one ought to behave in the household of God, which is the church of the living God, a pillar and buttress of the truth. 16 Great indeed, we confess, is the mystery of godliness: He was manifested in the flesh, vindicated by the Spirit, seen by angels, proclaimed among the nations, believed on in the world, taken up in glory. (1 Timothy 3:14-16, ESV)

At a GLANCE

In this chapter, we addressed three paradoxes of leadership in the church:

1. *Servant leaders love God's household even though sometimes she acts like a dysfunctional family (3:15).*
2. *Servant leaders love the church of the living God even though sometimes she appears dead (3:15).*
3. *Servant leaders love the church which is the pillar and foundation of the truth, even though sometimes she appears in disrepair (3:15).*

"Servant leaders must see God from a large and unique point of view ... What we as servant leaders see changes us."

GAUGE Your Response

As you meet with your group and/or trusted friend this week, examine your leadership in light of the paradoxes listed above. Then, create dialogue about the following questions:

1. Do I lovingly lead throughout the whole family (even the dysfunctional people / situations)?

2. Do I genuinely see life and speak life in the church even in seasons when she appears lifeless?

3. Do I look to pillars and foundations apart from Christ on which to build?

"The church's two-fold purpose was and is to hold firmly to the truth of Jesus Christ – that's our foundation – and to hold up the truth of the Gospel for everyone to see – that's our pillar. Ultimately both purposes point us to Jesus."

If an inspector was to evaluate the foundation and pillar of your ministry and life, would he/she see Christ through and through? Would there be other supplemental structures that would not pass the test?

Study Guide

CHAPTER 6
Servant Leadership's Hard Side

---

[1] *Now the Spirit expressly says that in later times some will **depart** from the faith by **devoting** themselves to deceitful spirits and teachings of demons,* [2] *through the insincerity of liars whose consciences are seared,* [3] *who **forbid** marriage and **require** abstinence from foods that God created to be received with thanksgiving by those who believe and know the truth.* [4] *For everything created by God is good, and nothing is to be rejected if it is received with thanksgiving,* [5] *for it is made holy by the word of God and prayer.* (1 Timothy 4:1-5, ESV)

At a GLANCE

In this chapter, we recognized that servant leaders are shaped in community by community. Sometimes, that very community is seduced by false teaching. These timeless words of Paul were for Timothy and are for us today. Four words define and describe the hard side of servant leadership:

1. *Depart (1 Timothy 4:1). For some, the Gospel seed had landed in the heart-soil of some and had not taken root. They abandoned the faith.*
2. *Devoting (1 Timothy 4:1). Some wander from the narrow way and pursue a life that appears more promising but end up enslaved and corrupted.*
3. *Forbid (1 Timothy 4:3). Some are "liars whose consciences are seared" (4:2). Their internal compass had been cauterized, and they were unable to think correctly about the things of God.*
4. *Require (1 Timothy 4:3). Some false teachers were commanding others to keep their distance from certain foods. Here, legalism resulted in the rejection of God's goodness toward us.*

Servant Leadership's Hard Side

GAUGE Your Response

This chapter is filled with challenging scenarios for the servant leader. Approach these topics humbly with your group and/or trusted friend in the faith.

1. Have you encountered someone who has "departed" from the faith? How do you guard against such false teaching? How do you guide others to remain in the faith?

2. Devoting (4:1 – prosecho) means to follow after. Is there someone in your life that you might lead down the path of righteousness? What path has your personal devotion?

3. How have you trained yourself to recognize false teachers who "forbid" things unforbidden and who perpetuate a suffocating legalism? How do you personally guard against becoming such a person?

4. Are there any "requirements" that have crept into your ministry that may be hindering another person's freedom in Christ? On the other side, are there any freedoms that you have that might cause another to stumble? Examine and discuss.

Study Guide

CHAPTER 7
The Servant Leader's Workout Routine

---

⁶ If you put these things before the brothers, you will be a good servant of Christ Jesus, being trained in the words of the faith and of the good doctrine that you have followed. ⁷ Have nothing to do with irreverent, silly myths. Rather train yourself for godliness; ⁸ for while bodily training is of some value, godliness is of value in every way, as it holds promise for the present life and also for the life to come. ⁹ The saying is trustworthy and deserving of full acceptance. ¹⁰ For to this end we toil and strive, because we have our hope set on the living God, who is the Savior of all people, especially of those who believe.

¹¹ Command and teach these things. ¹² Let no one despise you for your youth, but set the believers an example in speech, in conduct, in love, in faith, in purity. ¹³ Until I come, devote yourself to the public reading of Scripture, to exhortation, to teaching. ¹⁴ Do not neglect the gift you have, which was given you by prophecy when the council of elders laid their hands on you. ¹⁵ Practice these things, immerse yourself in them, so that all may see your progress. ¹⁶ Keep a close watch on yourself and on the teaching. Persist in this, for by so doing you will save both yourself and your hearers.

¹ Do not rebuke an older man but encourage him as you would a father, younger men as brothers, ² older women as mothers, younger women as sisters, in all purity. (1 Timothy 4:6-5:2, ESV)

At a GLANCE

Every servant leader need a workout routine!

Four Coaching Tips:

1. *Creativity is good, but sticking to the basics is better (4:6).*
2. *Trying is good, but training is better (4:7-8).*
3. *Youthful energy is good, but mature commitment is better (4:9-14).*
4. *Keeping the big picture is good, but monitoring the details is better (4:15-5:2).*

GAUGE Your Response

Review the four coaching tips above. Which message do you most need to hear today?

Regarding Swindoll's "Signposts on the Road to Maturity," and discuss the following questions with your group and/or trusted friend:

1. Am I living an exemplary life (4:12)?

2. Do I understand what is essential (4:13)?

3. Am I capitalizing on my strengths (4:14)?

4. Have I thrown myself into my calling (4:15)?

5. Will I stay at it regardless (4:16)?

Study Guide

CHAPTER 8
Only Multi-Generational Servant Leaders Will Do

---

³ *Honor widows who are truly widows.* ⁴ *But if a widow has children or grandchildren, let them first learn to show godliness to their own household and to make some return to their parents, for this is pleasing in the sight of God.* ⁵ *She who is truly a widow, left all alone, has set her hope on God and continues in supplications and prayers night and day,* ⁶ *but she who is self-indulgent is dead even while she lives.* ⁷ *Command these things as well, so that they may be without reproach.* ⁸ *But if anyone does not provide for his relatives, and especially for members of his household, he has denied the faith and is worse than an unbeliever.*

⁹ *Let a widow be enrolled if she is not less than sixty years of age, having been the wife of one husband,* ¹⁰ *and having a reputation for good works: if she has brought up children, has shown hospitality, has washed the feet of the saints, has cared for the afflicted, and has devoted herself to every good work.* ¹¹ *But refuse to enroll younger widows, for when their passions draw them away from Christ, they desire to marry* ¹² *and so incur condemnation for having abandoned their former faith.* ¹³ *Besides that, they learn to be idlers, going about from house to house, and not only idlers, but also gossips and busybodies, saying what they should not.* ¹⁴ *So I would have younger widows marry, bear children, manage their households, and give the adversary no occasion for slander.* ¹⁵ *For some have already strayed after Satan.* ¹⁶ *If any believing woman has relatives who are widows, let her care for them. Let the church not be burdened, so that it may care for those who are truly widows.*

¹⁷ *Let the elders who rule well be considered worthy of double honor, especially those who labor in preaching and teaching.* ¹⁸ *For the Scripture says, "You shall not muzzle an ox when it treads out the grain," and, "The laborer deserves his wages."* ¹⁹ *Do not admit a charge against an elder except on the evidence of two or three witnesses.* ²⁰ *As for those who persist in sin, rebuke them in the presence of all, so that the rest may stand in fear.* ²¹ *In the presence of God and of Christ Jesus and of the elect angels I charge you to keep these rules without prejudging, doing nothing from partiality.* ²² *Do not be hasty in the laying on of hands, nor take part in the sins of others; keep yourself pure.* ²³ *(No longer drink only water, but use a little wine for the sake of your stomach and your frequent ailments.)* ²⁴ *The sins of some people are conspicuous, going before them to judgment, but the sins of others appear later.* ²⁵ *So also good works are conspicuous, and even those that are not cannot remain hidden.*

¹ *Let all who are under a yoke as bondservants regard their own masters as worthy of all honor, so that the name of God and the teaching may not be reviled.*

[2] *Those who have believing masters must not be disrespectful on the ground that they are brothers; rather they must serve all the better since those who benefit by their good service are believers and beloved.* (1 Timothy 5:3-6:2, ESV).

At a GLANCE

There are many issues facing the church today. Among the more complex issues are the ways in which we care for one another. In this section of Scripture, Paul gives practical instruction to Timothy regarding our multi-generational service opportunities.

1. *Multi-generational servant leaders look like people who know when to care and how to care for marginalized people (1 Timothy 5:3-16).*
2. *Multi-generational servant leaders look like people who know who to support financially and how to support them (1 Timothy 5:17-20).*
3. *Multi-generational servant leaders look like people who know what to do and what not to do about "self-care" (1 Timothy 5:21-25).*
4. *Multi-generational servant leaders look like people who know what to say and how to say it in difficult work settings (1 Timothy 6:1-2).*

GAUGE Your Response

Review the "At A Glance" section above and discuss the following questions with your group and/or trusted friend:

1. In what way does your ministry intentionally care for the marginalized? What precautions are addressed in 1 Timothy 5:3-16 about the delicate interplay between family and church support? How have you sought to minister to "the least of these"?

Study Guide

2. How do elders, teachers, and leaders in the church experience our support? In what ways do you contribute to the support of these faithful leaders? Have you seen the consequences of failure in this area? Explain.

3. Review 1 Timothy 5:21-25. Are you quick to address "self-care" issues in your life? Is there an area of caution that needs to be addressed? Explain.

4. What does this chapter say about our support and submission? Are there some transferable truths for your current situation? Please share these insights.

This section of Scripture (and this eighth chapter) are easy to understand but some of the most difficult to apply. Don't rush to the next chapter without marinating in the application of these important concepts!

CHAPTER 9
Servant Leaders Beware

Teach and urge these things. ³ *If anyone teaches a different doctrine and does not agree with the sound words of our Lord Jesus Christ and the teaching that accords with godliness,* ⁴ *he is puffed up with conceit and understands nothing. He has an unhealthy craving for controversy and for quarrels about words, which produce envy, dissension, slander, evil suspicions,* ⁵ *and constant friction among people who are depraved in mind and deprived of the truth, imagining that godliness is a means of gain.* ⁶ *But godliness with contentment is great gain,* ⁷ *for we brought nothing into the world, and we cannot take anything out of the world.* ⁸ *But if we have food and clothing, with these we will be content.* ⁹ *But those who desire to be rich fall into temptation, into a snare, into many senseless and harmful desires that plunge people into ruin and destruction.* ¹⁰ *For the love of money is a root of all kinds of evils. It is through this craving that some have wandered away from the faith and pierced themselves with many pangs.* ¹¹ *But as for you, O man of God, flee these things. Pursue righteousness, godliness, faith, love, steadfastness, gentleness.* ¹² *Fight the good fight of the faith. Take hold of the eternal life to which you were called and about which you made the good confession in the presence of many witnesses.* ¹³ *I charge you in the presence of God, who gives life to all things, and of Christ Jesus, who in his testimony before Pontius Pilate made the good confession,* ¹⁴ *to keep the commandment unstained and free from reproach until the appearing of our Lord Jesus Christ,* ¹⁵ *which he will display at the proper time—he who is the blessed and only Sovereign, the King of kings and Lord of lords,* ¹⁶ *who alone has immortality, who dwells in unapproachable light, whom no one has ever seen or can see. To him be honor and eternal dominion. Amen.*

¹⁷ *As for the rich in this present age, charge them not to be haughty, nor to set their hopes on the uncertainty of riches, but on God, who richly provides us with everything to enjoy.* ¹⁸ *They are to do good, to be rich in good works, to be generous and ready to share,* ¹⁹ *thus storing up treasure for themselves as a good foundation for the future, so that they may take hold of that which is truly life.*

²⁰ *O Timothy, guard the deposit entrusted to you. Avoid the irreverent babble and contradictions of what is falsely called "knowledge,"* ²¹ *for by professing it some have swerved from the faith.*
Grace be with you. (1 Timothy 6:3-21, ESV)

Study Guide

At a GLANCE

In this chapter, we addressed some essential cautions for servant leaders:

1. Beware of heretical teachers (1 Timothy 6:3-5),
2. Do I subject my thoughts to Scripture or do I subject Scripture to my thoughts?
3. Does the text master me?
4. Am I growing in my submission to the word?
5. Beware of greedy Christians (1 Timothy 6:6-10),
6. Guard against the temptation of having possessions that possess you.
7. Contentment is based upon Christ's sufficiency, not self–sufficiency.
8. Contentment is found in romancing the Divine, not in the dollar.
9. Beware of personal compromise (1 Timothy 6:11-16 and 6:20-21).
10. Vigorous verbs are used to caution and to encourage Timothy toward authentic ministry and apprenticeship with Jesus: Flee (6:11), pursue (6:11), fight (6:12), take hold of (6:12), command (6:17), and guard (6:20) are all imperatives.
11. On three separate occasions in Paul's closing comments, he speaks of the importance of the faith (6:10, 12, and 21).
12. Beware of trusting things.
13. God is generous, and so we should be as well.
14. Be aware of Jesus' heart and way and serve accordingly.

GAUGE Your Response

What do you need to be aware of in your servant leadership? Take a quick glance at the four areas we should "beware of" listed above, and then devote yourself to further examination and application.

Take a moment to reflect on the "vigorous verbs" used to caution and to encourage young Timothy. Which of these words do you need to hear today? Why?

Paul begins and concludes his letter to Timothy with a word of "grace" (1:2, 6:21). Who needs to hear a word of grace from you today?

Discuss these items with your group / trusted friend. Additionally, look for ways to beware of leadership pitfalls while being increasingly aware of the servant leadership exemplified in Jesus Christ.

Study Guide

CHAPTER 10
Shaping the Servant Leader's Character

---

¹ *Paul, an apostle of Christ Jesus by the will of God according to the promise of the life that is in Christ Jesus,*

² *To Timothy, my beloved child:*

Grace, mercy, and peace from God the Father and Christ Jesus our Lord.

³ *I thank God whom I serve, as did my ancestors, with a clear conscience, as I remember you constantly in my prayers night and day.* ⁴ *As I remember your tears, I long to see you, that I may be filled with joy.* ⁵ *I am reminded of your sincere faith, a faith that dwelt first in your grandmother Lois and your mother Eunice and now, I am sure, dwells in you as well.* ⁶ *For this reason I remind you to fan into flame the gift of God, which is in you through the laying on of my hands,* ⁷ *for God gave us a spirit not of fear but of power and love and self-control.*

⁸ *Therefore do not be ashamed of the testimony about our Lord, nor of me his prisoner, but share in suffering for the gospel by the power of God,* ⁹ *who saved us and called us to a holy calling, not because of our works but because of his own purpose and grace, which he gave us in Christ Jesus before the ages began,* ¹⁰ *and which now has been manifested through the appearing of our Savior Christ Jesus, who abolished death and brought life and immortality to light through the gospel,* ¹¹ *for which I was appointed a preacher and apostle and teacher,* ¹² *which is why I suffer as I do. But I am not ashamed, for I know whom I have believed, and I am convinced that he is able to guard until that Day what has been entrusted to me.* ¹³ *Follow the pattern of the sound words that you have heard from me, in the faith and love that are in Christ Jesus.* ¹⁴ *By the Holy Spirit who dwells within us, guard the good deposit entrusted to you.*

¹⁵ *You are aware that all who are in Asia turned away from me, among whom are Phygelus and Hermogenes.* ¹⁶ *May the Lord grant mercy to the household of Onesiphorus, for he often refreshed me and was not ashamed of my chains,* ¹⁷ *but when he arrived in Rome he searched for me earnestly and found me—*¹⁸ *may the Lord grant him to find mercy from the Lord on that Day!—and you well know all the service he rendered at Ephesus.* (2 Timothy 1:1-18, ESV)

At a GLANCE

In this chapter, we noted that servant leadership is ongoing character training. Here are the five significant tools God uses for our character formation:

1. *Calling (2 Timothy 1:1,9)?*
2. *Home (2 Timothy 1:3,5)*
3. *Friendship (2 Timothy 1:2,4)*
4. *Giftedness (2 Timothy 1:6)*
5. *The Gospel (2 Timothy 1:8-18)*

Regarding "friendship" in particular, we've given four critical questions that must be asked of every friend and friendship:

1. Will this friend stand by me? (Proverbs 17:17)
2. Will this friend tell me the truth? (Proverbs 27:6)
3. Will this friend keep a confidence? (Proverbs 17:9)
4. Will this friend cause me to love God more? (Proverbs 22:24-25)

GAUGE Your Response

Take a moment to discuss the "four critical questions" on friendship above. Who has exemplified this kind of friendship for you in the past?

Of the five significant tools God uses for character formation, which has left the most profound impression on your life? Explain.

Consider these five significant tools one more time. How would servant leadership suffer if any of these tools had not left its mark?

Study Guide

CHAPTER 11
Finding Your Servant Leader Metaphor

---

*¹ You then, my child, be strengthened by the grace that is in Christ Jesus, ² and what you have heard from me in the presence of many witnesses entrust to faithful men who will be able to teach others also.³ Share in suffering as a good **soldier** of Christ Jesus. ⁴ No soldier gets entangled in civilian pursuits, since his aim is to please the one who enlisted him. ⁵ An **athlete** is not crowned unless he competes according to the rules. ⁶ It is the hard-working **farmer** who ought to have the first share of the crops. ⁷ Think over what I say, for the Lord will give you understanding in everything.*

*⁸ Remember Jesus Christ, risen from the dead, the offspring of David, as preached in my gospel, ⁹ for which I am suffering, bound with chains as a **criminal**. But the word of God is not bound! ¹⁰ Therefore I endure everything for the sake of the elect, that they also may obtain the salvation that is in Christ Jesus with eternal glory. ¹¹ The saying is trustworthy, for:*

If we have died with him, we will also live with him;

¹² if we endure, we will also reign with him;

if we deny him, he also will deny us;

¹³ if we are faithless, he remains faithful—

For he cannot deny himself. (2 Timothy 2:1-13, ESV)

At a GLANCE

In this chapter, we contemplate the use of metaphors throughout the Scriptures. Four significant metaphors are selected by Paul to convey the essence of servant leadership.

1. *Servant leadership looks like a good soldier (2:3). The Roman soldier modeled a life of difficulty, not ease. All Jesus-followers are soldiers on active duty.*

> 2. *Servant leadership looks like an honest athlete (2:5). No one can become the servant leader God desires without submitting to an ordered way of life.*
> 3. *Servant leadership looks like a hardworking farmer (2:6). There is no glamour in this. No large crowds will gather that would generate applause and recognition. One farmer toiling with persistence eventually experiences deep satisfaction.?*
> 4. *Servant leadership looks like a chained criminal (2:9). Paul might be chained, but the Scriptures were not. Paul might be confined, but the Word was not.*
>
> As we noted in this chapter, the power of a metaphor is its ability to instill perseverance and stamina. Find yours.

GAUGE Your Response

As you discuss these metaphors with a group or a trusted friend,

1. Talk about the metaphor for servant leadership that most resonates with you. Why are you drawn to this one above the others?

2. Was there anything in this chapter or in the Scripture that expanded your understanding of this metaphor?

3. Are there other metaphors in Scripture that help you to grasp complex Biblical concepts? Explain.

4. Journal this week about the metaphor that inspires you in your servant leadership. Look for additional Scriptures that speak to this word picture, while leaving room to reflect creatively on ways to apply these insights to your areas of leadership.

Study Guide

CHAPTER 12
The Servant Leader's Long Obedience

---

[14] *Remind them of these things, and charge them before God not to quarrel about words, which does no good, but only ruins the hearers.* [15] *Do your best to present yourself to God as one approved, a **worker** who has no need to be ashamed, rightly handling the word of truth.* [16] *But avoid irreverent babble, for it will lead people into more and more ungodliness,* [17] *and their talk will spread like gangrene. Among them are Hymenaeus and Philetus,* [18] *who have swerved from the truth, saying that the resurrection has already happened. They are upsetting the faith of some.* [19] *But God's firm foundation stands, bearing this seal: "The Lord knows those who are his," and, "Let everyone who names the name of the Lord depart from iniquity."*

[20] *Now in a great house there are not only **vessels** of gold and silver but also of wood and clay, some for honorable use, some for dishonorable.* [21] *Therefore, if anyone cleanses himself from what is dishonorable, he will be a **vessel** for honorable use, set apart as holy, useful to the master of the house, ready for every good work.*

[22] *So flee youthful passions and pursue righteousness, faith, love, and peace, along with those who call on the Lord from a pure heart.* [23] *Have nothing to do with foolish, ignorant controversies; you know that they breed quarrels.* [24] *And the Lord's **servant** must not be quarrelsome but kind to everyone, able to teach, patiently enduring evil,* [25] *correcting his opponents with gentleness. God may perhaps grant them repentance leading to a knowledge of the truth,* [26] *and they may come to their senses and escape from the snare of the devil, after being captured by him to do his will. (2 Timothy 2:14-26, ESV)*

At a GLANCE

In this chapter, we considered the "long obedience" of the servant leader. In many ways, this chapter continues where the previous one ended. Three more metaphors are used by Paul to assist his younger partner in ministry:

> 1. *Workman (2 Timothy 2:15). The ideal workman "correctly handles the word of truth." Literally, the phrase means "to cut rightly."*
> 2. *Instrument (2 Timothy 2:20-21). Instruments are to be ready for use anytime, anywhere, however, wherever, and whenever needed. Tools that are clean and ready for use is the essential idea.*
> 3. *Servant (2 Timothy 2:24). The word for servant here (doulos) is the most common one in the New Testament (used 100 plus times). It paints a portrait of a slave without rights.*
>
> Scripture will not let us pick and choose the places where we conduct ourselves as good workmen, ready instruments, and humble servants. Servant leadership is a long obedience through squabbles, but it is also a long obedience through everyday life.

GAUGE Your Response

If you have not done so already, re-read the passage above and prayerfully reflect on the concept of "long obedience" in the life of a servant leader.

Notice the three metaphors listed in the "At a Glance" section above. How might these three be received in our secular workforce today? Are these concepts demonstrated in your workplace?

Is "long obedience" a character trait that is encouraged in our society? Is it recognized in our churches? Is it accounted for in our approach to discipleship? Explain.

Take another look at the Scripture above and circle the many vivid words and situations that might clash with a servant leader's intent to live a life of "long obedience." Recognize the many obstacles that lie in the path of the servant leader!

Do you see yourself more naturally as a workman, an instrument, or a servant? Which of the three requires the most intentionality on your part?

Study Guide

CHAPTER 13
What Wise Servant Leaders Know

---

[1] *But understand this, that in the last days there will come times of difficulty.* [2] *For people will be lovers of self, lovers of money, proud, arrogant, abusive, disobedient to their parents, ungrateful, unholy,* [3] *heartless, unappeasable, slanderous, without self-control, brutal, not loving good,* [4] *treacherous, reckless, swollen with conceit, lovers of pleasure rather than lovers of God,* [5] *having the appearance of godliness, but denying its power. Avoid such people.* [6] *For among them are those who creep into households and capture weak women, burdened with sins and led astray by various passions,* [7] *always learning and never able to arrive at a knowledge of the truth.* [8] *Just as Jannes and Jambres opposed Moses, so these men also oppose the truth, men corrupted in mind and disqualified regarding the faith.* [9] *But they will not get very far, for their folly will be plain to all, as was that of those two men.* (2 Timothy 3:1-9, ESV)

At a GLANCE

In this chapter, we addressed some of the things that wise servant leaders keep in mind. Paul wanted his young disciple to understand the times and to know what to do. In essence, he taught:

1. *Wise servant leaders know these are the last days, and these days are stressful (3:1).*
2. *Wise servant leaders know these are the last days and that these days are sin-filled (3:2-7).*
3. *Wise servant leaders know these are the last days, and these days are seductive (3:8-9).*

This entire section of Scripture reflects the teachings of Jesus when He said, "And the gates of Hades will not overcome it" (Matthew 16:18). Servant leadership is tethered to that grand truth!

GAUGE Your Response

There is little doubt that these days are stressful! We are reminded that the Greek term (chalepos) is only used in this text and in Matthew 8:28, describing the demoniac who fiercely terrorized the people of that region.

In what ways are you alert to the times and responding in a Jesus-honoring way?

Do you tend to run from difficult (stressful) times or to honor Christ within such times?

In 2 Timothy 3:2-7, we see nineteen different sin-filled examples listed by Paul. Then and now, we are in sinful times.

How are you leading in a sin-stained world? Are you more prone to embrace brokenness, reflecting on your own? Do you shrink back from messy lives and misplaced affections?

Servant leaders recognize that these days are seductive. They see that folly and lawlessness abound. They see the alluring nature of sin, but resolve to stand with the Savior.

Do you become weary when you consider the seductive nature of these days? How do you remain motivated when the opposition appears overwhelming?

Study Guide

CHAPTER 14
What Kingdom-Driven Servant Leaders Really Look Like

---

¹⁰ *You, however, have followed my teaching, my conduct, my aim in life, my faith, my patience, my love, my steadfastness,* ¹¹ *my persecutions and sufferings that happened to me at Antioch, at Iconium, and at Lystra—which persecutions I endured; yet from them all the Lord rescued me.* ¹² *Indeed, all who desire to live a godly life in Christ Jesus will be persecuted,* ¹³ *while evil people and impostors will go on from bad to worse, deceiving and being deceived.* ¹⁴ ***But as for you****, continue in what you have learned and have firmly believed, knowing from whom you learned it* ¹⁵ *and how from childhood you have been acquainted with the sacred writings, which are able to make you wise for salvation through faith in Christ Jesus.* ¹⁶ *All Scripture is breathed out by God and profitable for teaching, for reproof, for correction, and for training in righteousness,* ¹⁷ *that the man of God may be complete, equipped for every good work.*

¹ *I charge you in the presence of God and of Christ Jesus, who is to judge the living and the dead, and by his appearing and his kingdom:* ² *preach the word; be ready in season and out of season; reprove, rebuke, and exhort, with complete patience and teaching.* ³ *For the time is coming when people will not endure sound teaching, but having itching ears they will accumulate for themselves teachers to suit their own passions,* ⁴ *and will turn away from listening to the truth and wander off into myths.* ⁵ ***As for you****, always be sober-minded, endure suffering, do the work of an evangelist, fulfill your ministry.* (2 Timothy 3:10-4:5, ESV).

At a GLANCE

All servant leaders "know" that Jesus is at the center of the universe and they are not!

There are three separate times the apostle Paul used the phrase "but you" in this text. Each offers clarity about what a servant leader looks like:

> 1. *A purpose driven servant leader looks like someone who has thoroughly investigated the cross life (3:10-13).*
> 2. *Purpose driven servant leaders look like people who passionately remain faithful to Scripture (3:14-4:4).*
> 3. *A purpose driven servant leader looks like someone who intentionally stays focused in every aspect of ministry (4:5).*

GAUGE Your Response

"But you" is an interesting refrain from Paul to Timothy. In this text, we are reminded that servant leaders look different than what might be common in this world.

Timothy was able to witness the cross-carrying life of Paul. In what ways have you thoroughly investigated "the cross life"? Do people close to you see evidence of cross-bearing in you?

What role does Scripture play in your ministry? Have you made a "lifelong commitment to devouring its content"? Explain.

Have you been proactive in maintaining your focus in every aspect of ministry? What patterns and practices have you woven into the fabric of your life that display this commitment? Are there any new holy habits that need to be formed in you?

Study Guide

CHAPTER 15
When Servant Leaders Must Step Up

---

⁶ *For I am already being poured out as a drink offering, and the time of my departure has come.* 7 *I have fought the good fight, I have finished the race, I have kept the faith.* ⁸ *Henceforth there is laid up for me the crown of righteousness, which the Lord, the righteous judge, will award to me on that Day, and not only to me but also to all who have loved his appearing.*

⁹ *Do your best to come to me soon.* ¹⁰ *For Demas, in love with this present world, has deserted me and gone to Thessalonica. Crescens has gone to Galatia, Titus to Dalmatia.* ¹¹ *Luke alone is with me. Get Mark and bring him with you, for he is very useful to me for ministry.* ¹² *Tychicus I have sent to Ephesus.* ¹³ *When you come, bring the cloak that I left with Carpus at Troas, also the books, and above all the parchments.* ¹⁴ *Alexander the coppersmith did me great harm; the Lord will repay him according to his deeds.* ¹⁵ *Beware of him yourself, for he strongly opposed our message.* ¹⁶ *At my first defense no one came to stand by me, but all deserted me. May it not be charged against them!* ¹⁷ *But the Lord stood by me and strengthened me, so that through me the message might be fully proclaimed and all the Gentiles might hear it. So I was rescued from the lion's mouth.* ¹⁸ *The Lord will rescue me from every evil deed and bring me safely into his heavenly kingdom. To him be the glory forever and ever. Amen.*

¹⁹ *Greet Prisca and Aquila, and the household of Onesiphorus.* ²⁰ *Erastus remained at Corinth, and I left Trophimus, who was ill, at Miletus.* ²¹ *Do your best to come before winter. Eubulus sends greetings to you, as do Pudens and Linus and Claudia and all the brothers.*

²² *The Lord be with your spirit. Grace be with you.* (1 Timothy 4:6-5:2, ESV).

At a GLANCE

In this final section of 2 Timothy, Paul challenges young Timothy to "step up" by exercising leadership in critical situations. Whether your season of life resembles that of Paul, Timothy, or somewhere in between, there are three different scenarios that must be considered.

Younger servant leaders should step up:

1. *When seasoned servant leaders will need to be replaced (4:6-8).*
2. *When current servant leaders feel alone and isolated (4:9-13 and 4:19-22).*
3. *When godly leaders are opposed by ungodly people (4:14-18).*

GAUGE Your Response

In this passage, Paul notes that he has "fought the good fight," he has "finished the race," and he has "kept the faith." Will your current trajectory in servant leadership afford you to say the same at the end of your life? What, if anything, requires some adjustments? Explain.

It is imperative to recognize that servant leadership is contingent upon trusted relationships. Notice the many names that are referenced in this final section of Paul's letter! Who ministers to you in your time of need? Who do you lean on when times get tough? Who have you empowered to journey with you and beyond your scope of ministry?

Paul sends a request for his coat, scrolls, and parchments (vs. 13) in his time of need. What are you longing for today?

When encountering hostile opposition, Paul asked for strength rather than exemption. Who stands by your side when you face opposition? Who are you standing beside as they encounter ungodly people? Look for opportunities to lock arms with partners in ministry this week by sharing words of encouragement and a supportive presence.

Study Guide

CHAPTER 16
The Servant Leader's Dance with God

¹ *Paul, a servant of God and an apostle of Jesus Christ, for the sake of the faith of God's elect and their knowledge of the truth, which accords with godliness,* ² *in hope of eternal life, which God, who never lies, promised before the ages began* ³ *and at the proper time manifested in his word through the preaching with which I have been entrusted by the command of God our Savior;* ⁴ *To Titus, my true child in a common faith: Grace and peace from God the Father and Christ Jesus our Savior.* (Titus 1:1-4, ESV)

At a GLANCE

In this opening section of Paul's letter to Titus, we have four questions that require further dialogue:

1. *What do we know about Crete?*
2. *What do we know about Titus?*
3. *What do we know about Paul?*
4. *What do we know about God?*

GAUGE Your Response

Crete is not just a distant island from a long-gone era. All servant leaders must know about their own Cretes. In what ways have you worked to understand the unique culture and people whom you serve? Are you careful to be a student of your unique environment in this divine assignment?

Titus is more than just a faithful servant in a fairytale. He is a tangible expression of real perseverance in a challenging time. Do you truly know the "Titus" in your life? Have you worked to know and to encourage him/her?

Paul is often seen as the incomparable example of servant leadership. Yet, he most often compared himself to a slave (doulos). Additionally, he refers to himself as an apostle of Jesus Christ while sharing other credentials. Do we truly know what it means to be both "servant" and "sent"? Do we bring "grace and peace" with us in our ministry contexts?

The nature of God is conveyed from Genesis to Revelation. But in this segment of Scripture, the term "Savior" is noted twice (along with four other occasions throughout the letter. In what ways do you demonstrate a trust in God's saving nature? Moreover, do you trust in His timing, might, and method by which He saves? Consider journaling about this as well as sharing these thoughts with a trusted friend and/or group.

CHAPTER 17
Standing Tall as a Servant Leader

---

⁵ This is why I left you in Crete, so that you might put what remained into order, and appoint elders in every town as I directed you—⁶ if anyone is above reproach, the husband of one wife, and his children are believers and not open to the charge of debauchery or insubordination. ⁷ For an overseer, as God's steward, must be above reproach. He must not be arrogant or quick-tempered or a drunkard or violent or greedy for gain, ⁸ but hospitable, a lover of good, self-controlled, upright, holy, and disciplined. ⁹ He must hold firm to the trustworthy word as taught, so that he may be able to give instruction in sound doctrine and also to rebuke those who contradict it.

¹⁰ For there are many who are insubordinate, empty talkers and deceivers, especially those of the circumcision party. ¹¹ They must be silenced, since they are upsetting whole families by teaching for shameful gain what they ought not to teach. ¹² One of the Cretans, a prophet of their own, said, "Cretans are always liars, evil beasts, lazy gluttons." ¹³ This testimony is true. Therefore rebuke them sharply, that they may be sound in the faith, ¹⁴ not devoting themselves to Jewish myths and the commands of people who turn away from the truth. ¹⁵ To the pure, all things are pure, but to the defiled and unbelieving, nothing is pure; but both their minds and their consciences are defiled. ¹⁶ They profess to know God, but they deny him by their works. They are detestable, disobedient, unfit for any good work. (Titus 1:5-16)

At a GLANCE

In this chapter, we consider Titus's difficult working conditions. The extensive portrait of evil detailed in 1:10-11 paints a picture of the challenges Titus would face. In this environment, Titus was encouraged to straighten out what was left unfinished and to cultivate and appoint shepherd leaders. This goal would require Titus to "stand tall" in at least three distinct ways:

1. *Servant leaders stand tall in the home (1:5-7).*
2. *Servant leaders stand tall in the heart (1:7).*

> *3. Servant leaders stand tall in holy habits (1:8).*
>
> As we noted in this chapter, the message is crystal clear – prioritize the home, watch the heart, and cultivate the mind for Christ!

GAUGE Your Response

Set apart some unhurried time to reflect on your "standing" privately. Then, once you've examined your home, heart, and holy habits, invite others into the examination of your patterns and practices:

1. How would you describe your home life as a child? In what ways do you influence those in your home today? Is there a gap between the current reality and what you sense God calling your "home life" to become? Explain.

2. Servant leaders have experienced spiritual heart surgery and continue to be under the Great Physician's care. Of the five heart ailments mentioned by Paul (1:7), which one could potentially wreck your life? What do you intend to do about this?

3. Has your life demonstrated a continual cultivation of holy habits? What are some specific habits that you have introduced into your life in the past 5 years? What unholy habits have you removed from your routine? How might your group or trusted friend provide accountability as you progress in this area?

Paul recognized that Crete was a difficult place, providing Titus with abundant challenges. Yet, he encouraged Titus to address matters of the home, heart, and habits with diligence and humility. As we lovingly lead in our own Crete, may we be found standing tall in the grace of our Lord.

Study Guide

CHAPTER 18
Saying What You Mean as a Servant Leader

---

¹ *But as for you, teach what accords with sound doctrine.* ² *Older men are to be sober-minded, dignified, self-controlled, sound in faith, in love, and in steadfastness.* ³ *Older women likewise are to be reverent in behavior, not slanderers or slaves to much wine. They are to teach what is good,* ⁴ *and so train the young women to love their husbands and children,* ⁵ *to be self-controlled, pure, working at home, kind, and submissive to their own husbands, that the word of God may not be reviled.* ⁶ *Likewise, urge the younger men to be self-controlled.* ⁷ *Show yourself in all respects to be a model of good works, and in your teaching show integrity, dignity,* ⁸ *and sound speech that cannot be condemned, so that an opponent may be put to shame, having nothing evil to say about us.* ⁹ *Bondservants are to be submissive to their own masters in everything; they are to be well-pleasing, not argumentative,* ¹⁰ *not pilfering, but showing all good faith, so that in everything they may adorn the doctrine of God our Savior.*

¹¹ *For the grace of God has appeared, bringing salvation for all people,* ¹² *training us to renounce ungodliness and worldly passions, and to live self-controlled, upright, and godly lives in the present age,* ¹³ *waiting for our blessed hope, the appearing of the glory of our great God and Savior Jesus Christ,* ¹⁴ *who gave himself for us to redeem us from all lawlessness and to purify for himself a people for his own possession who are zealous for good works.*

¹⁵ *Declare these things; exhort and rebuke with all authority. Let no one disregard you.* (Titus 2:1-15)

At a GLANCE

In this chapter, we hear Paul's emphasis on self-control (2:2, 5,6, and 12), purpose statements (2:4,5,8,10,12, and 14), and teaching. To summarize, we will look at three things servant leaders are "saying."

1. Servant leaders are saying "no" to anything that dishonors Jesus.
2. Servant leaders are saying "yes" to everything that honors Jesus.
3. Servant leaders are saying "Mission matters."

> Titus, like Timothy, was reminded to "not let anyone despise" him. The primary way that happens is through the servant leader's saturation in trustworthy speech soaked in the person of Christ.

GAUGE Your Response

As you discuss these items with a group or a trusted friend,

1. Talk about the things you once said "yes" to but now say "no" to because of Christ's redeeming work in you. Are you finding that you are becoming increasingly aware of what might dishonor Christ?

2. How big is your "yes" in honoring Jesus? Are you stingy about yielding to His ways, looking for the minimum requirements? Are you zealous about discovering more avenues for saying "yes" to Christ? Explain.

3. Take another look at the "so that" passages in this text (2:4, 2:5, 2:8, 2:10, 2:12, and 2:14). Is your mission clear? Does this mission matter to you? In the past 3 months, how has your mission been pursued and prioritized?

Journal this week about what your lifestyle is "saying." Take time to create three short lists:

1. Top Seven Things That Require a "Yes"
2. Top Seven Things That Require a "No"
3. Top Seven Things That Encapsulate My "Mission"

Study Guide

CHAPTER 19
The "Doing Good" Reminder of Servant Leadership

---

¹ *Remind them to be submissive to rulers and authorities, to be obedient, to be ready for every good work,* ² *to speak evil of no one, to avoid quarreling, to be gentle, and to show perfect courtesy toward all people.* ³ *For we ourselves were once foolish, disobedient, led astray, slaves to various passions and pleasures, passing our days in malice and envy, hated by others and hating one another.* ⁴ *But when the goodness and loving kindness of God our Savior appeared,* ⁵ *he saved us, not because of works done by us in righteousness, but according to his own mercy, by the washing of regeneration and renewal of the Holy Spirit,* ⁶ *whom he poured out on us richly through Jesus Christ our Savior,* ⁷ *so that being justified by his grace we might become heirs according to the hope of eternal life.* ⁸ *The saying is trustworthy, and I want you to insist on these things, so that those who have believed in God may be careful to devote themselves to good works. These things are excellent and profitable for people. (Titus 3:1-8)*

At a GLANCE

In this chapter, we examine the needed bridge between Jesus-followers and those who do not yet know Him. Paul gives Titus some encouragement to "do good" in three distinct ways:

1. *Servant leaders remind people that their public lives becomes their pulpits (Titus 3:1-2).*
2. *Servant leaders remind people that their stories becomes their songs (Titus 3:3-5a).*
3. *Servant leaders remind people that their salvation becomes their service (3:5b-8).*

Doing good saturates the entire letter (1:8, 1:16, 2:3, 2:7, 2:14, 3:1, 3:8, and 3:14). His reminders become our reminders as we explore this text and these tasks.

The "Doing Good" Reminder of Servant Leadership

GAUGE Your Response

Prayerfully examine yourself in light of this Scripture and chapter. Then, set apart some time to discuss the following:

1. How we approach our public work will either attract or detract from the cause of Christ. In what ways are you reminded of this reality? How do you remind others?

2. Notice the list of sins that characterizes our past in Titus 3:3. Then, consider the remarkable rescue described in Titus 3:4. Has this rescue story become stale in you? How long has it been since you've marveled at His grace as it is extended to you? In what ways does your life "sing" of this remarkable work of redemption?

3. We are "blessed to be a blessing." Are you ever tempted to try to earn grace? Do you tend to be a cul-de-sac or a conduit of the blessings you receive? Explain.

4. Were there any additional insights from this chapter that would be helpful to highlight once more?

Study Guide

CHAPTER 20
Dying Daily as a Servant Leader

---

⁹ But avoid foolish controversies, genealogies, dissensions, and quarrels about the law, for they are unprofitable and worthless. ¹⁰ As for a person who stirs up division, after warning him once and then twice, have nothing more to do with him, ¹¹ knowing that such a person is warped and sinful; he is self-condemned.

¹² When I send Artemas or Tychicus to you, do your best to come to me at Nicopolis, for I have decided to spend the winter there. ¹³ Do your best to speed Zenas the lawyer and Apollos on their way; see that they lack nothing. ¹⁴ And let our people learn to devote themselves to good works, so as to help cases of urgent need, and not be unfruitful.

¹⁵ All who are with me send greetings to you. Greet those who love us in the faith. Grace be with you all. (Titus 3:9-15)

At a GLANCE

In this chapter, we recognized that servant leaders die daily. Some literally perish in the name of Jesus, while others wrestle with the paradoxical truths of losing to gain, dying to live, and saving by spending. How do servant leaders die daily?

1. Servant leaders die daily to winning silly Bible arguments (3:9).
2. Servant leaders die daily to getting along with everyone (3:10-11).
3. Servant leaders die daily to many of our own needs (3:12-15).

In his final words to Titus, Paul continues to instruct and to encourage his disciple to stay the course and lovingly to lead those entrusted to him. We will do well to revisit these principles and poignant truths uttered in this letter!

Dying Daily as a Servant Leader

GAUGE Your Response

Consider the difficult task of writing a meaningful letter to a loved one, anticipating that this may be the last correspondence you'll ever have together. With a sense of urgency and sobriety, consider these challenges to Titus:

1. Know your Scripture, but die daily to winning silly Bible arguments. Make a list of "arguments" that should be avoided. Additionally, note the need for loving instruction in sound doctrine. How does this challenge you?

2. Are there any unreconciled relationships in your life? If so, what are your plans to reconcile? As you consider Titus 3:10-11 and Matthew 18, are there any limits or guidelines in this effort? Are there any other Scriptural guidelines that come to mind when you pursue God-honoring relationships with people?

3. There is something profoundly selfless about servant leaders. They die to many of their own needs as they pursue a calling beyond their own. What have you laid to rest from your previous life? What still needs to be left behind? Don't rush this process of discovery, and don't look for the trite answer. What needs to die?

4. Before you do anything else, mark your calendar for a date in the future when you can enjoy several hours of solitude as you prayerfully reflect on this entire study of Scripture. What lessons were most helpful? Are there any holy habits that have formed as a result of this study? What are your next steps as you continue in this life of servant leadership?

References

Augustine. (1960). *The Confessions of St. Augustine.* New York: Image Books.

Barclay, William. (1970). *The Daily Study Bible Series: The Letters to Timothy, Titus, and Philemon* (Rev ed.). Philadelphia: Westminster Press.

Barrett, C.K. (1963). *The Pastoral Epistles.* Oxford: Clarendon Press.

Barton, Ruth Haley. (2008). *Strengthening the Soul of Your Leadership.* Downers Grove: IVP.

Berry, Wendell. (2002). "The Peace of Wild Things." *Good Poems.* Ed. Garrison Keillor. New York: Viking.

Bowling, John C. (2000). *Grace-Full Leadership: Understanding the Heart of a Christian Leader.* Kansas City: Beacon Hill Press.

Dickson, John. (2011). *Humilitas: A Lost Key to Life, Love, and Leadership.* Grand Rapids: Zondervan.

Dungy, Tony. (2009). *Uncommon: Finding Your Path to Significance.* Carol Stream: Tyndale.

Dwight, Timothy. (1968). "I Love Thy Kingdom Lord." *Favorite Hymns of Praise.* Cincinnati: Standard Publishing.

Foster, Richard. (1978). *Celebration of Discipline.* San Francisco: Harper.

Guinness, Os. (Ed.). (1999). *Character Counts.* Grand Rapids: Baker Books.

References

Guthrie, Donald. (1990). *The Tyndale New Testament Commentaries: The Pastoral Epistles.* Grand Rapids: Eerdmans.

Harmless, William. (2004). *Desert Christians: An Introduction to the Literature of Early Monasticism.* New York: Oxford University Press.

Hybels, Bill. (2002). *Courageous Leadership.* Grand Rapids: Zondervan.

James, Carolyn Custis. (2011). *Half the Church: Recapturing God's Global Vision for Women.* Grand Rapids: Zondervan.

Keller, Timothy. (2009). *The Centrality of the Gospel.* Retrieved June 1, 2013, from redeemercitytocity.com.

Kinnaman, David. (2011). *You Lost Me: Why Young Christians Are Leaving Church and Rethinking Faith.* Grand Rapids: Baker.

Lamott, Anne. (1999). *Traveling Mercies: Some Thoughts on Faith.* New York: Anchor Books.

Liefeld, Walter L. (1999). *The NIV Application Commentary: 1&2 Timothy-Titus.* Grand Rapids: Zondervan.

McNeal, Reggie. (2000). *A Work of Heart: Understanding How God Shapes Spiritual Leaders.* San Francisco: Jossey-Bass.

McNeal, Reggie. (2009). *Missional Renaissance: Changing the Scorecard for the Church.* San Francisco: Jossey-Bass.

Nietzsche, Friedrich. (1907). *Beyond Good and Evil.* Trans. Helen Zimmern. London: Macmillan Publishing.

References

Nouwen, Henri. (2001). *In the Name of Jesus: Reflections on Christian Leadership.* New York: Crossroad Publishing.

Ortberg, John. (1997). *The Life You've Always Wanted.* Grand Rapids: Zondervan.

Peterson, Eugene. (2002). *The Message.* Colorado Springs: NavPress.

Peterson, Eugene. (2005). *Christ Plays in Ten Thousand Places: A Conversation in Spiritual Theology.* Grand Rapids: Eerdmans.

Peterson, Eugene. (2007). *The Jesus Way: A Conversation on the Ways that Jesus is the Way.* Grand Rapids: Eerdmans.

Ryken, Leland, Wilhoit, James C., & Longman III, Tremper. (1998). *Dictionary of Biblical Imagery.* Downers Grove: IVP.

Sanders, J. Oswald. (1986). *Spiritual Leadership.* Chicago: Moody.

Spurgeon, Charles. (1863). *Paul: His Cloak and His Books* from the Metropolitan Tabernacle Pulpit. Sermon No.542. Retrieved June 15, 2013, from http://www.spurgeon.org/sermons/0542.htm.

Stanley, Andy. (2003). *Next Generation Leader.* Colorado Springs: Multnomah Publishers.

Stedman, Ray. (2009). *The Fight of Faith.* Grand Rapids: Discovery House Publishers.

Stewart, James S. (1978). *A Faith to Proclaim.* Grand Rapids: Baker Book House.

Stott, John R.W. (1973). *The Message of 2 Timothy: The Bible Speaks Today.* Downers Grove: IVP

Stott, John R.W. (1996). *The Message of 1 Timothy & Titus.* The Bible Speaks Today. Downers Grove: IVP.

Thurston, Bonnie Bowman. (1989). *The Widows: A Women's Ministry in the Early Church.* Minneapolis: Augsburg Fortress Press.

Tozer, A.W. (1985). *Whatever Happened to Worship.* Harrisburg: Christian Publications.

Tucker, Ruth. (2008). *Leadership Reconsidered: Becoming a Person Influence.* Grand Rapids: Baker Books.

Wake, William & Lardner, Nathaniel. (1996). *Apocryphal New Testament.* Whitefish: Kessinger Publishing.

Willard, Dallas, Averbeck, R., & Bock, D. (1999). *Biblical Theological Foundations for Spiritual Formation.* Spiritual Formation Conference conducted at Trinity Evangelical Divinity School, Deerfield, IL.

Witherington, Ben. (2006). *Letters and Homilies for Hellenized Christians. Volume 1: A Social-Rhetorical Commentary on Titus, 1-2 Timothy, and 1-3 John.* Downers Grove: IVP Academic.

Wright, N.T. (2004). *Paul for Everyone: The Pastoral Letters.* Philadelphia: Westminster John Knox Press.